From Auntie [illegible]
Christmas 1990.

The Forester's Companion

BY THE SAME AUTHOR

Working Plans for Estate Woodlands
Notes on Estate Forestry
An Experiment in Forestry
The Trees of Bicton
The Arboriculturalist's Companion
A Book of Trees (An Anthology)
Before the Echoes Die Away
A History of English Forestry
A Forestry Centenary: History of the Royal Forestry Society of England, Wales and Northern Ireland
Gunners at Larkhill
Plain Soldiering

The Forester's Companion

Fourth Edition

N. D. G. JAMES

BASIL BLACKWELL

First Edition 1955
Second edition 1966
Reprinted in paperback 1979
Third Edition 1982
Reprinted 1983, 1986, 1987
Fourth Edition 1989

Basil Blackwell Ltd
108 Cowley Road, Oxford OX4 1JF, England

Basil Blackwell Inc.
432 Park Avenue South, Suite 1505
New York, NY 10016, USA

British Library Cataloguing in Publication Data

A CIP catalogue record for this book is available from the British Library.

Library of Congress Cataloging in Publication Data

James, N. D. G.
The forester's companion / N. D. G. James. — 4th ed.
p. cm.
Bibliography: p.
Includes index.
ISBN 0–631–16724–2 — ISBN 0–631–16258–5 (pbk.)
1. Foresters and forestry—Great Britain—Handbooks, manuals, etc.
I. Title.
SD179.J348 1989
634.9—dc19

Typeset by Columns of Reading
Printed and bound in Great Britain by
Billings & Sons Ltd., Worcester

Foreword

BY THE EARL OF YARBOROUGH, DL

President of the Royal Forestry Society of England, Wales and Northern Ireland

To welcome this new edition of *The Forester's Companion* is like greeting an old friend. A familiar with whom one is at ease and whose worth one knows.

Mr N. D. G. James is to be congratulated on having chosen the original concept for this book nearly 35 years ago and for so assiduously keeping it up to date in successive editions, while preserving the essential format. Nowhere else is such a wealth of practical information ready to hand, so conveniently available, without recourse to libraries. There can be little doubt that this publication has achieved its original purpose. That this is the fourth edition is testimony to, and speaks for, itself. Generations of foresters have used it over the years and I am sure that present and future generations will do likewise and be thankful for it.

The Royal Forestry Society of England, Wales and Northern Ireland is proud of its association with this work from the beginning and we can whole-heartedly recommend its use to our membership and to anyone else engaged in the business of forestry.

Contents

CHAPTER VI
Silviculture

CHAPTER VII
Coppice and Underwood

CHAPTER VIII
Forest Management

CHAPTER IX
Timber Measuring

CHAPTER X
The Elements of Forest Surveying

CHAPTER XI

Forest Protection

CHAPTER XII

Diseases and Pests

CHAPTER XIII

Forest Roads and Rides

CHAPTER XIV

Felling, Extraction and Transport

CHAPTER XV

Sawmills and Conversion

CHAPTER XVI

Utilization

CHAPTER XVII

Timber Seasoning and Preservation

CHAPTER XVIII

The Valuation and Sale of Timber

CHAPTER XIX

Gates and Fencing

CHAPTER XX

Hedges and Shelter Belts

CHAPTER XXI

Amenity Planting

CHAPTER XXII

Forestry and Shooting

CHAPTER XXIII

Trees and the Law

CHAPTER XXIV

Grants and Felling Licences

CHAPTER XXV
The Forestry Commission

CHAPTER XXVI
The State Forest Service in Northern Ireland

CHAPTER XXVII
Societies, Organizations, Establishments and Trusts Concerned with Forestry

CHAPTER XXVIII
Forest Gardens and Forest Parks

CHAPTER XXIX
Education and Training

CHAPTER XXX
Publications, Periodicals and Libraries

CHAPTER XXXI
Machinery and Equipment

CHAPTER XXXII
Safety in Forestry

CHAPTER XXXIII

Preface to Fourth Edition

SINCE the previous edition was published in 1982 a considerable number of changes have taken place in forestry. Some of these are concerned with administration—a new system of forestry grants, the withdrawal of the Dedication Scheme, fundamental changes in taxation and the introduction of the Farm Woodlands Scheme. The structure of the Forestry Commission has also undergone several alterations, not only at Headquarters but also in the Conservancies which have been reduced in number and increased in size. The formation of the Forestry Industry Committee of Great Britain in 1987 which is supported by bodies representing every aspect of modern forestry is an event of major importance.

Changes have also taken place at some of the universities where the teaching of forestry has been merged with biology or ecological science. At the same time, there is a far greater interest in conservation. This is reflected in this edition, by the inclusion of information relating to several bodies whose interests in conservation have a bearing on forestry.

N.D.G.J.

BLAKEMORE HOUSE
KERSBROOK
BUDLEIGH SALTERTON
DEVON
July 1988

Acknowledgements for the Fourth Edition

I WISH to record my thanks to the following who have helped in various ways during the preparation of this new edition. I am also very grateful to the Forestry Commission for allowing me to draw on the contents of many of their publications and, in several cases, to include extracts from them.

Mr R. H. Adam, Managing Director, Scottish Woodlands Ltd.; Mrs H. Austin, Forestry Commission; Mr R. Brookes, Administrator, British Wood Preserving Association; Mr M. Brown, Technical Manager, Omark UK Ltd.; The Director, The Building Research Establishment; Mr D. A. Burdekin, Chief Research Officer (South), Forestry Commission; Dr J. Burley, Director, The Oxford Forestry Institute; Mr E. S. Carter, CBE, Farming and Wildlife Trust; The Secretary, The Countryside Commission; The Secretary, The Countryside Commission for Scotland; Mrs M. W. Dick, Secretary, The Institute of Chartered Foresters; Mr J. Eadie, Director, Scottish Forestry Trust; Mr D. Elgy, Forestry Commission; Mr R. Gray, Secretary, The Society of Consultant Foresters of Scotland; Mr R. Gregor, Editor, *Slasher*; Mr H. Hart, Forestry Commission; Mr E. H. M. Harris, Director, The Royal Forestry Society of England, Wales and Northern Ireland; Dr O. W. Heal, Director, Institute of Terrestrial Ecology (North); Dr J. C. Hetherington, University College of North Wales; Mr S. F. Hodgson, Operations Director, British Trust for Conservation Volunteers; The Secretary, The Home Timber Merchants' Association of Northern Ireland; Mr G. B. Jones, Planning Officer, Forest Service Northern Ireland; Mr J. M. Josephi; Mr M. G. July, Nature Conservancy Council; Miss M. M. Lewis, Secretary, Forestry Safety Council; Mr J. F. Lindsay, Head of Information, Forestry Commission; The Director, Long Ashton Research Station; The Secretary, The Men of the Trees; Mr D. M. Macarthur, Secretary, The Home Timber Merchants' Association of Scotland; Dr E. J. Parker, Technical Publications Officer, Forestry Commission; Dr J. A. Petty, University of Aberdeen; Mr A. G. Phillips, Secretary, Association of Professional Foresters; Mr C. Pugsley, The Countryside Commission; Mr A. O. Reardon, Editor, *Forestry and British Timber*; Maj-Gen. T. A. Richardson, CB, MBE, Secretary, British Christmas Tree Growers' Association; Mr H. B.

Roberts, Secretary, The British Timber Merchants' Association (England and Wales); Mr G. Robertson, Technical Secretary, Forestry Training Council; The Secretary, The Royal Scottish Forestry Society; Mr R. M. Rutherford, Secretary, Dwyfor Woodlands Ltd.; The Hon. Secretary, The Society of Irish Foresters; Mrs S. M. Stirling, Librarian, The Devon and Exeter Institution; Mr K. G. Stott, Long Ashton Research Station; Mr H. A. Thomas, Director, The Welsh Agricultural Organization Society Ltd; The Secretary, The Timber Research and Development Association; Mr D. R. Tracey, Forestry Commission; The Secretary, The Tree Council; Mr R. Van Oss, Director, The Game Conservancy Trust; Mr W. B. Walker, Managing Director, Flintshire Woodlands; Mr P. H. Wilson; Mr A. R. Williams, Chief Executive, Timber Growers United Kingdom Ltd.; Mr M. R. W. Williams, Secretary, The Central Forestry Examination Board and Dr T. W. Wright, Editor, *The Quarterly Journal of Forestry*.

CHAPTER I

Forest Trees Grown in Britain

THIS chapter contains short notes on the characteristics and site requirements of those trees which may be grown for timber production and is divided into two main sections—namely broadleaved species and conifers. Although, in the past, the common elm has proved to be a valuable source of timber, in view of the devastating effect of elm disease during recent years and consequently the uncertain future of this species, it has been omitted. For more detailed information, reference should be made to the following publications of the Forestry Commission which also contain particulars of other species which are not included in this chapter:

Bulletin No. 14, *Forestry Practice*.

Bulletin No. 62, *Silviculture of Broadleaved Woodlands*.

1. BROADLEAVED SPECIES

Species	*Soil*	*Suitable sites*	*Conditions to avoid*	*Wind-firm or -weak*	*Frost-hardy or -tender*	*Light-demanding or shade-bearing*	*Remarks*
ASH (*Fraxinus excelsior*)	Well watered yet well drained deep loams, particularly calcereous loams. Will also grow on the deeper soils over limestone and chalk.	Moist sheltered situations free from spring frosts.	Frost hollows; poor, dry, or shallow soils; exposed sites; grassland, heather, and moorland; badly drained sites and very heavy soils.	Wind-firm.	Frost-tender.	Shade-bearing for about first 7 years, but then becoming very light-demanding.	A species which is very particular as to its requirements, needing ideal conditions for best results. Unsuitable for wholesale planting, and generally only suitable for establishment in groups. Naturally regenerates freely. Best quality ash commands a high price.
BEECH (*Fagus sylvatica*)	Chalk and lime-stone. Can grow reasonably well on any soil other than peat and heavy clay.	Most old woodland sites, provided they are well drained.	Very exposed sites. Heather-covered land; badly drained sites; frost hollows; infertile, dry sands.	Wind-firm, except on shallow soils overlying rock.	Frost-tender	Very shade-bearing.	Best results are obtained by planting beech with a nurse, such as Scots pine, which is later removed as thinnings. Difficult to establish as a first crop on grassland. Valuable for underplanting. May be seriously damaged by grey squirrels.
BEECH, SOUTHERN (*Nothofagus obliqua, Nothofagus procera*)	Both will grow on a wide range of soils. *N. procera* appears to dislike calcareous soils but *N. obliqua* is more accommodating in this respect. Avoid very heavy clays for either species.	*N. procera* grows best in higher rainfall areas while *N. obliqua* prefers the drier sites and seems to be less demanding as to site requirements. Sheltered situations are best.	Sites liable to be affected by heavy frosts, exposed situations and inadequately drained areas.	Wind-firm on suitable sites.	Both may be damaged by heavy frosts.	Both species are very light-demanding.	Very fast-growing species with a high volume production although details of their requirements have not yet been fully assessed. See Forestry Commission Forest Record No. 122—*Nothofagus in Britain*.

BIRCH (*Betula verrucosa. B. pubescens*)	Will grow on most soils, but prefers the lighter and drier soils.	Very accommodating as to site, and will grow in most places.	It is sometimes difficult to establish on sites which have not previously carried a crop of trees.	Wind-firm.	Very frost-hardy.	Light-demanding.	The chief value of birch lies in its use as a nurse crop. There is some demand for birch poles in the turnery trade. If grown as nurses, failure to remove may result in damage caused by whipping.
CHESTNUT, SWEET OR SPANISH (*Castanea sativa*)	Deep fertile soils. Light loams over gravel are suitable for coppice.	Well-drained, unexposed sites.	Very wet or very dry soils. Heavy clays. Calcareous or poor soils. Exposed sites and frost hollows.	Wind-firm.	Frost-tender.	Shade-bearing for about first 7 years, but then becoming light-demanding.	Grown as coppice in Kent, Sussex, and Hereford. Large timber is very liable to be shaken, and there is considerable risk in growing it on untried soils.
OAK, PENDUNCULATE OAK (*Quercus robur*) SESSILE OAK (*Q. petraea*)	Deep, fresh fertile soils. Drained clays. Deep loam over chalk. Light sandy loams if moist.	Woodlands in a good agricultural district.	Exposed areas, frost hollows, soils of poor fertility; shallow and badly drained soils.	Very wind-firm.	Frost-tender. Pedunculate oak is more frost-tender than sessile oak.	Light-demanding, but sessile oak will stand more shade than pedunculate oak.	Sessile oak has a better form as a forest tree than pedunculate, and suffers less from defoliation and mildew. Good oak always sells well; poor oak seldom.
POPLAR (*Populus gelrica*) (*P. robusta*) (*P. serotina*) (*P. eugenei*) (*P. laevigata*) (*P. tacamahaca* × *trichocarpa* 32) (*P.* × *euramericana*)	Deep rich soils, especially of alluvial origin. Ample water supply, yet well drained.	The bottom of river valleys, river banks and low-lying sheltered sites.	Exposed sites, high elevation, shallow or acid soils, stagnant water.	Moderately wind-firm.	Frost-hardy.	Very light-demanding.	No longer in demand for matches and chip baskets but now used for plywood, pulp and pallets. Poor firewood.

1. BROADLEAVED SPECIES

Species	*Soil*	*Suitable sites*	*Conditions to avoid*	*Wind-firm or -weak*	*Frost-hardy or -tender*	*Light-demanding or shade-bearing*	*Remarks*
SYCAMORE (*Acer pseudoplatanus*)	Probably grown best on soils suitable to ash, i.e. well drained, deep, moist calcareous loams, but will also grow well on most soils, provided they are not very dry or very wet.	Ideally moist, sheltered sites, but will grow in exposed situations and on sites open to the sea.	Very dry or very wet sites; heather and moorland.	Very wind-firm.	Moderately frost-hardy.	Shade-bearing for about the first 7 years, but then becoming light-demanding.	A useful, but rather neglected, species. Regenerates easily on most sites, but is subject to considerable damage by grey squirrels. Veneer class sycamore commands a high price.
WILLOW, CRICKET BAT (*Salix alba var. coerulea*)	Deep alluvial soil.	On the banks of streams and watercourses in which the water is moving.	Any other sites than those described in the last column. Especially should waterlogged sites and stagnant water be avoided. Avoid frost hollows.	Moderately wind-firm.	Moderately frost-tender. Subject to injury by late frosts, in frost hollows, or where exposed to cold winds.	Very light-demanding.	The raising and growing of cricket bat willows is very specialized work.

2. CONIFERS

Species	*Soil*	*Suitable sites*	*Conditions to avoid*	*Wind-firm or -weak*	*Frost-hardy or -tender*	*Light-demanding or shade-bearing*	*Remarks*
CEDAR, WESTERN RED (*Thuya plicata*)	Deep fresh soils, good loams; moderately heavy loams. Will grow on chalky soil, limestones, and shallow soils.	Moist slopes and valleys; districts of high rainfall and cool temperatures. Sheltered sites but will succeed where more exposed.	Dry, hot sites; sour or peaty soils; frosty situation; loose sands.	Wind-firm.	Moderately frost-tender.	Very shade-bearing.	Valuable for under-planting. A good hedge plant, but subject to *Didymascella* (*syn. Keithia*) *thujina* (Leaf dieback) when young. See Chap. XII. Liable to butt rot.
CYPRESS, LAWSON (*Chamaecyparis lawsoniana*)	Deep fertile soils and heavy loams, but will grow on a variety of soils if not too wet.	Sheltered situations; high rainfall areas.	Hot, dry soils and heather-covered sites.	Moderately wind-firm, but may suffer where growth is fast.	Moderately frost-hardy.	Very shade-bearing.	Very good for under-planting; valuable for hedging; may produce forked growth. Very free from disease.
FIR, DOUGLAS (*Pseudotsuga menziesii*)	Deep firm soils, but lighter rather than heavier. Shales and rocky soil.	Sheltered, well-drained sites and sides of valleys.	Exposed situations; wet, soft, or shallow soils; smoke and fumes; heather land; chalk and limestone; poor, infertile soils.	Moderately wind-firm, except on the moister sites, but liable to windblow if suddenly exposed or when under-thinned.	Moderately frost-hardy, but may suffer damage on low-lying sites.	Moderately shade-bearing, especially when young.	Only plant Oregon or Green Douglas. Requires frequent thinning. Fast growing and useful in converting coppice to high forest.
FIR, GRAND (*Abies grandis*)	Well-drained fertile loams.	Sheltered sites.	Poor, thin, or acid soils; frosty sites; exposed sites.	Reasonably wind-firm.	Very frost-tender.	Very shade-bearing.	Grows very quickly on suitable sites, and produces large quantities of timber. Very suitable for underplanting.

2. CONIFERS

Species	*Soil*	*Suitable sites*	*Conditions to avoid*	*Wind-firm or -weak*	*Frost-hardy or -tender*	*Light-demanding or shade-bearing*	*Remarks*
HEMLOCK, WESTERN (*Tsuga heterophylla*)	Light or heavy loams, of reasonable fertility, but of good depth; but will grow well on the wetter and drier sites.	Sheltered, but will grow on moorland sites.	Dry, sandy soils and heather covered sites.	Very wind-firm.	Moderately frost-hardy, but needs shelter throughout its first year. Frost hollows should be avoided.	Exceptionally shade-bearing.	Very useful for under-planting. Risk of heart rot on sites previously carrying conifers.
LARCH, EUROPEAN (*Larix decidua*)	Deep, fresh, moist, but porous loams.	Open, but not exposed situations.	Exposed situations. Badly drained or very dry sites. Thin soils over chalk, peat, grass, or heather. Frosty sites or near the sea. Smoke and fumes.	Very wind-firm.	Moderately frost-hardy, but frost hollows should be avoided.	Light-demanding.	If planted on unsuitable sites, larch canker (*Lachnellula willkommii*) will occur. Scottish seed is best.
LARCH, JAPANESE (*Larix kaempferi*)	Peats, if well drained. Heavier soils than European larch. Loams over chalk and limestone.	Old woodland sites; grass and heather slopes. Higher rainfall areas. Withstands smoke.	Dry sites; districts with less than 30 inches rainfall. Exposed situations. On very fertile soils growth is so rapid that younger trees lack rigidity, and often produce 'corkscrew' leaders.	Very wind-firm.	Moderately frost-hardy, but frost hollows should be avoided.	Light-demanding.	Virtually free from larch canker. Very useful for planting when converting coppice to high forest. Hybrid larch (*Larix* × *eurolepsis*) has similar characteristics, but is often a faster grower.

PINE, AUSTRIAN (*Pinus nigra var. nigra*)	Poor, light, shallow soils; sands; chalk; limestones.	Exposed situations; near the sea.	Moorlands in north and west.	Very wind-firm.	Frost-hardy.	Light-demanding.	Should never be planted for its timber, but only in shelter belts or as nurse. Will grow on practically pure chalk. Like all pines, it is very subject to honey fungus (*Armillaria mellea*).
PINE, CORSICAN (*Pinus nigra var. maritima*)	Light, sandy soils; chalk; limestone (if not shallow); heavy clays.	Low elevations; near sea; south and east England. Low rainfall district. Withstands smoke.	High elevations; exposed sites if ground is soft.	Very wind-firm.	Frost-hardy.	Light-demanding.	Seedlings develop long tap roots very quickly, and may be difficult to establish in the forest. Plant in late spring, as 1 yr 1 yr. Useful for planting on sand dunes.
PINE, LODGE POLE (*Pinu contorta*)	Poor soils generally.	Will grow on poor, wet soils and heather sites.	Normally only grown on very poor sites where Scots pine fails.	Wind-firm.	Frost-hardy.	Light-demanding, but will stand a certain amount of shade.	On the better soils more valuable species should be grown. Very good pioneer crop; resistant to sea winds. Severely attacked by pine shoot moth (*Ryacionia buoliana*) in south of England and by pine beauty moth (*Panolis flammea*) in north of Scotland.
PINE, MONTEREY (*Pinus radiata*)	Deep, sandy soils.	In districts where the climate is mild, e.g. Devon and Cornwall, near the sea.	Any other than those referred to in the two preceding columns.	Wind-firm.	Very frost-tender.	Light-demanding.	Grows rapidly in districts to which it is suited, but produces coarse timber. Withstands salt-laden winds.
PINE, SCOTS (*Pinus sylvestris*)	Sandy and light soils.	Heather and bilberry sites. Low rainfall areas. Low elevations.	High elevations. Smoke and fumes. Chalks and limestones, except as a nurse.	Wind-firm,	Very frost-hardy.	Light-demanding.	Will grow under varying conditions, and often regenerates naturally without difficulty. Useful as a nurse to beech on calcareous soils.

2. CONIFERS

Species	*Soil*	*Suitable sites*	*Conditions to avoid*	*Wind-firm or -weak*	*Frost-hardy or -tender*	*Light-demanding or shade-bearing*	*Remarks*
REDWOOD (*Sequoia sempervirens*)	Deep and fertile; moist, but not wet.	High rainfall areas. Sheltered valleys.	Low rainfall districts; poor soils; exposed sites; frost hollows.	Moderately wind-firm.	Frost-tender when young, becoming hardier.	Very shade-bearing.	Will produce coppice shoots and can be propagated on a commercial scale by cuttings, as well as by seed. The Wellingtonia (*Sequoiadendron giganteum*) will grow under conditions similar to the redwood, but will withstand drier and more acid conditions than the redwood.
SPRUCE, NORWAY (*Picea abies*)	Most reasonably fertile soils; moist loams; shallow peats; heavy clays.	Old woodland sites; grassy or rushy land. On the whole a very accommodating species.	Dry sites; frost hollows; heather covered land; smoke and fumes; chalk; poorly drained sites; posed situations.	Very wind-weak, owing to shallow rooting system.	Moderately frost-tender. Frost hollows should be avoided.	Moderately shade-bearing.	Very liable to conifer heart rot (*Heterobasidion annosum* formerly *Fomes annosus*) if grown on unsuitable sites. Mound planting advisable on peats and wet sites. A very shallow rooting species. The commonest species grown for Christmas trees.
SPRUCE, SITKA (*Picea sitchensis*)	Peats, loams, deep moist soils.	Exposed situations; damp sites; areas subject to smoke and fumes. High rainfall districts; poorer moorland sites.	Frosty sites; dry sites; old woodland sites (owing to risk of honey fungus). Low rainfall areas.	Wind-firm.	Frost-tender.	Moderately shade-bearing, but less so than Norway spruce.	Mound planting on wet sites should be adopted. A fast grower under suitable conditions.

CHAPTER II

Nursery Work

1. *Propagation of Trees*

TREES can be propagated by seed, cuttings, layering, or suckers.

(a) Seed
The most usual method of propagation, for details of which see Section 3 below.

(b) Cuttings
Chiefly used for the propagation of shrubs and ornamental trees, but not usually for forest trees, except willows and poplars (see Section 5 of this chapter).

(c) Layering
Used in propagating shrubs and ornamental trees, but in forestry chiefly used for filling vacancies in sweet or Spanish chestnut coppice, and hazel coppice.

Procedure: Vigorous growing stool shoots are cut, nicked, or twisted (so that bark breaks), in one or up to three places. The shoot is then bent over and pegged down securely and covered with earth at points of rupture. Provided the soil remains moist, roots should form within a year, and when these have developed the young plant is separated from the parent by severing with a knife.

Two points essential for success:
(i) The soil around the break must be kept moist.
(ii) The layered shoot must be fixed immovably.

(d) Suckers
Adventitious buds may occur on the roots of trees and give rise to shoots which form suckers. These can be utilized by severing them at a point as close to the parent root as possible. They should then be lined out in the nursery and left for 1 to 2 years before removal to their permanent position.

The following species are particularly prone to produce suckers:
Common elm (*U. procera*), aspen, white and balsam poplars, birch, false acacia (*R. pseudacacia*).

2. *The Forest Nursery*

Detailed information on all the aspects of forest nurseries and their management will be found in Forestry Commission Bulletin No. 43, *Nursery Practice*.

(a) Sources from which trees can be obtained

Supplies of trees can be obtained in three ways:

(i) Trees are raised in the nursery from seed.
(ii) Seedlings are bought and lined out in the nursery for 1 or 2 years.
(iii) Transplants are bought and planted in the wood direct.

Note: The above does not apply to poplars, which can be raised in the nursery from cuttings or purchased as rooted or unrooted setts and lined out in the nursery or planted in the wood direct (see Section 5—Propagation of poplars).

(b) Types of nursery

There are two types of nursery:

(i) *Permanent*

With this type of nursery trees are raised for planting out on the whole estate. Where trees are raised from seed, the seed beds will normally be located in the permanent nursery.

(ii) *Temporary*

These nurseries are non-permanent and decentralized, and are often supplementary to a permanent one. They may be established in or near planting areas which lie some distance from the permanent nursery.

The advantage of temporary nurseries are that the cost of transporting large numbers of plants from the main nursery to a distant planting site is avoided or greatly reduced, and there is less delay between lifting and planting. The chief disadvantage is that labour is more scattered, and consequently supervision is more difficult.

(c) Selecting a site for a nursery

The following points should be considered in selecting the site of a permanent nursery, although it is unlikely that a single site will fulfil all these requirements:

(i) The soil should be easy to work, of good depth, clean and in good heart. The soil conditions of a forest nursery should be moderately acid (pH 4·5 to 5·5).
(ii) The site should not be a frost hollow or subject to frost.
(iii) Wet, damp sites must be avoided.

(iv) North and north-west aspects are preferable. Sites with a south aspect are liable to be dried out by the sun; while in frosty weather too quick a thaw may occur. South-west aspects are often subject to excessive wind and driving rain, while east aspects are open to very cold winds. Avoid north aspects for poplars.
(v) A slightly inclined site is best.
(vi) A water supply should be available.
(vii) As far as possible the nursery should be located: (1) in the centre of the estate; (2) close to the head forester's house; (3) close to the woodmen's cottages.
(viii) If adjacent to old hardwood areas, the risk of cockchafer attack may be increased; while if sited near the timber yard, pine weevils may cause damage.
(ix) Where a new nursery is to be formed on old meadow land, the increased cost of cleaning, and presence of wireworms and cockchafer grubs, should be borne in mind.
(x) The nursery must be adjacent to a hard road to give easy access for lorries.
(xi) Nurseries situated on heathland have much to commend them. They produce first quality plants and owing to their comparative freedom from weeds, are easy to keep clean. Plant indicators of such sites are heather or ling, with some bracken and wavy-hair grass (*Deschampia flexuosa*). When clearing such sites the vegetation should be removed and not burnt on the site.

(d) Size of nurseries

(i) The size of the nursery should be based on the number of plants which it is intended to produce each year. On an estate which is concerned with raising stock for planting in its woodlands rather than for sale, the amount of stock to be raised will depend on the area to be planted or re-planted annually.
(ii) It is unlikely that the formation of an estate nursery would be justified unless at least 8 hectares (20 acres) of woodland were to be planted each year.
(iii) The Forestry Commission consider that about 0·4 hectares (1 acre) of nursery is needed to produce between 70,000 and 100,000 young trees for planting out and that a nursery would be uneconomical if less than 25,000 plants are produced annually (Bulletin No. 43).

(e) Layout of nurseries

(i) When laying out a nursery, the best shape is a square or rectangle, since this is the most economical in fencing and can be easily divided into convenient beds.
(ii) A permanent rabbit fence should be erected around the site.

Even if rabbits are not present such a fence will keep out or discourage unauthorized persons, hares, cats, dogs and so on. For details of such a fence see Chapter XIX.

(iii) Hedges may be planted around the boundaries if the site is subject to strong winds but internal hedges restrict the use of machinery, require attention, may compete with nursery stock and can encourage weeds. Information on hedges will be found in Chapter XX but the use of Western red cedar (*Thuya plicata*) should be avoided as it may be attacked by the fungus *Didymascella thujina* (*syn. keithia*) and the disease transmitted to nursery stock.

(iv) In laying out the nursery attention should be paid to the following points: (1) arrangement of internal roads and paths; (2) entrances; (3) turning points (if necessary); (4) site for tool shed, etc.

(v) Provision should be made to enable vehicles and machinery to be driven into the nursery. A road about 5 m (15 ft) wide laid up the centre may be sufficient in small nurseries but in large ones additional roads should be provided. These should subdivide the area into blocks or sections of about an acre but in nurseries which are mainly mechanized these blocks will be considerably larger.

(vi) The land lying between the roads may be divided into smaller plots by paths 1·2 m (4 ft) wide and spaced about 9 m (30 ft) apart.

(vii) The roads and permanent paths should have hard surfaces; in the case of the former sufficient to enable vehicles to be used during the winter.

(viii) For information regarding manuring, green cropping and fallowing, see Section 6—Fertility in nurseries.

3. *Seeds and Sowing*

(*a*) *Formation of seed beds*

(i) Approximately one-tenth of the nursery should be reserved for seed beds.

(ii) They should be sited on the lightest and most easily worked soil, since a fine tilth is essential. All stones should be removed.

(iii) Seed beds should be 0·9 m (36 in.) to 1·06 m (42 in.) wide, and divided by alleyways or narrow trodden paths 38 cm (15 in.) to 48 cm (18 in.) wide. The beds should be about 7·5 cm (3 in.) higher than the paths, and this can be achieved by heaping some of the soil from the alleyways on to the bed.

(iv) Seed beds may be surrounded by impregnated boards or small mesh wire netting sunk below ground as a protection against mice.

(v) In nurseries which are 8 hectares (20 acres) or more in area, much of the work will normally be carried out by machinery.

(b) Supplies of seed

(i) Seed can be purchased from a forest seed merchant or from the Forestry Commission through their Seed Officer at the Commission's Research Station, Alice Holt Lodge, Wrecclesham, Farnham, Surrey, GU10 4LH.

(ii) It can also be collected from suitable trees growing on the estate but the need to obtain seed only from the best type of parent trees cannot be over-emphasized.

(iii) Under *The Forest Reproductive Material Regulations* 1977, the Forestry Commission is responsible for keeping a National Register of approved seed orchards, seed stands and stool beds in respect of European silver fir, European and Japanese larch, Norway and Sitka spruce, Austrian, Corsican, Scots and Weymouth pine, Douglas fir, pedunculate, red and sessile oak, beech and poplar. The Regulations only allow seed or poplar cuttings from such sources to be sold in the United Kingdom or other countries within the European Economic Community. The seller must provide the buyer with a Supplier's Certificate where material from any of the above fifteen species is to be sold and the appropriate parts of the Certificate must be completed.

(iv) Seed collection can be carried out by climbing, with stick and bag, by collecting the larger seeds after they have fallen or from felled trees.

(v) Further information on seed collection will be found in Forestry Commission Bulletin No. 43, *Nursery Practice*, and on seed origins in Bulletin No. 66, *Choice of Seed Origins for the Main Forest Species in Britain*.

(vi) The Forest Seed Association was terminated in 1973 after this country joined the European Economic Community.

(c) Collection of seed

The following is a guide to the time of year when seed should be collected, but the exact time may vary with the season and the location of the estate:

(i) *May–June*: Wych elm.

(ii) *August*: Ash (if sown immediately after gathering), but see paragraph (iii) of sub-section *(e) Storage of seed*.

(iii) *August–September*: Birch, hornbeam, Lawson cypress, silver firs (*Abies grandis* and *A. procera*), Western hemlock (*Tsuga heterophylla*), Western red cedar (*Thuya plicata*).

(iv) *September–October*: Sycamore, Douglas fir, hybrid and Japanese larch, Sitka spruce.

(v) *October–November*: Alder, ash, beech, hawthorn, holly, hornbeam, maple, oak, sweet chestnut, lodgepole pine, Norway spruce, Serbian spruce (*Picea omorika*).

(vi) *November–January*: European larch, holly.

(vii) *January–February*: Austrian pine, Corsican pine, Scots pine.

(d) Seed extraction

(i) In most cases cones require heating before the seeds can be extracted. The sun or the heat of a room may be sufficient for some species, but more heat may be needed in other cases.

(ii) Large-scale extraction needs a kiln and extractor, but it may be possible to make arrangements for a nurseryman or the Forestry Commission to undertake this work.

(iii) The chief danger in kiln extraction is overheating.

(iv) The extraction of European larch seed is difficult.

(e) Storage of seed

The method adopted depends on the species, some requiring to be kept dry and well ventilated, while others should be stratified by mixing with sand. Stratification is dealt with in Section *(f)* below—*Treatment of seed before sowing*.

(i) *Beech and oak*: Can be stored from time of collection until the time of sowing in the following spring. During this period they should be kept reasonably dry and ventilated, and the storage conditions should be similar to those needed for corn storage. Where large quantities are to be dealt with, a pit 60 cm (2 ft) deep with thatched roof (height of 2 m (6 ft) above floor of pit) should be constructed. For further information, see Forestry Commission Bulletin No. 43, *Nursery Practice*.

(ii) *Sweet chestnut*: May be spread out on dry floor and turned periodically to avoid heating. The seed must be protected from mice, and an alternative method is to place in sacks and hang up in a dry, cool shed.

(iii) *Ash, maple, sycamore*: The treatment of these seeds is described in Bulletin No. 43. Ash may be sown immediately after collection or stratified and sown about 17 months after collection. Sycamore and Norway maple can be sown as soon as harvested or stratified for 6 weeks before sowing in the spring.

(iv) *Hawthorn, holly, hornbeam*: The best results will be obtained if these seeds are stratified after collection and sown in the spring, 18 months or so later.

(v) *Conifers*: The seed of most conifers can be stored for up to three years if placed in airtight containrs and kept in a dry cool place.

(f) Treatment of seed before sowing

(i) *Stratification*

This consists of mixing the seeds of those species listed below with two to three times as much sand (by volume) as the seeds concerned.

The mixture is then placed in a pit or wooden seed boxes which hold about 0·028 cubic metres (1 cubic foot). Small quantities of mixed seeds may also be placed in polythene bags or sealed tins which should be stored in a cool place.

The following species may be treated by stratification:

ash	hawthorn	lime	Douglas fir
birch	holly	maple	silver fir
cherry	hornbeam	sycamore	

Silver fir has also given good results when sown in January and February without being stratified.

(ii) *Seed treatment*
In the past seed was often treated with red lead as a deterrent to birds and mice, and although red lead does not achieve this object, seeds which have been so treated can be seen more easily. Better results will be obtained by using a dressing based on thiram, which is primarily a fungicide, but as it can cause irritation of the skin and eyes, care should be used in handling it. Details will be found in Bulletin No. 43.

(iii) *Soaking of seed*
The wetting and drying of seed before sowing adversely affects germination and seed should be sown dry except for those species which require stratification (see paragraph (i) above).

(g) Germination

(i) *The germination percentage* of a sample of seed indicates the proportion which will germinate under optimum conditions (see tables on p. 20 for details of various species).

(ii) *The germination energy* of a particular quantity of seed is the percentage which will germinate within a given time, e.g. 20 days at a given temperature (generally 75°F. or 24°C.).

(iii) *The plant per cent* is the average number of seedlings produced per hundred seeds sown.

(h) Methods of sowing

(i) There are five methods: broadcast; in bands; in drills; dibbling; in small containers.

(ii) *Broadcast*
(1) suitable for conifers and small hardwood seeds; (2) seed can be sown by hand, with a perforated tin (as a 'pepper pot'), or with a 'bounding board' (seed thrown against a board held vertically so that it richochets off the board); (3) after sowing, seeds should be covered with fine grit distributed with a sieve.

(iii) *In bands*
(1) miniature 'trenches' 15 cm (6 in.) wide and up to 5 cm (2 in.)

deep (according to the size of the seed to be sown) are formed 15 cm (6 in.) apart; (2) care should be taken to avoid sowing seeds too thickly and the following is a guide: chestnuts, acorns—4–5 cm ($1\frac{1}{2}$–2 in.) apart; ash, beech, sycamore—2·5 cm (1 in.) apart; (3) after sowing, the seeds are covered with soil.

(iv) *In drills*
(1) drills can be made with the back of a rake, by pressing a board on edge into the soil, or by the use of slatted boards or rollers (the slats having been fixed at the correct distances); (2) after sowing, the seed is covered with grit which passes a 2 mm ($\frac{1}{16}$ in.) or 3 mm ($\frac{1}{8}$ in.) mesh.

(v) *Dibbling*
(1) only used for sowing the larger seeds, such as acorns, chestnuts, etc.; (2) seeds dibbled at about 5 cm (2 in.) apart and sown at a depth approximately equal to the length or diameter of the seed.

(vi) *In small containers*
These are of two types: tubes and paper pots, which include Japanese Paper Pots or JPPs. In the first type, seedlings (referring to as 'tubelings') are raised in small plastic tubes which are planted in the forest without removing them from the tubes. They survive well on ploughed peats but suffer from frost lift in mineral soils. With their use the rate of planting has increased tremendously while it is possible to continue planting until late August. A full description of their production and use is given in Forestry Commission Bulletin No. 43. *Nursery Practice.*

(i) Time for sowing
The normal time for sowing seeds is from the middle of March to the middle of April. If planted too late the young seedlings will never make up lost time.

The following hardwoods can also be planted as soon as they have been collected (see Section 3(*c*) of this chapter for times):

ash	sweet chestnut
birch	sycamore
Norway maple	wych elm
oak	

Silver fir has also given good results when sown in January and February without being stratified (see Section 3(*f*) of this chapter).

(j) Protection of seed beds
(i) Seed beds (especially some conifers) need protection during their first summer against the sun in hot weather. (An hour of

very hot sun when seedlings are coming through may kill a very large proportion of them.)

(ii) Protection may also be needed against frost.

(iii) Shelter can be provided by: (1) Branches of foliage arranged to form an arch over the seed bed (conifer branches should be avoided, since the needles fall; broom is probably the best). (2) Wooden laths 2·5 cm (1 in.) wide nailed 1·25 cm (½ in.) apart to canvas strips or flexible wire which can be rolled up or unrolled as required. They are supported about 23–30 cm (9–12 in.) above seed bed by wires nailed to the tops of short stakes driven in on either side of the bed. (3) Wooden laths nailed to movable wooden frames. (4) Chestnut-pale fencing, 13 mm (½ in.) interval between pales. (5) A 'hedge' of birch brushwood 0·9 m (3 ft) high (held in position by two horizontal wires fixed to posts) erected parallel to one side of the seed bed, so as to cast a shadow over the bed during the sunniest period of the day.

(k) Weeding seed beds

(i) Seed beds must be kept free of weeds and this can be done either by using herbicides (chemical weedkillers) or by hand weeding.

(ii) Although hand weeding is expensive, it is effective and may have to be adopted when spraying cannot be undertaken. In such cases weeding should begin as early as possible and should continue at intervals of 3 to 4 weeks according to conditions.

(iii) Herbicides can be applied either before the seedlings appear (pre-emergence) or afterwards (post-emergence) and a summary of information relating to the spraying of seedbeds is given in the tables on pp. 18–19). However, full details relating to the use of sprays in nurseries and their application will be found in Forestry Commission Bulletin No. 43, *Nursery Practice*, on which these two tables are based.

(l) Seeds and germination

The two tables on p. 20 provide information relating to the seeds and germination of broadleaved species and conifers. The metricated figures have been produced by the kindness of the Forestry Commission.

(m) Seed orchards

In recent years seed orchards have been establshied which consist of trees on which cuttings from specially selected 'plus trees' are grafted. The seeds produced by these grafts are harvested in due course. Full details of these were given in Forestry Commission Bulletin No. 54, *Seed Orchards* (1975) but in 1987 this was out of print.

PRE-EMERGENCE SPRAYS

Type	Application rates		Precautions
	Imperial	*Metric*	
Vaporizing oil	60 gallons per acre. ½ gallon to 40 sq. yd.	700 litres per hectare. 1 litre to 14 sq. m.	Spray up to 4 days before seedlings emerge but not in a drought or hot weather. Advisable to test on small area before starting large operation.
Paraquat	2 pints in 40 gallons water per acre. ¼ pint in 5 gallons to 605 sq. yd.	2·5 litres in 400 litres water per hectare. ½ litre in 80 litres to 2000 sq. m.	Spray up to 4 days before emergence. Use rubber gloves and face shields; do not inhale vapour; keep locked up and away from children.
Simazine	4 lb (50% powder) in 60 gallons water per acre. ¼ lb in 3¾ gallons per sq. yd.	4·5 kg in 600 litres water per hectare. ½ kg in 66 litres per 1,100 sq. m.	Only use on hardwoods when seed covered by at least 25 mm (1 in.) soil. Do NOT use on conifer seed beds.

POST-EMERGENCE SPRAYS

Type	Application rates		Species if applicable	Precautions
	Imperial	Metric		
White spirit	25 gallons per acre. 1 pint to 25 sq. yd.	275 litres per hectare. $\frac{1}{4}$ litre to 9 sq. m.	Scots and Corsican pine Norway and Sitka spruce Western red cedar Lawson cypress	Do not use until 4 weeks after completion of germination. Do not spray hardwood beds with any oil or use vaporizing oils for post-emergence sprays.
White spirit	15 gallons per acre. 1 pint to 40 sq. yd.	165 litres per hectare. $\frac{1}{4}$ litre to 15 sq. m.	Lodgepole pine Larch Douglas fir Western hemlock Silver firs	
Simazine	2 lb (50% wettable powder) in 40 gallons water per acre.	2 kg in 400 litres water per hectare.	Can be used on 2nd-year seed beds of all species (EXCEPT ash, Japanese larch and *Picea omorika*) provided they are over 5 cm (2 in.) high.	Do not spray 1st-year conifer seed beds or undercut seedbeds.
	$\frac{1}{4}$ lb in 5 gallons water to 605 sq. yd.	$\frac{1}{4}$ kg in 50 litres water per 1250 sq. m.		
Paraquat	—	—	—	NEVER use as a post-emergence spray.

BROADLEAVED SEEDS

Species	Approx. no. of viable seeds		No. of m² required for 1 kg of seed	No. of yd² required for 1 lb of seed	Approx. no. of 1-year usable seedlings produced	
	per kg	*per lb*			*per kg*	*per lb*
Ash	9,000	4,000	22·50	12·20	4,500	2,040
Beech	2,800	1,270	4·75	2·60	1,500	680
Hornbeam	9,200	4,170	15·25	8·25	3,700	1,675
Oak	220	100	·75	·40	150	68
Sycamore	5,300	2,400	17·50	9·50	3,000	1,360
Sweet chestnut	180	82	1·00	·55	100	45

CONIFER SEEDS

Species	Approx. no. of viable seeds		No. of m² required for 1 kg of seed	No. of yd² required for 1 lb of seed	Approx. no. of 1-year usable seedlings produced	
	per kg	*per lb*			*per kg*	*per lb*
Cedar, Western red	500,000	226,500	210	114	175,000	79,275
Cypress, Lawson	230,000	104,190	155	84	115,000	52,100
Fir, Douglas	70,000	31,710	70	38	31,000	14,000
Fir, grand	20,000	9,060	25	14	10,000	4,350
Fir, noble	12,000	5,450	12	6	5,000	2,265
Fir, silver	2,000	900	2	1	1,000	450
Hemlock, Western	375,000	170,000	155	84	145,000	65,700
Larch, European	60,000	27,200	60	32	36,000	16,300
Larch, hybrid	50,000	22,650	50	27	27,000	12,230
Larch, Japanese	100,000	45,300	110	60	65,000	29,450
Pine, Corsican	55,000	25,000	90	49	36,000	16,300
Pine, lodgepole	270,000	122,300	225	122	121,000	54,800
Pine, Scots	140,000	63,420	115	62	63,000	28,540
Spruce, Norway	110,000	50,000	80	43	55,000	24,915
Spruce, Sitka	320,000	145,000	190	103	160,000	72,480

4. *Transplanting*

(a) Lifting seedlings

(i) Seedlings can be lifted either at the end of their first or second year, the latter being more usual.

(ii) Lifting may be carried out with a fork or spade, according to the soil, care being taken to avoid the roots being stripped.

(iii) On lifting, seedlings should be sorted and counted after any poor specimens have been thrown out. Those less than 4 cm (1½ in) should be discarded.
(iv) After lifting, seedlings must be protected from the sun and cold, drying winds.

(b) Lining out

(i) This consists of replanting the seedlings in rows which are normally 17·5, 20 or 22·5 cm (7, 8 or 9 in.); apart, with the plants at distances of 3·7, 5 or 7·5 cm (1½, 2 or 3 in.) in the rows.
(ii) The number of plants per 100 sq. m. and 100 sq. yd. at these spacings is given in the following table.
(iii) Season for lining out. Probably the best times are: south of the Border, late February and March; north of the Border, March and early April.
(iv) Lining out can be done by hand, with a plough or with a transplanting machine.
(v) When carried out by hand, the work is greatly facilitated by the use of transplanting boards which are usually 3 m (10 ft) or 2 m (6 ft 4 in.) in length.
(vi) The use of a light plough will eliminate much of the manual work and the Forestry Commission have evolved ploughs which are specially designed for lining out seedlings.
(vii) The employment of transplanting machines for lining out seedlings has been somewhat restricted, on account of certain operating problems and the fact that they work at very slow speeds.

(c) Undercutting

(i) This consists of cutting the long roots which develop while the young plant is growing in the nursery. It is particularly

NUMBER OF TRANSPLANTS PER 100 SQUARE METRES/YARDS

Per 100 sq. metres				*Per 100 sq. yards*			
Distance between plants in row (cm)	*Distance between rows*			*Distance between plants in row (in.)*	*Distance between rows*		
	17·5 cm	*20 cm*	*22·5 cm*		*7 in.*	*8 in.*	*9 in.*
3·75	15,250	13,300	11,850	1½	12,340	10,800	9,600
5	11,400	10,000	8,900	2	9,250	8,100	7,200
7·5	7,600	6,650	5,900	3	6,170	5,400	4,800

applicable to those species which develop a deep root system such as pines, Douglas fir and oak.

(ii) The object is to encourage the young plant to produce a compact root system and thereby avoid the need for transplanting.

(iii) Although originally practised with a sharp spade, undercutting is now generally done with a cutting bar mounted on a tractor which acts as a knife when it is drawn through the soil. The most effective depth is 8–10 cm (3–4 in.) for seedlings and 10–15 cm (4–6 in.) for transplants.

(iv) Undercutting produces the best results if done early in the growing season but it can be carried out more than once during the year. Seedlings which have been undercut are claimed to be as good as transplants. At the end of the second year such seedlings are known as 1–u–1,, i.e. 1 year–undercut–1 year.

(d) Grading seedlings

(i) Although in the past seedlings were normally graded before being lined out, the value of doing so is now rather doubtful, although in any case it is essential to discard all poor-quality seedlings.

(ii) If it is decided to grade them, they should be divided into two classes; (1) very good; (2) ordinary; and each class should be lined out separately.

5. *Propagation of Poplars*

The following is a brief account of one method by which poplars may be raised; for further information reference should be made to Forestry Commission Bulletin No. 43.

(*a*) Cuttings 23 cm (9 in.) long and 1 cm ($\frac{3}{8}$ in.) thick are taken from 1-year-old shoots.

(*b*) These are planted by pushing them vertically into really well-cultivated soil in rows 45 cm (18. in.) apart and 38 cm (15 in.) apart in the row, so that the top of the cutting is flush with the soil.

(*c*) This may be done at any time during the usual planting season, i.e. November–March.

(*d*) If more than one shoot is produced, these should be reduced to one when the new shoots are 23–30 cm (9–12 in.) long.

(*e*) At the end of the first year the plants should be 1·5–2·5 m (5–8 ft) tall and are known as 1-year rooted cuttings (C1 + 0). If transplanted for 1 year they are known as C1 + S1, the letter C indicating that they are cuttings and S that they have been stumped back.

(*f*) Those which are not big enough to be moved to the planting area at the end of the first year, should be lifted and transplanted at a distance of 0·6 m (2 ft) within the rows and 0·9 m (3 ft) between the rows. The roots should be pruned and the shoot cut back to within 2·5 cm (1 in.) of the root collar. The portion which is removed can be used for further cuttings.

6. *Fertility in Nurseries*

(a) General

(i) Fertilizers which are used in forest nurseries can be divided into two main groups: inorganic fertilizers and organic manures.

(ii) Inorganic fertilizers can be classified according to the nutrients which they supply, the most important being nitrogen (N), phosphorus (P), potassium (K) and magnesium (Mg).

(iii) Organic manures include hop waste and composts of various types.

(iv) In addition green crops are grown in some nurseries.

(b) Inorganic fertilizers

(i) Forestry Commission Bulletin No. 43 provides detailed information on the use of those fertilizers which were commonly used in forest nurseries in 1972, but improvements are continually being made in the production of fertilizers and proprietary names change in course of time.

(ii) Those who are concerned with the management of forest nurseries or who wish to become more fully acquainted with the subject should refer to Bulletin No. 43 and to the manufacturers of the fertilizers concerned.

(c) Organic manures

(i) The use of farmyard manure in forest nurseries has now been discontinued, largely on account of the weed seeds which it invariably contains.

(ii) Hop waste is now used as an organic manure and can be applied directly to the soil without composting.

(iii) The most successful compost would appear to be that made from bracken and hop waste which should be applied at a rate of 50 tonnes per hectare (20 tons per acre).

(d) Green cropping

(i) In the past it was common practice to rest a section of the nursery each year by growing a green crop on it; after this had been ploughed in the ground was left fallow for the rest of the season.

(ii) With the increased use of inorganic fertilizers the value of green manuring has diminished to a great extent, although in some nurseries a green crop is still grown primarily as a 'smother crop' to suppress weeds.

(iii) Three green crops are recommended by the Forestry Commission which should be sown at the following rates.

Oats	400–500 kg per hectare (3–4 cwt per acre)
Lupins	450 kg per hectare ($3\frac{1}{2}$ cwt per acre)
Rye grass	
For summer crop	
Perennial	33 kg per hectare (30 lb per acre)
For autumn crop	
Perennial	22 kg per hectare (20 lb per acre)
Italian	11 kg per hectare (10 lb per acre)

Mustard is no longer considered to be suitable as a green crop.

7. *Dunemann Seed Beds*

This method of raising seedlings, which was first practised in Germany about 1937 by Adolf Dunemann, consisted of sowing seeds on beds of conifer needles which are often spruce.

The beds, which are kept in place by wooden frames 30 cm (12 in.) deep and 2 m (6 ft 6 in.) wide, must be watered regularly and provided with adequate shade if they are to be successful. Shade is generally provided by lath screens or branches and in some cases by permanent canopies.

The advantages claimed for the Dunemann system are:

(*a*) Bigger and better seedlings.
(*b*) Little or no weed growth.
(*c*) No frost lift.
(*d*) Little or no adverse influence of the weather.

The seed beds should be about 30 cm (12 in.) deep; after sowing, the seeds should be covered with sifted beech mould or sharp sand to a depth of about 0·6 cm ($\frac{1}{4}$ in.).

8. *Labour Requirements*

The labour requirements for a nursery will vary from one man per 0·4 hectares (1 acre) in small nurseries to one man per 1·6 hectares (4 acres) for larger areas. The intensity of labour also depends on the extent to which mechanization has been adopted.

Nursery management has now become a very specialized business and those in charge must be fully trained in this work, if the nursery is to be a success.

9. *Packing Nursery Plants*

If plants are sent long distances by rail or road, the packing should not only protect them but also prevent them from becoming dry, and at the same time ensure that they do not 'heat' in the bundle.

Plants should be made up into bundles of convenient size for handling. After lifting, all soil should be removed and the plants tied in bundles of 50, 100, or 200, according to size.

Until the introduction of the polythene bag young plants were normally packed in straw or bracken and then made up into bales held together by sacking. Polythene bags now provide an easy and satisfactory method of packing.

Plants may be kept in these bags for 2–6 months according to the species, provided that the points which are set out in Bulletin No. 43 are observed. Information relating to the cold storage of seedlings and transplants will also be found in this Bulletin.

10. *Tools and Equipment for the Nursery*

The following list includes some of the tools and items of equipment which are needed in a forest nursery.

(*a*) *Hand tools*
Forks, spades, rakes, dutch hoes, mattocks, cuffing boards, secateurs, pruning knives.

(*b*) *Equipment*
Transplanting boards, hand sprayers, garden lines, buckets, watering cans, wheelbarrows.

(*c*) *Miscellaneous items*
Twine, canvas or hessian, trestles, labels, polythene bags, first-aid outfit.

(*d*) *Mechanical equipment*
In the larger nurseries mechanical equipment will greatly assist

production and should reduce costs. Such equipment would include:

Wheeled tractor, plough, cultivator, harrow, rotavator, roller, undercutting blade and tractor-mounted sprayer.

In smaller nurseries a garden type of mechanical cultivator with the usual accessories will be found to be extremely useful.

11. *Nursery Pests*

See Chapter XII.

CHAPTER III

Preparations for Planting

1. *Preparation of the Planting Area*

THE preparation of an area before it can be planted may be considered under four headings: namely, clearing, draining, fencing, and the destruction of rabbits, if there are any present.

(a) Clearing

(i) Clearing may be carried out by hand, by machine, or by a combination of both.
(ii) Hand clearing is very costly, especially if the area is overgrown derelict woodland.
(iii) Machines used in clearing include bulldozers, and specially designed land-clearance equipment.
(iv) Any saleable produce, such as cordwood, should be sold if possible, to reduce cost of clearing.
(v) The cost of clearing derelict woodland sites may be reduced by cutting lanes through the area in which young, fast-growing conifers are planted. (See also Chapter VII regarding this matter.)

(b) Draining

(i) An area may be drained by: preventing an excessive amount of water flowing onto the area; removing excess water from the area.
(ii) Intercepting channels cut across a slope above an area to be planted is an example of the first method.
(iii) A system of open drains should deal with the second case.
(iv) Forest drains should always be open (since pipes will become blocked by tree roots), and may be classified as: mains, leaders (secondaries), feeders (minors).
(v) Mains should be about 14–18 m (15–20 yd) apart, according to the soil and circumstances.
(vi) Feeders should be 45–75 cm (18–30 in.) in depth, depending on conditions.
(vii) Open drains should be about one-third wider at the top than at

the bottom, the smallest being a spade's width at the bottom, or about 8 in. (20 cm).

(viii) The importance of drainage cannot be over-emphasized especially on the heavier soils. Poor drainage retards tree growth and may prove fatal. It is one of the chief causes of windblow.

(c) Fencing

(i) When an area is being replanted the opportunity should be taken to attend to the boundary fences, if any adjoin the site. The work would include cutting and laying a live hedge, and making good any gaps. Post and rail or post and wire fences should be repaired and banks made up.

(ii) Where rabbits are present, a rabbit-proof fence should be erected, of which the following type will be found suitable:

Stakes or spiles. About 5 cm (2 in.) top diameter and 1·5 m (5 ft) long (driven in with a beetle) at 3 m (10 ft) apart.

Straining posts. About 15 cm (6 in.) top diameter and 1·8 m (6 ft) long, dug and rammed with a strut on either side, used at intervals of 90 m (100 yd) or at any point at which the fence materially changes direction.

Wire netting. 105 cm (42 in.) wide, 3·1 cm (1¼ in.) mesh, 1·25 mm (18) gauge. The bottom 15 cm (6 in.) either turned outwards at an angle of 60° and buried in a shallow trench or turned outwards at an angle of 90° and held down by turf or sods of earth placed on the bottom 15 cm (6 in.) at intervals of 30–45 cm (12–18 in.).

Top straining wire. 3·15 mm (8) gauge wire fixed 15 cm (6 in.) above the top of the netting. This may be replaced by barbed wire where there is a risk of trespass and damage.

Tying wire and staples. Between the stakes, the wire netting may be fastened to the top straining wire with light tying wire or wire netting fasteners.

The straining posts with 3·14 cm (1¼ in.) 10 gauge staples. If required 3·8 cm (1½ in.) 8 gauge staples may be used for the straining wire.

Note. The subject of fencing is also dealt with in Chapter XIX.

(d) Tree shelters

Plastic tubes for protecting trees, which are generally referred to as tree shelters, are described in Chapter XXI, Section 5.

2. *The Treatment and Planting of Sand Dunes*

(*a*) If sand dunes are to be planted, the work should proceed in three stages: firstly, checking the movement of the sand; secondly, fixation of the sand; and thirdly, the actual planting of trees.

(*b*) Briefly, sand may be checked by encouraging the formation of artificial dunes, which may be brought about by erecting two lines of wattle hurdles; the first about 6 m (20 ft) in front of the second. As the sand reaches the top of the hurdles a fresh line is erected above them, and so on, until the required height is reached.

(*c*) Fixation of the surface is brought about by establishing surface vegetation on the dune. Suitable plants are marram grass, creeping willow, everlasting pea, etc. The Forestry Commission has successfully fixed the surface of dunes at Culbin, Morayshire, by 'thatching' sandhills with birch branches.

(*d*) When fixation has been achieved the area may be planted, and the following species are most suitable

Corsican pine, Scots pine, lodgepole pine (*P. contorta*), maritime pine (*P. pinaster*), Monterey pine (*P. radiata*).

The two last-named species are only suitable for the milder parts of the country.

CHAPTER IV

Planting and Establishment

1. *The Age for Planting*

(*a*) On the whole young trees are better than older ones, since they withstand the shock of transplanting better than older trees, whose root system is more developed.

(*b*) Trees, however, should not be too small, or: (i) they may be overwhelmed by weed growth; (ii) weeding costs will be high, owing to the time taken to find them; (iii) losses may be heavy during weeding.

(*c*) Young trees are cheaper to buy, cheaper to raise, and cheaper to plant (more trees planted per man per day).

(*d*) The following list gives the ages at which trees are commonly planted. Two points should be noted: firstly that age in itself is no criterion of the suitability of a tree for planting and secondly that owing to improved nursery technique during recent years, 2-year-old trees are sometimes as big as 3-year-olds.

A. Broadleaves

Ash	2 year 1 year transplants.
Beech	2 year 1 year transplants.
Birch	1 year transplants, or 2 year 1 year transplants.
Chestnut, sweet	2 year seedlings, or 2 year 1 year transplants.
Oak	1 year seedlings (if well grown), 2 year seedlings, or 1 year 1 year transplants.
Poplar	1 year, 2 year or 3 year rooted cuttings.
Sycamore	2 year 1 year transplants.
Willow, cricket bat	Rooted or unrooted setts, 10 to 12 ft long.
Other hardwoods	2 year 1 year transplants, or 2 year 2 year transplants.

B. Conifers

(The following trees are transplants)

Cedar, western red	2 year 1 year, or 2 year 2 year.
Cypress, Lawson	2 year 1 year, or 2 year 2 year.

Cypress, Nootka	2 year 1 year.
Fir, Douglas	1 year 1 year, or 2 year 1 year.
Fir, European silver	2 year 2 year.
Fir, grand	2 year 1 year, or 2 year 2 year.
Fir, noble	2 year 1 year, or 2 year 2 year.
Hemlock, western	2 year 1 year, or 2 year 2 year.
Larch	1 year 1 year, or 2 year 1 year.
Pine, Austrian	1 year 1 year, or 1 year 1 year 1 year.
Pine, Corsican	1 year 1 year, or 1 year 1 year 1 year.
Pine, lodgepole	2 year 1 year.
Pine, Monterey	1 year 1 year.
Pine, Scots	1 year 1 year, or 2 year 1 year.
Redwood	2 year 2 year.
Spruce, Norway	2 year 1 year, or 2 year 2 year.
Spruce, Serbian	2 year 2 year.
Spruce, Sitka	1 year 1 year, or 2 year 1 year.
Wellingtonia	2 year 2 year.

2. *The Time for Planting*

(*1*) During the period of winter rest, when the trees have 'hardened off', i.e. November–March (inclusive).

(*b*) It is sometimes possible to start planting towards the end of October, and to continue it until the middle of April if the weather, season, and locality permit.

(*c*) In January and February the weather is often too hard for planting and this should be borne in mind when drawing up a planting programme.

(*d*) Planting before Christmas:

(i) Trees are well established, and should start growth in the spring with the least set-back;

(ii) *but*, they are more liable to suffer from frost, snow, and wind during the winter.

(*e*) Planting after Christmas:

(i) trees escape most of the rigours of the winter in their new positions;

(ii) *but*, if there is a spell of dry weather just after planting, losses may be heavy.

(*f*) Although no definite rules can be laid down as to the best months for planting, the following views are frequently held:

plant before Christmas: Broadleaved trees and larch.
plant after Christmas: Conifers (except larch).
plant as late as possible, i.e. March or April: Corsican pine.

(*g*) However, with a large planting programme, a shortage of labour, and risk of hard weather, planting should start as early as possible, i.e. as soon as conditions permit.

(*h*) Never plant: (i) in frost; (ii) in a cold wind; (iii) in waterlogged ground.

(*i*) With the introduction of tubed seedlings and container plants the planting season can be extended over a much longer period. The Forestry Commission have found that when tubed seedlings as used in peat, planting can be continued from April to August.

3. *The Number of Trees per Unit of Area*

(*a*) The number of trees per hectare or per acre, i.e. the distance between the planted trees, depends on several factors including the following:

(i) The species used and its rate of growth.
(ii) The persistence of side branches.
(iii) The soil and site conditions, e.g. wider planting can be undertaken on the better sites in the higher rainfall areas.
(iv) General economic conditions: low labour costs tend to favour close planting; high labour costs favour wide planting.

(*b*) *Planting distances*

(i) At the beginning of this century it was usual to plant most species of conifers at a distance of 1 m (3 ft) but since then planting distances have gradually increased.
(ii) A distance of 2 × 2 m (6 ft in. × 6 ft 6 in.) is now commonly used for conifers and under favourable conditions this can be increased to 2·1 m (7 ft). The implications of extending this to 2–4 m (8 ft) in the case of the fastest-growing conifers, are also being examined.
(iii) Owing to the fact that most hardwoods other than poplars do not begin their initial height growth as quickly as conifers, they

PLANTING DISTANCES

Species	*Spacing (metres)*	*No. of trees per hectare*	*Spacing (feet)*	*No. of trees per acre*
Ash	1·35	5,490	4½	2,150
Beech	1·20	6,945	4	2,722
Oak	1·2 × 0·9	9,260	4 × 3	3,630
Sycamore	1·35	5,490	4½	2,150
Willow	9·0	123	29½	50
Conifers	2·0	2,500	6½	1,030
	2·1	2,268	7	890

Information relating to poplars is given in Section 11 of this chapter.

are planted at closer intervals so as to encourage upward rather than side growth in the early years.

(c) Square planting

(i) By this method trees are planted in rows, the distance between each tree in a row and the distance between the rows being the same. If the position of each tree is joined by an imaginary line, squares will be formed thus:

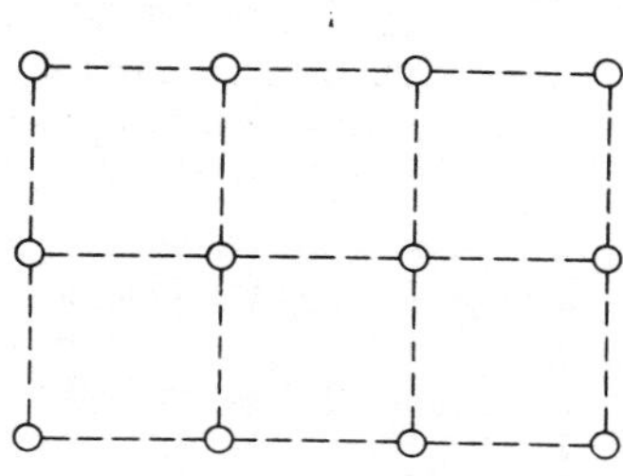

TREES PER HECTARE/ACRE—SQUARE PLANTING

Distance apart (metres)	*No. of trees per hectare*	*Distance apart (feet)*	*No. of trees per acre*	*Distance apart (metres)*	*No. of trees per hectare*	*Distance apart (feet)*	*No. of trees per acre*
1·2	6,944	4	2,722	2·4	1,736	8	680
1·4	5,102	4½	2,151	2·7	1,371	9	537
1·5	4,444	5	1,742	3·0	1,111	10	435
1·6	3,906	5½	1,440	3·6	771	12	302
1·8	3,086	6	1,210	4·2	567	14	222
2·0	2,500	6½	1,031	4·8	434	16	170
2·1	2,267	7	889	5·5	330	18	134
2·3	1,890	7½	775	6·1	268	20	109

(ii) To calculate the number of trees per hectare for planting on the square reduce the area to be planted to square metres. Divide the result by the square of the planting distance and the result will give the number of trees per hectare.

Example: Planting distance 2m

Square metres in one hectare = 10,000

Then $\dfrac{10{,}000}{2 \times 2} = 2{,}500$ trees per hectare.

(iii) A similar calculation is used in the case of feet and acres.

Example: Planting distance 6 ft

Square feet in one acre = 43,560

Then $\dfrac{43{,}560}{6 \times 6} = 1{,}210$ trees per acre.

(d) Rectangular or line planting

(i) In this system trees are planted at equal distances in the line, but a different distance between the lines is adopted so that trees are planted in rectangles, thus:

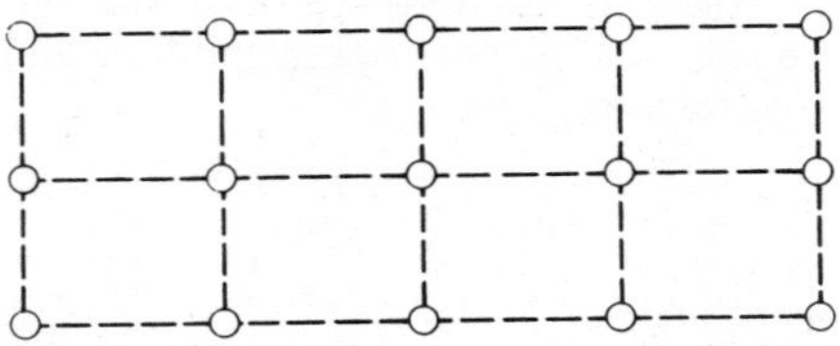

(ii) To calculate the number of trees per hectare, the number of square metres in a hectare (10,000) is divided by the distance in the lines multiplied by the distance between the lines.
Example: Planting distance 1·5 m by 2 m

$$\text{Trees per hectare} = \frac{10{,}000}{1{\cdot}5 \times 2} = 3{,}333$$

(iii) For Imperial measure the calculation would be as follows:
Example: Planting distance 5 ft by 6 ft

$$\text{Trees per acre} = \frac{43{,}560}{5 \times 6} = 1{,}452$$

TREES PER HECTARE/ACRE—RECTANGULAR PLANTING

Distance between plants in the row (metres)	*Distance between rows (metres)*	*No. of trees per hectare*	*Distance between plants in the row (feet)*	*Distance between rows (feet)*	*No. of trees per acre*
1·2	1·5	5,555	4	5	2,178
1·2	1·8	4,630	4	6	1,815
1·2	2·1	3,968	4	7	1,555
1·5	1·8	3,703	5	6	1,452
1·5	2·1	3,175	5	7	1,244
1·8	2·1	2,645	6	7	1,037

(e) Triangular planting

(i) In triangular planting, or ‘planting on the triangle’, each tree is equidistant from its neighbour, and a series of equilateral triangles are formed if an imaginary line is drawn between each tree, thus:

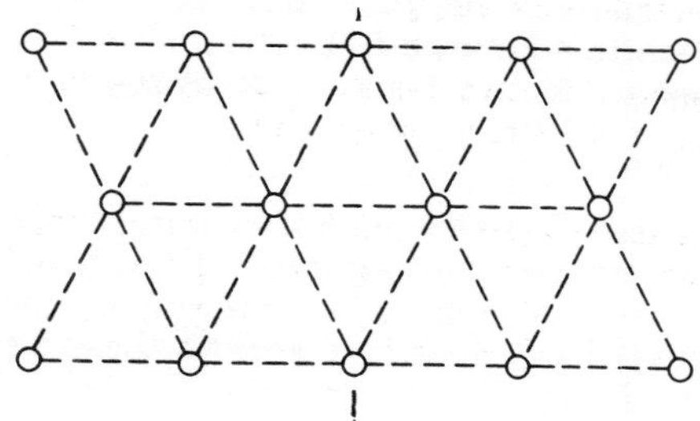

TREES PER HECTARE/ACRE—TRIANGULAR PLANTING

Distance between trees (metres)	*Distance between rows (metres)*	*No. of trees per hectare*	*Distance between trees (ft in.)*	*Distance between rows to the nearest inch (ft in.)*	*No. of trees per acre*
0·91	0·78	14,085	3 0	2 7	5,590
1·06	0·91	9,625	3 6	3 0	4,106
1·22	1·06	7,803	4 0	3 6	3,144
1·37	1·22	6,416	4 6	4 0	2,484
1·52	1·32	5,020	5 0	4 4	2,012
1·67	1·44	4,124	5 6	4 9	1,663
1·83	1·60	3,447	6 0	5 3	1,398
1·98	1·70	2,946	6 6	5 7	1,191
2·13	1·83	2,566	7 0	6 0	1,026
2·43	2·10	1,957	8 0	6 11	785
2·74	2·36	1,540	9 0	7 9	620
3·04	2·64	1,255	10 0	8 8	502
4·57	3·96	550	15 0	13 0	223
6·09	5·25	313	20 0	17 4	125
7·62	6·60	198	25 0	21 8	80
9·14	7·92	138	30 0	26 0	55

(ii) To calculate the number of trees per hectare, the number of square metres in a hectare (10,000) is divided by the square of the planting distance (i.e. the side of one triangle squared) and the result multiplied by a constant of 1·155.

Example: Planting distance 2m

Square metres in 1 hectare = 10,000

Then $\frac{10,000}{2 \times 2} \times 1{\cdot}155 = 2,888$ trees per hectare.

(iii) For Imperial measure the calculation would be as follows:
Example: Planting distance 5 ft
Square feet in 1 acre = 43,560

$$\text{Then } \frac{43{,}560}{5 \times 5} \times 1{\cdot}555 = 2{,}012 \text{ trees per acre.}$$

(iv) It will be noticed that this method requires more trees per unit of area than square planting and that although the distance between the trees is equal to the planting distance, the shortest distance between the lines is less. Both these figures are given in the table on page 35.

(f) Quincunx planting

(i) This method is a modification of square planting, an additional tree being planted in the centre of every four trees planted on the square. If the positions of the trees originally planted on the square are joined by a solid line, and those of the additional trees by a broken line, the following diagram is provided:

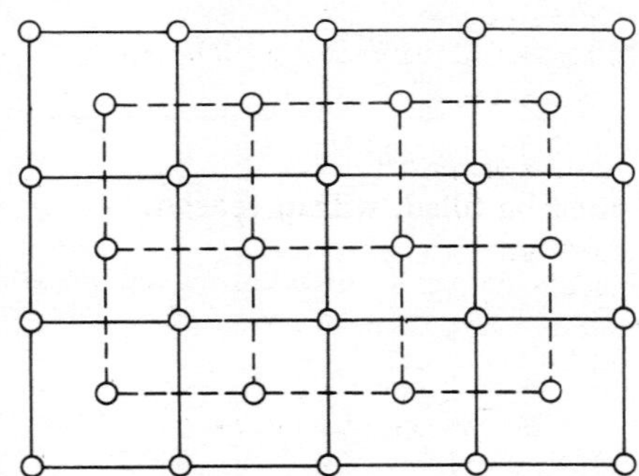

(ii) To calculate the number of trees per unit of area, follow the procedure as described for planting on the square and multilply the results by two.
Example: Planting distance 2 m
No. of trees required for square planting = 2,500
No. of trees required for quincunx method = 2,500 × 2
= 5,000

4. *Close and Wide Planting*

The advantages and disadvantages of planting trees close together or wide apart are outlined below.

(a) Advantages of close planting

(i) A large number of thinnings can be removed, and with some species, e.g. larch, these can provide a useful financial return early in the rotation.

(ii) There is less need to fill vacancies, i.e. to beat up the area.
(iii) Natural pruning is more effective.
(iv) There are more poles from which to choose when thinning.

(b) Disadvantages of close planting

(i) Since more trees are planted per acre, the planting costs are higher.
(ii) Failure to thin at the right time results in greater damage than in the case of wider planting.
(iii) There is greater risk of disease in the case of some species, such as European larch, especially if the area if under-thinned.
(iv) If the early thinnings from the species which have been planted are unremunerative, the cost of removing them may be heavy.

(c) Advantages of wide planting

(i) Cheaper: less plants are required.
(ii) Thinning costs are reduced.
(iii) Less damage is caused if thinning is delayed.
(iv) Risk of disease is reduced.

(d) Disadvantages of wide planting

(i) All vacancies must be filled, within reason.
(ii) Less natural pruning.
(iii) Thicket stage takes longer to develop except possibly with the fastest-growing species on favourable sites.

5. *Choice of Species*

(a) Considerations

The considerations which govern the choice of a particular species will include the following:

(i) Soil.
(ii) Climate.
(iii) Silvicultural requirements of species.
(iv) Wishes of the owner.
(v) Special considerations other than those of a silvicultural nature, e.g. shelter or amenity.

(b) Surface vegetation as a guide to soil and species

The surface vegetation growing on a site is often a useful guide as to the soil and the species which may be expected to grow well on that soil. It cannot be over-emphasized, however, that the presence or absence of these plants must not be taken as conclusive evidence, but should be treated only as signs which must be interpreted in the light of other evidence.

(c) Soil indicators

(i) Damp, wet soils: rushes, sedges, iris, kingcup, cotton grass.
(ii) Heavy, moist clays: ferns, horsetails (*Equisetum* spp.).
(iii) Limestone and chalk: dog's mercury, wood sanicle, rock rose, wild strawberry, wild thyme, garlic, yew, wayfaring tree, spindle, juniper, wild clematis or old man's beard.
(iv) Fertile soils: nettle, foxglove, bramble, bracken, rosebay willow-herb, bluebell (*Scilla non-scripta*).
(v) Poor soils: ling (*Calluna vulgaris*), cross-leaved heather (*Erica tetralix*) (this may also indicate a need for drainage), bell heather (*Erica cinerea*), bilberry (*Vaccinium myrtillus*) mat grass (*Nardus stricta*).

(d) Species indicators

(i) *Hardwoods*

Ash.
Dog's mercury, garlic, wood sanicle.
Beech.
Dog's mercury, ferns, spurge laurel, wood sanicle.
Oak.
Bramble, bluebell (wild hyacinth), ferns, primrose.

(ii) *Conifers*

Douglas fir.
Bracken, bramble, ferns, grass.
European larch.
Bracken, ferns, grass.
Japanese larch.
Bracken, heather (*Calluna vulgaris*), ferns, grass.
Scots pine and lodgepole pine.
Heather (*Calluna vulgaris*)
Norway spruce and Sitka spruce.
Rushes, purple moor grass (*Molinia caerulea*), other grasses.
Corsican pine.
Heather (*Calluna vulgaris*) in southern districts.

(e) For requirements of individual species, see Chapter I.

6. *Methods of Planting*

(a) General

(i) The method adopted will depend on:
(*a*) the soil; (*b*) the size of the growing trees to be planted; (*c*) the site: a steep hillside may require a different treatment to a level site.

(ii) *Heeling in*

As soon as the trees arrive on the planting area they should be heeled in or sheughed in. If tied in bundles, these *must* be untied, or heating will occur, and the plants put in a vertical position along the edge of the open trench. The trench is then partly filled in so as to cover the roots. Young trees may remain heeled in for several weeks without damage, providing that growth does not commence during this period.

(iii) *Planting depth*

Trees should be planted at the same depth as they were growing in the nursery before lifting. A mark known as the 'root-collar' can usually be seen, and indicates soil level.

(iv) *Planting rate*

The number of trees a man can plant in a day depends on: (*a*) soil: light or heavy; (*b*) cleanliness of site at time of planting; (*c*) weather conditions during planting; (*d*) size of the plants; (*e*) method of planting adopted; (*f*) experience, age, and energy of labour employed; (*g*) supervision and organization of labour.

(v) *Supervision of planting personnel*

Much depends on the proper organization of the planting gang. Where several men are actually engaged in planting, arrangements should be made to keep them supplied with plants, so that they do not waste time collecting these from a distant point. In the larger areas trees should be heeled in at several different points, so as to save walking time.

(vi) *Treading*

It is most important that trees are planted firmly in the first place, and that they are systematically firmed by treading at least once during the first few weeks after planting. If heavy frost occurs, or if the newly planted trees are blown about after planting, treading will have to be carried out more frequently. In doing so the heel should be used, care being taken to avoid scraping the bark of the young tree.

(vii) Trees must be planted in an upright position, and when planting or treading care must be taken to avoid them being forced out of the vertical.

(viii) *Screefing*

On planting sites which are covered by a thick mat of grass this should be removed before planting, by 'screefing'. This can be done most easily with a mattock and a patch of about 45 cm (18 in.) in diameter should be cleared.

(b) Notch planting

Basically this consists of making a slit or notch in the ground and inserting a tree into the cut. There are several variations, depending on the tool used, and these are referred to below.

(i) *With a planting spade*

(1) Slits are made with a straight-backed planting spade, in the form of an 'L', 'T', 'V', or, less frequently, an 'H', one of the corners formed by an intersection being levered up and the plant inserted in the slit.

(2) The tree is inserted rather too deeply, and then pulled upwards slightly to straighten the roots. If this is done too violently, stripping of the roots may occur.

(ii) *With a mattock*

It is important to use a mattock the head of which has both an axe face and a pick face. These faces are set at right-angles to each other, which enables an 'L' notch to be made by turning the haft through 180°. In the south-west of England a mattock is also known as a 'two bill'.

(iii) *With a 'Schlich' or 'Mansfield' spade*

(1) The Schlich spade is roughly the shape of a shield, the bottom forming a point.

(2) At about half the distance from the top of the space (where the socket for the handle joins the face) the thickness of the face is slightly increased for about 5 cm (2 in.). This has the effect of forming a ridge or bulge across the face of the spade when seen from the front.

(3) The Mansfield spade is somewhat similar, but the end of the spade face is straight instead of pointed, as in the case of the Schlich spade.

(4) The object of the bulge is to form a recess which gives additional root space.

(5) In use, the spade is driven into the earth and worked to and from the planter, so as to make a wide notch. The tree is dropped in, and the notch is closed by again inserting the spade a little behind the first notch and forcing the adjoining soil towards the tree to close the first slit. If necessary, the second slit is closed by another insertion, or by treading with the foot.

(iv) *With a dibble or planting arrow*

(1) This method is suitable only for small plants, and on very light soils or sands. It is now seldom used.

(2) A notch or hole is made with the dibble or arrow, and the plant put in.

(3) The arrow is a small short-handled tool, about 18 in. long, with heart-shaped iron head. It is a single-handed tool.

Dibbling is not strictly notch planting, but is sufficiently related to it to be included.

(c) Pit planting

(i) In pit planting (or 'pitting') the young tree is placed in a hole, as opposed to a slit in the case of notch planting.

(ii) Holes are generally dug with one of the following tools: (1) garden spade; (2) mattock; (3) semi-circular spade.

(iii) Pit planting is generally confined to the heavier soils, on which other methods are not suitable. It is, however, the slowest, and therefore the most expensive, method, and, although less beating up should be necessary, treading is even more important than in other methods.

(iv) Pitting with a spade or mattock.

(1) Holes about 25 cm (10 in.) deep and square are dug.

(2) When planting, care is taken to ensure the roots are spread out.

(3) On heavy clay soils, holes may be dug about four weeks before planting, so that weathering of the soil can take place. If opened too long before planting, the holes may fill with water.

(d) Turf and mound planting

These two methods have been devised for planting peat and low lying areas in conjunction with a system of drainage.

(i) *Turf planting*

(1) Turfs approximately 30 cm (12 in.) square and 10–15 cm (4–6 in.) thick are cut out and placed upside-down where each tree is to be planted.

(2) Most of the turfs can be obtained from the drains which should be cut, usually at about 7·5 cm (25 ft) apart.

(3) In planting, a notch is cut in the side of the turf on the side facing the prevailing wind and the tree inserted so that its roots lie between the bottom of the inverted turf and the ground.

(4) An alternative method is to cut thicker turfs, about 23 cm (9 in.) thick, and plant the trees *in* them.

(5) Conditions will usually be improved by an application of ground mineral phosphate (GMP) at the rate of 42 g (1½ oz) per tree.

(ii) *Mound planting*

(1) This method is used where trees are to be planted at a higher level than in turf planting.

(2) Instead of turfs being cut, loose peat and soil are heaped up in a mound and the tree planted in it. Before planting the mound should be firmed as much as possible.

Note. When afforesting large areas of moorland the Forestry Commission first plough the site with specially designed ploughs. These cut and invert a large furrow so as to form a ridge and on this the young trees are planted. On the poorer types of peat, tubed seedlings can be planted successfully provided that a 'step' or shelf is cut in the side of the ridge, and this can be done by fitting an attachment to the mould board known as a sock.

(e) Mechanized planting
Planting machines have never been used to any great extent in this country although several types, usually based on the design of an agricultural cabbage-planting machine, have been tried from time to time.

7. *Planting Rates*

The number of trees which a man can plant in a day depends on the factors set out in Section 6(*a*)(iv), and since these factors are themselves variable, the figures given below can only be regarded as a guide.

Notch planting	.. ..	500–700 per man per day
Mattock	.. ..	500–700 „ „ „ „
Schlich spade	.. ..	500 „ „ „ „
Dibble or spear	.. ..	800–900 „ „ „ „
Pit planting	.. ..	200–300 „ „ „ „
Tubed seedlings	.. ..	4000 „ „ „ „

8. *Direct Seeding*

(*a*) Although for several hundred years the planting of acorns was common practice, at the present time direct seeding is usually confined to Scots and Corsican pine.

(*b*) Seeds of these two species should be sown with a matrix of sawdust to assist in the even distribution of the seed which is sown by hand.

(*c*) The following sowing rates have produced satisfactory results but these may have to be increased where conditions are less receptive:

Scots pine: 1·6 kg of seed per hectare (1½ lb per acre)
Corsican pine: 1·1 kg of seed per hectare (1 lb per acre)

(*d*) Before sowing the ground should be harrowed or otherwise cultivated and, when possible, rolled after sowing is completed.

9. *Beating Up*

(*a*) Beating up or beeting is the work of replacing any trees which have died, and should be carried out during the first year after planting.

(*b*) It is necessary only if more than 15% of the trees originally planted die, but this will depend on the planting distance and whether deaths occur in groups or patches.

(*c*) It is adivsable to use a good sample tree for this purpose, which will hold its own with trees planted a year earlier. Special care should be taken in planting these replacements, so as to give them every assistance.

(*d*) In certain cases beating up may have to be carried out in the second year after planting, but this should be avoided if possible.

10. *Weeding*

(*a*) In forestry the term 'weeding' refers to the control of vegetation which may compete with young trees. It is generally necessary during the first 2 years after planting, although in some cases it may be extended to 3.

(*b*) 'Weeds' comprise those plants which are found growing in newly planted or regenerated areas and which interfere with the development of the young trees. Examples are grass, bracken, gorse, rhododendron and heather.

(*c*) The amount of weeding necessary depends on:

(i) Soil. The more fertile, the heavier the weed growth.
(ii) Season. Warm, wet weather encourages weed growth.
(iii) Condition of the site when planted.
(iv) Size of trees when planted. The smaller the tree, the more weeding is generally necessary.
(v) Shade-bearing characteristic of the species. Shade-bearing species can withstand certain types of heavy weed growth better than light-demanders.

(*d*) A certain amount of controlled weed growth is beneficial to some species, since it protects the young trees from drought, sun scorch and drying winds.

(*e*) There are three basic methods of weeding:

(i) By hand.
(ii) By machine.
(iii) With herbicides.

(*f*) Hand weeding is usually carried out with a short-handled grass hook or a long-handled brushing hook, known in some districts as a staff hook.

(*g*) For mechanical weeding three types of machine can be used:

(i) Brush cutters or clearing saws operated by one man and carried by means of a harness.
(ii) Motor scythes, usually mounted on two wheels, the cutting mechanism generally being a reciprocating knife or rotating blades, the operator walking behind the machine.
(iii) Tractor-mounted machines operating flails or tractor-towed rollers or breaking bars.

(*h*) The use of herbicides has increased very considereably in recent years and they are now widely used, especially where large areas have to be weeded.

(i) Some herbicides can be obtained in granular form but the majority are applied as a liquid. Spraying equipment is of three kinds:
   medium-volume sprayers (MV)
   low-volume sprayers (LV)
   ultra low-volume sprayers (ULV)
(ii) The lower the volume, the smaller the quantity of liquid is required, the ULV sprayer only needing about 2·5% of the amount necessary for the MV sprayer per hectare or acre, in order to produce the same effect.
(iii) Many points have to be considered when using herbicides, and detailed information on their composition and application, together with the necessary equipment and safety precautions will be found in the following publications:
Forestry Commission
   Handbook No. 2, *Trees and Weeds* (1987)
   Booklet No. 51, *The Use of Herbicides in the Forest* (1986)
Forestry Safety Council
   Guide No. 2, *ULV Herbicide Spraying*
   3, *Application of Herbicide by Knapsack Spraying*
   4, *Application of Granular Herbicides*
   7, *Planting*

11. *Poplar Planting*

(*a*) For some 50 years the cultivation of poplar in this country was directed towards the production of match-making and, later, chip baskets. To achieve the quality required by the manufacturers a planting distance of up to 8 m (26 ft) was necessary and grants by the Forestry Commission for planting poplars were conditional upon wide spacing.

(*b*) In January 1970 Messrs Bryant & May announced that they were discontinuing the manufacture of chip baskets and wood veneer packaging and in October the Commission stated that for the production of pulpwood a spacing of less than 7·3 cm (24 ft) might be approved.

(*c*) In the following years Messrs Bryant & May advised growers that due to falling sales it was unlikely that they would buy timber resulting from planting carried out in or after 1972. Later in 1978 they announced that they were not seeking further supplies of home-grown timber.

(*d*) In 1958 the Forestry Commission began experiments on the close planting of poplars and these showed that an espacement of 2–1 m (7 ft) produced relatively clean poles with little taper and a forest floor clear of competing growth. These poles appeared to be ideal for pulpwood.

(*e*) Further trials were carried out by coppicing poplar 7 years after planting and the best results were obtained from a spacing of 2·1 m (7 ft). It was estimated that on a 15-year rotation one to three poles would be produced from each stool, resulting in a yield equal to 1½ times that produced by an uncoppiced area. Details of these experiments will be found in 'Poplar growing at close spacing' by R. C. Stern, *Quarterly Journal of Forestry*, vol. LXVI, 1972.

(*f*) The cultivation of poplars in association with farm crops has been described by A. Beaton in 'Poplars and agroforestry', *Quarterly Journal of Forestry*, vol. LXXXI, 1987.

CHAPTER V

The Tending of Woods and Plantations

1. *Cleaning*

(*a*) After planting, beating up, and weeding a plantation, the next operation to be carried out will be cleaning, and this will be necessary after the young crop has entered the 'thicket stage', i.e. when the side branches of adjoining trees have become interlaced. Normally this can be expected to occur from 8 to 10 years after planting.

(*b*) Cleaning consist of cutting out all undesirable growth on the site, and such growth can be classified as follows:

(i) Tree weeds, i.e. undesirable tree species other than those planted or purposely regenerated.

Examples are: blackthorn, hawthorn, sallow, birch, and stool shoots from felled hardwoods or coppice.

(ii) Wolf trees, i.e. those trees of the planted or regnerated crop which have grown more quickly than their associates, and have developed an overlarge crown, defective shape, and general coarseness.

(iii) Climbing weeds, e.g. honeysuckle, wild clematis or traveller's joy, and ivy. Bramble, although not a climber, may, for practical purposes, be included in this class.

(*c*) Although described in these notes as two operations, cleaning and brashing (see below) are normally carried out at the same time, and, in fact, it is impossible to clean without at the same time brashing.

(*d*) If cleaning and brashing are delayed as long as is reasonably possible, compound interest on the cost will be accordingly reduced.

2. *Brashing*

(*a*) Brashing, or brushing up, consists of removing the side branches of young trees up to 'head height', or as high as a man can comfortably reach, which may be taken as about 2 m (6 ft).

(*b*) Brashing is carried out after the thicket stage has been reached and before thinning is attempted. The age when brashing should be put in hand depends on the rate of growth, but it usually 10–12 years after planting.

(*c*) Apart from the cost of doing so, brash is a source of humus and should not be removed unless there is a risk of fire or in order to facilitate the removal of thinnings.

(*d*) Some of the results of brashing are:

(i) The crop can be inspected and marked for thinning without difficulty.
(ii) The timber is improved, since the removal of the lower branches reduces the extent of any knots.
(iii) If the brash is removed, the risk of fire is reduced.

(*e*) Although brashing is frequently carried out by hand with a pruning saw or chisel-edged tool, increasing use is being made of light-weight chainsaws. There is, however, considerable risk of damage to the tree unless action is taken to protect it, and this can be done by fixing a strip of wood or aluminium to the sides of the saw guide bar. When a chainsaw is used it is most important that the operator wears a safety helmet, visor, gloves and ear protectors. This subject has been covered in an article entitled 'Chainsaw brashing', by R. G. M. Lamb, *Timber Grower*, No. 51, February 1974.

(*f*) Whatever tools are used the branches should be removed by cutting as close to the stem as possible.

(*g*) Dead branches of larch may be removed with a stick, but if this method is used on anything but the smallest, the end of the branch may be pulled out of the tree, leaving an empty socket up to 1·2 cm (½ cm) deep.

(*h*) On some estates the space between every fourth or fifth row of trees was sometimes cleared of brash so as to facilitate the removal of thinnings, the operation being known as 'drifting'. However with the introduction of modern methods of extraction, such as the use of skylines and forwarders, as well as the greatly increased cost of labour, the drifting of brash can seldom be regarded as economic or necessary.

(*i*) In the past it has been common practice to brash virtually every tree in a plantation but as this is an expensive and time-consuming operation, it is prudent to take some action to reduce the cost of which the following are examples:

(i) By making the maximum use of chain saws instead of hand tools.
(ii) By reducing the number of trees to be brashed. At the least, any trees which would be removed during the first thinning such as small suppressed trees and those which are dead, dying, badly damaged or mis-shapen should be omitted.
(iii) By leaving the plantation unbrashed except for the provision of inspection racks.

(*f*) However, totally unbrashed plantations have the following disadvantages:

(i) They form a greatly increased fire hazard.
(ii) If the crop is to be grown for 'saw timber', the presence of a number of large knots in the best length may well detract from the value of the timber although this is a matter on which some authorities disagree.
(iii) From a shooting point of view unbrashed plantations are impossible to drive unless a large number of racks are cut.

(*k*) Attention is drawn to Forestry Safety Council Guide No. 9, *Brashing and Pruning with Handsaw.*

3. *Thinning*

(a) General

(i) Except in the case of stands which are grown on short rotations solely for pulpwood, thinning is an operation which should always be carried out.
(ii) When planted at 2 m apart there are 2,500 trees per hectare but this number will be greatly reduced as the crop increases in age.

(b) The objects in thinning

The normal practice is to remove some of the trees (that is to say a proportion of the standing volume) at intervals over a period of years so as to achieve the following:

(i) To reduce the number of trees growing on a site so that those remaining have more growing space and less root competition, thus assisting in their subsequent development.
(ii) to obtain an intermediate financial return between planting and maturity.
(iii) To reduce the risk of disease and pests, by removing diseased, dying, and dead trees, and to remove other trees which are harmful to the crop, e.g. whips and wolf trees.
(iv) To ensure a reasonably equal distribution of final crop trees throughout the area.

(c) The thinning regime

The thinning or cutting regime which is applied to a stand is made up of three components: the thinning intensity, the thinning cycle and the thinning type.

(i) The thinning intensity is the frequency at which thinnings are carried out, or the rate at which the volume which is attributable to the thinnings is removed.
(ii) The thinning cycle is the number of years between each consecutive thinning.
(iii) The thinning type relates to the category of the trees which are removed during a thinning operation and is based on the relative dominance of the trees within the stand.

(d) Thinning intensity

(i) The higher the intensity, i.e. the heavier the thinnings, the more trees will be removed and the greater will be the space for those which remain.

(ii) Up to a point the more space which is provided for the trees which are left, the greater will be their response. However, if too much space is given them, i.e. the stand is over-thinned, the volume production will fall.

(iii) The maximum thinning intensity which can be acheived without loss in volume production is known as the *marginal thinning intensity*. Research by the Forestry Commission has established that the marginal intensity is approximately equal to an annual removal of 70% of the yield class. The marginal thinning intensity of a stand of yield class 10 would therefore be 7 cubic metres per hectare per annum.

(e) Classification of trees

(i) The following is a classification of the types of trees which may be found in a stand of timber:

(1) Dominant. (2) Co-dominant. (3) Sub-dominant.
(4) Suppressed. (5) Wolf trees. (6) Whips.
(7) Dead and dying.

(ii) Dominant trees are the tallest trees; co-dominant are not so tall as dominant; while sub-dominants are less tall again.

(iii) Suppressed trees are those which grow below the crowns of the other trees in the stand.

(iv) Wolf trees are large, coarse, misshar[illegible] trees.

(v) Whips have tall, thin stems, and are [illegible] unstable that they may cause damage to other trees when they sway.

(f) Types and grades of thinning

(i) There are two main types of thinnings:

(1) *Low thinning*. This is the removal of trees which are falling behind in the struggle for existence, so that the final crop is selected from the fastest growing and strongest members of the crop.

(2) *Crown thinning*. In this case thinning is carried out mainly amongst the dominant classes, so as to favour the best individuals. Many dominated stems, except dead, dying, or diseased, are retained so that the forest floor and soil conditions are preserved, thus aiding the growth of the best stems.

(ii) Low thinning may be divided into the following three grades:

(1) *Light thinning*. This does not break the canopy to any extent.

(2) *Moderate thinning*. This makes a definite break in the canopy, so that looking up at the crowns after such a

thinning, one-fifth of the sky immediately overhead can be seen.

(3) *Heavy thinning*. This causes a general breaking-up of the canopy, so that looking up at the crowns after such a thinning, one-third of the sky immediately overhead can be seen.

(g) *When to thin*

(i) The following table shows the standard thinning ages, which are the ages when the first thinnings are normally carried out in the stated yield classes.

(ii) This is based on a table in Field Book No. 2 (previously Booklet No. 54), *Thinning Control*, by kind permission of the Forestry Commission. This Field Book also deals with thinning procedures, yields and control and those who require more information on these matters are strongly advised to acquire a copy.

AGES AT WHICH FIRST THINNINGS ARE NORMALLY CARRIED OUT

Species	*Spacing*		*Yield class*													
	m	*ft*	*30*	*28*	*26*	*24*	*22*	*20*	*18*	*16*	*14*	*12*	*10*	*8*	*6*	*4*
Scots pine	1·4	4·6									21	23	25	29	33	40
	2·0	6·5									22	24	27	31	35	45
	2·4	7·8									24	26	29	34	39	49
Corsican pine	1·4	4·6						18	19	20	21	23	25	28	33	
	2·0	6·5						19	20	21	22	24	27	30	36	
	2·4	7·8						20	22	23	25	27	30	34	41	
Lodgepole pine	1·5	4·9									19	21	23	26	31	40
	2·0	6·5									20	22	25	28	34	44
	2·4	7·8									21	24	27	31	38	48
Sitka spruce	1·7	5·5				18	18	19	20	21	22	24	26	29	33	
	2·0	6·5				18	19	20	21	22	23	25	27	30	35	
	2·4	7·8				19	20	21	22	24	25	28	30	34	40	
Norway spruce	1·5	4·9					20	21	22	23	24	26	28	31	35	
	2·0	6·5					21	22	23	25	26	29	31	35	41	
	2·4	7·8					23	24	25	27	28	31	34	39	46	
European larch	1·7	5·5										18	20	22	26	32
Japanese larch Hybrid larch	1·7	5·5									14	15	17	19	22	26
	2·0	6·5									15	16	18	20	23	27
	2·4	7·8									16	17	19	21	25	30
Douglas fir	1·7	5·5				16	17	17	18	19	21	23	25	28		
	2·0	6·5				16	17	18	19	20	22	24	27	30		
	2·4	7·8				17	18	19	20	22	24	27	30	34		
Western hemlock	1·5	4·9				19	20	21	22	24	26	28				

Western red cedar/ Lawson cypress	1·5	4·9				21	22	23	24	26	28	30				
Grand fir	1·8	5·9	19	20	20	21	21	22	23	24	25					
Noble fir	1·5	4·9					22	23	25	27	29	31				
Oak	1·2	3·9												24	28	35
Beech	1·2	3·9											26	29	32	37
Sycamore/ ash/birch	1·5	4·9										14	15	17	20	24

(h) Thinning control

(i) Thinning control is the action which should be taken so as to ensure that the correct volume is removed during thinning operations. Control is necessary in order to avoid a stand being over-thinned or under-thinned.

(ii) The procedure which should be followed is set out in Field Book No. 2, *Thinning Control.*

(i) Observations on thinning

The following are general observations on thinning:

(i) It is often necessary to retain certain trees in a crop temporarily, in order to maintain the canopy, to prevent deterioration of the forest floor, or to avoid the risk of the wind-blow. Such trees will never form the final crop, but nevertheless, they have an important duty to perform in the development of the plantation.

(ii) In neglected plantations, where trees have become drawn up and are not wind-firm, thinning must be carried out cautiously, on the principle of 'little and often'.

(iii) Trees which are to be removed should be clearly marked on at least two sides.

(iv) When the crop has reached a sufficiently advanced stage of development, prospective final crop trees may be marked with, for example, a band of red paint at breast height.

(v) An indication as to whether a stand requires thinning may be obtained from:

(1) The crown proportion. This is the proportion of the total height of a tree which bears living branches. If the crown proportion of the dominant trees becomes too small they cannot 'maintain' vigour. The dominants in larch plantations should have a crown proportion of about two-thirds up to a height of 40 ft, and about one-half subsequently. With other conifers it may be one-half to one-third up to 40 ft, and may be reduced to one-quarter as the trees become old.

(2) The condition of the forest floor.

(3) Management tables.
(4) The judicious use of Pressler's borer.

(j) Line thinning

(i) The following is a short account of line thinning but for a full description of the operation, reference should be made to Forestry Commission Leaflet No. 77—*Line Thinning* (1980).

(ii) Basically there are two forms of thinning:
(1) Selective thinning in which individual trees are removed at undefined distances throughout the stand.
(2) Systematic thinning in which trees are removed in 'sections' according to a plan or system which has been previously laid down and which is irrespective of the individual merits of the trees removed.

(iii) Line thinning is an example of systematic thinning and trees can be removed by the following methods.
(1) By rows when lines of trees as planted, are removed.
(2) By strips when rows of trees are removed but not in accordance with the rows which were planted.
(3) By chevrons or strips cut diagonally through the crop, irrespective of the planted lines. These emanate from a central rack and commence opposite each other.
(4) By staggering chevrons which emanate from the central rack at alternate intervals.

(iv) *Advantages*
(1) Marking is reduced to a minimum.
(2) Felling is quicker.
(3) Extraction is much easier.

(v) *Disadvantages*
(1) Since a line contains both large and small trees, some of the better trees are felled which in a selective thinning would have been retained. Consequently a smaller number of the better trees are left and this may affect the final crop and result in a loss of volume.
(2) Only those trees growing next to the line which is removed, will benefit from this form of thinning.
(3) The removal of lines of trees may increase the risk of windblow.

(vi) *Limitations*
(1) Normally the line method is only used for first thinnings.
(2) Not more than two adjacent rows should be removed and the Forestry Commission have adopted the removal of:
1 row in 2, 3 or 4 rows
2 rows in 4 or 5 rows.

(3) Line thinning is most satisfactory in stands of reasonably even growth which do not contain a great variation in the size of individual trees. It is less satisfactory in stands that have a limited number of good trees which will be further reduced by this type of thinning.

4. *Pruning*

(a) The advantages of pruning

(i) The quality of the timber is improved by preventing the formation of knots.

(ii) The appearance of the tree is enhanced, which should encourage prospective buyers.

(b) Species

(i) Fast-growing conifers are probably the most economic species to prune.

(ii) On the whole, broadleaved species, if properly grown, will not require much pruning. Poplar planted 5·5–7·3 m (18–24 ft) apart is, however, an exception.

(c) Size to prune

(i) Within reason, the sooner pruning can be started the better, since the smaller will be the central knotty core.

(ii) Since brashing (see Section 2 of this chapter) consists of the removal of the lower branches; pruning, in fact, starts with this operation.

(iii) The earlier a tree is pruned, the smaller will be the knotty core at maturity. Pruning should start before the tree exceeds 10 cm (4 in.) diameter at breast height, and may be carried out in three to four stages up to a height of 6–7·3 m (20–24 ft).

(d) Season to prune

During the winter months is probably best. It is inadvisable to prune when the sap is rising.

(e) The height to prune

(i) The maximum height for pruning is usually about 6–7·3 m (20–24 ft), although several owners have successfully pruned trees to a greater height.

(ii) As the height to which a tree is pruned increases, so also increases:

(1) The difficulty of the work.

(2) The cost.

(3) The risk of accidents.

(f) Tools for pruning

Pruning tools can be divided into three classes: firstly, hand saws; secondly, chisel-edged tools and thirdly, chainsaws.

(i) *Saws*

(1) The advantage claimed for pruning saws is that they are easy to use, and therefore very suitable for novices.

(2) The disadvantages which are put forward are that they leave a rougher cut surface which does not heal over so quickly as a chisel-cut surface, and that rate of progress is slower.

(3) There are several types of pruning saws, of which the following are a selection:

(*a*) Straight single-handed pruning saw.

(*b*) Curved single-handed 'Grecian' saw with pistol-grip handle.

(*c*) Two-handed saws. These are usually fitted with curved blades 30–40 cm (12–16 in.) long which can be attached to handles of varying lengths. Those 1–1·2 m (3–4 ft) long being used for brashing and those 3–3·6 m (10–12 ft) long for high pruning.

(ii) *Chisel-edged tools*

These are claimed to be quicker, neater, and to give better healing surface than saw-edged tools.

(iii) *Chain saws*

The remarks on the use of chain saws for brashing which are contained in Section 2 of this chapter also apply to their use for pruning. However special care must be exercised when the operator leaves the ground and attention is drawn to the following Forestry Safety Council Guides:

No. 10, *The Chainsaw*
12, *Chainsaw Snedding*
18, *Tree Climbing and Pruning.*

(g) General notes on pruning

(i) Whatever type of pruning tool is chosen, it should always be kept as sharp as possible.

(ii) Most men have a personal preference for a particular type of tool; the best results are achieved if they are allowed to use the tool they like.

(iii) When pruning, the cut should be made flush with the main stem of the tree. On no account should 'snags' be left.

(iv) Differing opinions are held on the subject of pruning live and dead branches, but the following facts emerge:

(1) Dead branches can always be removed.

(2) Two objections to pruning live branches which are sometimes put forward are firstly the risk of excessive 'bleeding'

and secondly that the reduction of the living crown will interfere with growth.

(3) It is very much easier to remove live branches of Lawson cypress and Western red cedar (*Thuya plicata*) than dead ones.

CHAPTER VI

Silviculture

1. *Silviculture and Arboriculture*

(*a*) The growing and cultivation of trees may be divided into two main divisions:

(i) Silviculture. (ii) Arboriculture.

(*b*) Silviculture is the commercial cultivation of trees for the production of timber.

(*c*) Arboriculture is the cultivation of trees so as to produce individual specimens of the greatest ornament and beauty, to provide shelter, to grow fruit, or for any purposes other than the production of timber as such.

2. *Silvicultural Characteristics*

(*a*) Silvicultural characteristics of a tree are the special features of the growth and site requirements of a species which affect its use in silviculture.

(*b*) The following are some of the points which should be taken into account in assessing the silvicultural characters of a species:

(i) Shape of the root system.
(ii) Shape of the crown.
(iii) Persistency of the side branches.
(iv) The demand for light, and ability to withstand shade.
(v) The demands in respect of soil, situation, and climate.
(vi) The rate of growth, and ultimate height attained.
(vii) The quantity and quality of timber produced.
(viii) The liability to disease, fungi, and insect attack.

(*c*) For the details regarding the silvicultural characteristics of individual species, reference should be made to recognized textbooks on forestry.

(*d*) Information regarding the requirements of species will be found in Chapter I.

(*e*) The silviculture, regeneration and establishment of the principal broadleaved species are described at length in Forestry Commission Bulletin No. 62, *Silviculture of Broadleaved Woodland.*

3. *Choice of Species*

Information will be found under Section 5 of Chapter IV, on Planting and Establishment.

4. *Pure and Mixed Woods*

(a) The advantage of pure woods

(i) The management is easier than in mixed woods.
(ii) The thinning of pure plantations needs less skill.
(iii) Natural pruning may be more effective in pure woods than in mixtures.

(b) The disadvantages of pure woods

(i) If the species is lightly foliaged, such as ash or larch, or has hard needles which do not easily decompose, such as Scots or Corsican pine, soil deterioration may occur.
(ii) The thinnings of some species, notably hardwoods, do not command a ready sale, and financial returns from early thinnings may be very low.
(iii) Where pure crops are attacked by pests or disease, control is often difficult, and the resulting damage greater than in the case of mixed woods.

(c) The advantages of mixed woods

(i) The risk of fire is less in a stand of conifers and broadleaved species than in a pure conifer crop.
(ii) If a species is found to be unsuited for a particular soil, it can be removed as thinnings.
(iii) Where soil conditions vary, a mixed plantation may result in irregular pure groups of those species which are adapted to local variations of soil.
(iv) The risk of wind-blow may be reduced by mixing shallow rooting with deeper rooting species.
(v) A species which will produce saleable thinnings may be mixed with one which is to form the final crop, but which in itself does not produce marketable thinnings.
(vi) Soil deterioration can be considerably reduced by introducing a soil-improving species in a lightly foliaged crop.

(d) The disadvantages of mixed woods

(i) Mixed woods are more difficult to manage than pure ones.
(ii) Natural pruning may be less effective.

(e) Types of mixtures

Mixtures can be divided into two main classes:

(i) Even aged mixtures.

(ii) Uneven aged mixtures.

and these are considered below.

(f) Even aged mixtures

There are four ways of making mixtures of even aged trees:

(i) *By single trees*

(1) In this case, mixing may be indiscriminate or systematic.

(2) This method will prove satisfactory only if the height growth of the species adopted are the same. Better natural pruning will also be obtained if the species have the same pruning capacity.

(ii) *By alternate rows*

As in the case of mixing by single trees, comparable height growth is essential for success.

(iii) *By strips*

(1) Making mixtures by planting several rows of a species in strips is a development of the alternate row method.

(2) A minimum of three adjacent rows of any one species should be planted.

(3) The proportion between the species can be adjusted by varying the number of rows of each. Thus, three rows of beech, followed by six rows of larch, and so on, would give a mixture in the proportion of one-third beech and two-thirds larch.

(iv) *By groups*

(1) The advantage of this method is that any difference in height growth or pruning capacities will only affect the outside of the group.

(2) A group should not be less than nine plants, and groups may very well be very much bigger if conditions warrant it.

(3) If, however, groups are more than a quarter of an acre they tend to produce a wood consisting of pure blocks of species, rather than a mixture.

(g) Uneven aged mixtures

(i) These may be formed by underplanting, or by natural regeneration, thus producing a 'two-storied forest'.

(ii) Either the upper storey must be very heavily thinned, or the under-storey must be composed of species which will tolerate shade.

5. *Natural Regeneration*

Broadly speaking, there are four principal conditions which are necessary for successful natural regeneration, and these are considered below.

(a) An adequate supply of seed

(i) The frequency of seed production varies according to the species and the season.

(ii) Most species produce seed in reasonable quantities every second, third, or fourth year.

(iii) Beech, however, is less prolific, and good seed years may only happen every 10 to 12 years, usually after a very hot summer.

(iv) Oak is rather uncertain, and crops of acorns are often irregular and vary considerably from district to district.

(v) An adequate supply of seed cannot be obtained unless seed trees are present, either on or immediately adjacent to the area to be regenerated.

(vi) Seed trees must be of the right age and type if satisfactory results are to be obtained.

(vii) The period of a tree's life when the best seed is produced has been defined by various authorities as during middle age or 10 to 20 years after principal height growth has been completed. Nevertheless, seed produced by quite young trees may be satisfactory.

(viii) P. T. Maw in *The Practice of Forestry* (1909) gives the following ages at which good seed can be expected in the case of hardwoods:

Alder	25 years	Hornbeam	40 years
Ash	30 „	Norway maple	35 „
Beech	60 „	Oak	60 „
Birch	25 „	Sycamore	35 „

(ix) The following species regenerate without difficulty, providing conditions are reasonably favourable:

Ash	Sycamore
Birch	Scots pine

(x) The following do not regenerate so readily as the foregoing, and may prove difficult unless conditions are very favourable:

Beech	Larch
Oak	Spruce
Sweet chestnut	

(b) A suitable seed bed

(i) Soil conditions which are unsuitable for natural regeneration include:

(1) A deep layer of undecayed humus, such as leaves or needles.

(2) Grass; especially if forming a matted layer.

(3) Excessive growth of surface vegetation, such as brambles, bracken, etc.

(ii) Where conditions are unsuitable, satisfactory results will often be obtained if some form of cultivation is adopted, or if the ground is scarified in some way. This may be brought about by the following:

(1) The use of disc harrows drawn by a light tractor.

(2) The use of market gardeners' light two-wheeled tractor fitted with discs or a rotary cultivator.

(3) The hauling of baulks of timber, about the size of a gate post, to which iron spikes have been fitted, or yew logs with branch snags left on. This method is particularly useful in areas of brambles.

(4) The use of unringed pigs. These can be kept within the necessary area by means of an electric fence, while the use of tethered pigs is possible under certain conditions.

(iii) Unless the roots of a seedling can reach mineral soil by the end of the first year it is unlikely to survive.

(c) An absence of predators

(i) Predators can be divided roughly into two classes: firstly, those which interfere with regeneration by eating the seeds; and secondly, those which eat the young seedlings.

(ii) Those which eat the seed include:

(1) Squirrels: chiefly grey, but the brown can also do damage.

(2) Birds: probably the two worst are wood pigeons and pheasants.

(3) Voles and mice.

(iii) Those which eat the young seedlings include:

(1) Rabbits: the greatest damage is caused by rabbits where they are present it is usually impossible to obtain satisfactory regeneration without erecting netting. (For details of a rabbit fence see Chapter III, Section 1(*c*).)

(2) Hares: the damage caused by hares is generally far less than in the case of rabbits. Hare damage is often very local.

(3) Voles and mice.

(4) Slugs: the amount of damage caused by slugs has not been accurately assessed.

(iv) The steps to be taken against injurious animals and birds is dealt with in Chapter XI—Forest Protection.

(d) Sufficient light for subsequent growth of seedlings

(i) Although light is not an essential for germination, development and growth cannot take place satisfactorily without a sufficient intensity of light.

(ii) If there is insufficient light it will be necessary to carry out a thinning of the mother trees.

(iii) When additional light is admitted, the effect may be fourfold, according to when the thinning is carried out:

(1) The seed-bearing capacity of the mother trees is improved, as more room is given for crown development.

(2) The decomposition of raw humus is accelerated.

(3) The growth of young seedlings is assisted.

(4) If too heavily thinned, weed growth may be stimulated so that the seedlings are choked.

6. *Underplanting*

(a) The objects of underplanting

Underplanting is carried out in order to:

(i) Improve the quality of the crop, and this is achieved in the following ways:

(1) By maintaining or improving soil fertility, and by preventing deterioriation of the forest floor by heavy weed growth.

(2) By preventing or severely curtailing the development of excessively large crowns and side branches.

(ii) Utilize to the full the site, by ensuring that the maximum amount of timber is grown on it.

(b) The requirements for underplanting

The following conditions are necessary for successful underplanting:

(i) The crop which is to be underplanted should be a lightly foliaged species which does not cast a dense shade.

(ii) The species which is to form the understorey must be a shade-bearer.

(iii) The existing crop should be of a sufficiently high quality as to be worth underplanting.

(iv) The existing crop should be young enough to be able to respond to the benefits which underplanting can produce.

(c) Species for underplanting

(i) The following species are amongst those which may be underplanted: ash, oak, and larch.

(ii) The following are suitable for planting under the species mentioned in the above paragraph: Lawson cypress, Grand fir (*Abies grandis*), Western hemlock (*Tsuga heterophylla*), Western red cedar (*Thuya plicata*), and beech.

(d) Treatment prior to underplanting
Before underplanting a stand, the overwood should be thinned. The intensity of the thinning will depend on the condition of the stand, and any doubtful trees should be removed.

(e) Age for underplanting
It is important that the overwood is young enough to respond to treatment. As a guide, oak should be between 35 and 50 years, and larch from 30 to 40 years; but site and growth conditions should be taken into account.

(f) Advantages of underplanting
(i) The main crop or overstorey is improved in quality.
(ii) The maximum output is obtained from the land.
(iii) Underplanting will greatly improve the game-holding capacity of an area.

(g) Disadvantages of underplanting
(i) If rabbits are present, wire netting will have to be erected, and the cost of this may be a serious item.
(ii) Difficulties may be experienced in felling the overstorey if this is to be removed before the understorey.

7. *Silvicultural Systems*

(a) General
(i) R. S. Troup has defined the term 'silvicultural system' as follows:
'The process by which the crops constituting a forest are tended, removed, and replaced by new crops, resulting in the production of woods of a distinctive form.'
(ii) There are a great number of systems, and these notes only deal briefly with those which may be found in this country. For full details reference should be made to *Silvicultural Systems*, by R. S. Troup (Oxford University Press), 2nd edition (1952).

(b) Notes on systems
(i) Of the systems referred to below, the only ones which are commonly found on estates in this country are: coppice, coppice with standards, the clear-cutting system, and sometimes an inexact form of the selection system.
(ii) The other systems which are mentioned cannot be described as common in this country, but a brief description of them may be useful for reference purposes.
(iii) The systems described below are:
(1) Coppice. (2) Coppice with standards. (3) Clear-cutting system: (*a*) Even-aged forest; (*b*) Two-storied high forest. (4)

Selection system. (5) Group system, (6) Strip system. (7) Uniform or Shelterwood compartment system. (8) Early final selection system.

(c) *Coppice*

(i) *Species*

(1) The following are the species which are usually found growing under this system:
Hazel, Spanish chestnut, ash, oak, alder, sycamore, hornbeam, birch.

(2) In addition, other species are often found growing mixed with the above, such as willow, dogwood, etc., but these are not recognized coppice species, and are generally regarded as weeds.

(ii) *Procedure*

(1) The crop is managed on a short rotation, the interval between cutting depending on the species and the market. The shortest rotation is probably 5 years in the case of ash, grown for walking-sticks, and the longest 25 years for alder, grown as large under-water piles.

(2) After cutting, the stools will produce fresh shoots or 'springs', which are allowed to grow for another 10, 15, or 20 years, according to the length of the rotation, when they are again cut and the procedure repeated.

(3) To calculate the area to be cut each year, the total area is divided by the rotation and the resulting figure, known as the annual cut or coupe, gives the area to be cut in any one year. Thus, if 18 hectares are managed on a 12-year rotation, the annual coupe will be 18/12 or 1·5 hectares. Similarly, if 30 acres are managed on a 15-year rotation, the annual coupe will be 30/15 or 2 acres.

(iii) *Notes on species*

(1) Hazel:

(*a*) Uses: pea and bean sticks; hedge stakes and hetherings: wattle hurdles; thatching spars, etc.; flower and tomato stakes, etc.

(*b*) Rotation: generally 8–12 years.

(*c*) Life of a stool: 80–100 years.

(2) Spanish chestnut:

(*a*) Uses: wirework poles (hop poles); cleft pale fencing; fencing stakes or 'spiles'; flower and tomato stakes, etc.

(*b*) Rotation: 9 years upwards for cleaving crops; 14–16 years for wirework poles.

- (*c*) Spanish or sweet chestnut coppice is chiefly grown in Kent, Sussex, and Hereford.
- (*d*) Life of a stool: about 100 years.

(3) Ash:
- (*a*) Uses: tool handles; sheep hurdles; fence rails; walking-sticks, etc.
- (*b*) Rotation: about 15 years, or rather longer rotation for large poles and a shorter one for smaller produce; walking-sticks 5 years.
- (*c*) Life of a stool: 40–50 years.

(4) Oak:
- (*a*) Uses: originally grown for the production of bark for tanning and for charcoal, and otherwise has little use, except for firewood or fencing material.
- (*b*) Rotation: 16 years for tanning bark, and up to 35 years for fencing.
- (*c*) Life of a stool: 100 years or more.

(5) Alder:
- (*a*) Uses: turnery; under-water piling; gunpowder.
- (*b*) Rotation: 10–25 years.

(6) Sycamore:
- (*a*) Uses: turnery; fencing material, if impregnated with preservative.
- (*b*) Rotation: 15–20 years.

(d) Coppice with standards

This system is a combination of coppice and high forest, consisting of coppice grown beneath an overwood of uneven-aged timber trees.

(i) *Species*

(1) The coppice consists of the species normally grown for coppice, and described in the last sub-section.

(2) The standards usually consist of a lightly foliaged species which does not cast much shade. Typically oak standards are grown, but the following are suitable species:

Oak, poplar, ash, larch, sweet chestnut.

(ii) *Procedure*

(1) The coppice is managed on a rotation suitable for the production of the necessary produce.

(2) The standards are managed on a rotation which is usually a multiple of the coppice rotation, thus:

Hazel coppice on 12-year rotation and oak standards on 120-year rotation, i.e. the standard rotation is ten times that of the coppice.

(3) Standards are propagated by natural regeneration, by allowing suitable stool shoots to grow on to form trees and by planting.

(4) According to Troup, the number of standards per acre should be 20–40, that is, 50–100 per hectare. If evenly spaced 66 trees per hectare (27 trees per acre) would be 12 m (40 ft) apart while 118 trees per hectare (48 trees per acre) would be 14·6 m (30 ft) apart.

(e) Clear-cutting system

The clear-cutting system can be divided into two sub-divisions; even-aged high forest and two-storied high forest.

(i) *Even-aged high forest*

(1) The principle of this system is that an area is planted with trees, and when these have reached the desired age on which the rotation is fixed the whole area is felled and then replanted. When these young trees reach the necessary age the procedure is repeated.

(2) To put this sequence of events on a systematic basis, a calculation similar to that described under 'Coppice' is made. The total area is divided by the rotation, and the result will give the area which theoretically ought to be cut each year, thus:

$$\begin{array}{c}\text{Area to be felled}\\\text{(or annual coupe)}\end{array} = \frac{\text{Total area}}{\text{Rotation}}$$

Example: If the total area is 85 hectares (210 acres) managed on a 70-year rotation, the amount to be felled each year will be 1·21 hectares (3 acres).

(3) In theory, if 1·21 hectares of this area of 85 hectares were felled each year and then replanted, at the end of 70 years the area would be divided into 70 blocks of 1·21 hectares each, aged consecutively from 1 to 70 years. Where such a state of affairs exists, it is known as a 'normal forest', but it is extremely unlikely that any 'normal forest' exists in Great Britain at the present time.

(4) The following figures are a rough guide as to the length of the rotation for the various species mentioned.

Oak	90–140 years	Conifers	40–80 years
Beech	90–140 ,,	Ash	50–70 ,,
Sycamore	60–80 ,,	Poplar	40–45 ,,

(ii) *Two-storied high forest*

Under this sub-division the crop consists in theory of two age classes; the overstorey and the understorey. This condition is usually produced by underplanting an older stand with young trees, as described in Section 6 of this chapter, and to which reference should be made.

(iii) *Advantages of the clear-cutting system*

The following are some of the advantages of this system:

(1) Simple to manage.
(2) Yield can be calculated with comparative ease.
(3) No damage is caused to younger trees, which is found in other systems when the crop is felled, since the whole area is cleared at one time. This presupposes that in the case of two-storied high forest the whole crop is felled together when the understorey has reached an economic size.
(4) The trees which form the final crop are more uniform in size, and are usually cleaner.
(5) Artificial replanting is more certain, and occupies a shorter period of time than natural regeneration, on which the other systems are normally dependent.
(6) Extraction of felled material is easier.

(iv) *Disadvantages of the clear-cutting system*

The following are some of the disadvantages of the system:

(1) Difficulties may occur in establishing a new crop on a completely bare site due to exposure, wind, forest, sun, etc.
(2) If the area is not planted very soon after it has been cleared, heavy weed growth will frequently occur, thereby further adding to the cost of re-establishment.
(3) Soil deterioration and drying, through loss of overhead cover.
(4) The risk of insect pests is greatly increased in certain cases when clear felling is adopted, e.g. pine weevil in pine areas.
(5) Increased risk of landslides, erosion, and so forth on steep slopes and hillsides.
(6) Even-aged forests are more susceptible to certain diseases and pests.
(7) Even-aged forests are less resistant to damage by wind and snow.
(8) The larger the area which is clear felled, the more are the disadvantages intensified.
(9) In the clear-cutting system the yield is based on the *area* to be felled. If this area is under-stocked through damage by disease, unsuitability of species, soil, etc., the calculated yield will prove incorrect. In the system described below the yield is based on the *volume* of timber and not *area*, and consequently the risk of mis-calculation from this source does not arise.

(f) Selection system

(i) In this system trees of all ages are scattered over the area, and are felled either singly or in twos or threes as and when it is considered necessary. The criterion as to this is dependent on the yield calculation, which is in turn based on the volume increment.

(ii) Ideal introduction of the youngest trees is by natural regeneration, but where natural seeding is difficult, or only attained at long intervals, it may be supplemented by planting.

(iii) *Advantages of the selection system*

(1) The site is never exposed, as in the clear-cutting system, and the difficulties experienced in the replanting of bare exposed sites do not arise.
(2) There are never unsightly cleared area.
(3) Soil deterioration is avoided.
(4) Risk of landslides and soil erosion is avoided.
(5) Excellent for ornamental woods, amenity woods, shelter belts, etc.
(6) The heavy cost of replanting cleared sites is avoided.
(7) The area produces a regular income, and the 'dead' period during the first 10 or 12 years with a young plantation is avoided.
(8) Risk of damage by snow, insect pests, and disease are avoided, or greatly reduced.
(9) As individual trees are isolated in later life they continue to grow rapidly; consequently they can be economically grown to a large size.
(10) A bigger proportion of the yield is in large timber, and a smaller proportion in thinnings. The money yield can therefore be higher than in an even-aged forest.

(iv) *Disadvantages of the selection system*

(1) Difficult to manage.
(2) Extraction of timber is difficult and expensive.
(3) Damage to young trees may occur during felling of the larger trees.
(4) Whether regeneration is dependent on natural or artificial means, the area must be protected against rabbits, if present.
(5) Most suitable for shade-bearing species.

(g) Group system

(i) This is a development of the selection system, in so far as the removal of one, two, or three trees is extended so that a small group of trees is felled.
(ii) The size of the groups depends on the species; the less shade-bearing the requirements, the larger the group.
(iii) Groups of 0·04–0·10 hectares ($\frac{1}{10}$–$\frac{1}{4}$ acre) may be taken as a guide to average requirements.
(iv) The initial groups are scattered over the area, and as

regeneration proceeds the groups are increased in size by further fellings, so that in due course the groups link up and the whole area is cleared of mother trees.

(v) In the case of heavy-seeded species, such as beech, if too large a group is formed the mast will not reach the centre, so that such groups will have a 'hollow' centre.

(vi) The groups are in course of time filled by naturally regenerated seedlings produced from seed which has fallen from the surrounding trees.

(h) Strip system

(i) Very briefly, this system consists of clearing a strip, instead of groups of trees.

(ii) The strip should be cut at right-angles to the prevailing wind, so that the seed may be blown by the wind from the trees on the windward side onto the strip.

(iii) As the strip is successfully regenerated it is increased in width by felling a further strip immediately adjoining it and to the windward. In effect, the existing strip is widened.

(iv) When this newly felled strip is regenerated, a further felling takes place, and this procedure is repeated until the whole of the area is restocked.

(i) Uniform or Shelterwood Compartment system

(i) Under the three previous systems the overwood is removed gradually, either by selecting individual trees, by removing groups of trees, or by the felling of strips. In the uniform system the overwood is removed uniformly over the whole of the area.

(ii) The overwood is removed in stages by means of a series of 'regeneration' fellings, of which there are two main classes: (1) the seeding felling; (2) secondary fellings.

(iii) The object of the seeding felling is to open up the canopy and admit sufficient light to enable the seedling trees to survive during their early stages of development. Under the secondary fellings, more light is admitted through the further removal of mother trees.

(iv) As regeneration proceeds, the number of mother trees is accordingly reduced, until ultimately they are all removed by a final felling.

(j) Oceanic system

(i) This system, which is sometimes referred to as the Early Final Selection system, was evolved by Maj.-Gen. D. G. Moore on his estate at Mountfield, Co. Tyrone, Northern Ireland in the late 1960s.

(ii) The object is to overcome wind-throw in stands of Sitka spruce growing on exposed sites.

(iii) This is achieved by adopting a rotation of about 30 years and by reducing the number of trees just as the canopy is closing in, which is known as 'respacing'.
(iv) If planted at 2 m ($6\frac{1}{2}$ ft) apart, i.e. 2,500 trees per hectare (1,030 per acre), this number would be reduced to about 1,000 per hectare (410 per acre) by decapitating the unwanted trees just above the lowest whorl of live branches.
(v) The stand receives no further attention, thinning or pruning until it is clear felled.

CHAPTER VII

Coppice and Underwood

1. *General*

(*a*) Coppice is the oldest form of forestry practised in this country, the word 'coppice' having its origin in the French word *couper*—to cut.

(*b*) Coppice may be divided into three main classes:

(i) Hazel. (ii) Chestnut. (iii) Other.

(*c*) Hazel coppice is the commonest class, and is found throughout the Midlands and Southern counties.

(*d*) Chestnut coppice refers to the Spanish or sweet chestnut, and this is chiefly found in Kent, Sussex, and Hereford. It also occurs elsewhere, but the largest areas are found in the three counties mentioned above, especially Kent and Sussex.

(*e*) Other types of coppice include oak, ash, sycamore, maple, birch, wych elm, alder, and mixtures of any of these species with or without hazel and chestnut.

(*f*) Chestnut coppice is a very specialized form, and, while most of the other species will grow under standards as coppice with standards, the best results will only be obtained by growing chestnut as coppice and not under the shade of standards.

(*g*) See also Chapter VI, under 'Silvicultural Systems', for further information regarding coppice rotations, etc.

2. *New Aspects of Coppice*

(*a*) During the past decade a number of changes have taken place in the growing and utilization of coppice.

(*b*) In some cases both the supply and demand for it has decreased for the following reasons.

(i) The difficulty in obtaining the services of those who are skilled at 'working up' coppice.

(ii) The replacement of coppice products by other materials. Examples of this are the use of plastics for china crates, thus eliminating the demand for crate rods, and also the effect of dutch barns and silage-making on the need for thatching spars.

(iii) The replanting of coppice areas as high forest or their conversion to agricultural land.

(*c*) At the same time the demand for coppice for some purposes has been maintained or has even increased, of which the following are examples:

(i) For garden items, such as wattle hurdles, wooden rakes and besoms and also for material for show and point-to-point jumps.
(ii) For firewood, largely as a result of the very considerable increases in the price of other fuels and the introduction of wood-burning stoves.
(iii) For pulpwood.
(iv) For game coverts.

3. *Coppice Production*

(*a*) *The production from 1 acre of hazel coppice (about 10 years old)*

(i) The following figures were kindly supplied by the late Mr G. C. Laws:

Hedge stakes	3,500	
Hetherings	96	bundles (20 per bundle)
Pea sticks	188	bundles (21 „ „)
Bean rods	127	bundles (21 „ „)
Barbed-wire stakes	148	
Faggots	70	
Clothes-line props	27	
Small firewood	1	ton

(ii) The equivalent out-turn from 1 hectare would be as follows:

Hedge stakes	8,645	
Hetherings	237	bundles
Pea sticks	464	„
Bean rods	313	„
Barbed-wire stakes	365	
Faggots	173	
Clothes-line props	66	
Small firewood	2½	tonnes

(*b*) *The production from 1 acre of chestnut coppice 14 years old*

(i) The following figures were made available through the kindness of the late Mr A. D. C. Le Sueur:

Cleft poles (2 ft 6 in.–6 ft in length)	29,000
Tree and fruit stakes (4 ft 6 in.–8 ft in length)	810
Tomato stakes (4 ft 6 in. in length)	4,320
Spiles (5 ft in length)	800
Thatchers' pins (5 ft in length)	2,400
Rails (12 ft in length)	36

(ii) The equivalent out-turn from 1 hectare would be as follows:

Cleft poles 0·7 m–1·8 m in length)	71,630
Tree and fruit stakes (1·3–2·4 m in length)	2,000
Tomato stakes (1·3 m in length)	10,670
Spiles (1·5 m in length)	1,976
Thatchers' pins (1·5 m in length)	5,928
Rails (3·6 m in length)	89

(c) Cutting and working up

The following figures are reproduced by kind permission of the late Mr C. Bruce Durham:

A skilled worker will:

(i) Cut down 1 acre of hazel coppice in 1 week (1 hectare in 2½ weeks).

(ii) Work up (i.e. cut out, sort, tie, and bundle) 1 acre of hazel coppice into crate rods, pea sticks, bean rod, etc., in 3–6 weeks, according to the density of the crop (1 hectare in 7–14 weeks).

(iii) Make up to 5 dozen sheep hurdles in 1 week.

(d) Other sources of information

Further information will be found in the following Forestry Commission publications:

Bulletin No. 62, *Silviculture of Broadleaved Woodland.*
Bulletin No. 64, *The Yield of Sweet Chestnut Coppice.*
Leaflet No. 83, *Coppice.*

4. *Treatment of Unproductive Coppice and Derelict Woodlands*

(a) Unproductive coppice

Coppice which comes into this category may be treated in two ways: firstly, by clearing (wholly or partially) and planting; and secondly, by selecting suitable coppice shoots or 'springs' and allowing them to grow on into timber trees.

(i) *Clearing and planting*

(1) Complete clearance: this is normally carried out by machinery such as bulldozers or land-clearance equipment.

(2) Partial clearance: this can be done by hand or machine and a considerable saving in cost can be effected. The following is a brief description of the *Lane method*:

(*a*) Narrow strips or lanes about 1 m (3 ft) wide are cut through the area;

(*b*) the distance between adjacent lanes is equal to the planting distance, e.g. 1·8 m (5 ft) and the young trees are planted in the lanes at this distance;

(c) this method is only suitable where the height of the coppice is less than 1·8 m. Japanese larch and Douglas fir are very suitable for this form of conversion.

(ii) *Selection of stool shoots*
This method can only be adopted when the coppice comprises a species which is able to grow into timber. It is therefore impossible to use this method for hazel.

In selecting coppice poles under this method, care should be taken to see that the stool is sound. First-class timber will never be produced by this method, but it is the cheapest way of dealing with areas of this kind, since neither planting nor rabbit fencing are necessary.

(b) Derelict woodlands
In truly derelict woodlands the only satisfactory methods are whole or partial clearance, as already described in the case of unproductive coppice.

5. *Osier Beds*

(a) General
The cultivation of osiers is sometimes considered to be an agricultural rather than a forestry matter and the following short notes are only in the nature of an introduction.

A full account of methods of growing basket willows and their utilization, entitled 'Cultivation and uses of basket willows' by K. G. Stott, will be found in the *Quarterly Journal of Forestry*, vol. L, April 1956, pp. 103–112.

(b) Species
The three most important species of willow which are used for basket making are those which are given below with some of their cultivars.

(i) *Salix triandra*
Cultivars: Black Maul, Champion, New Kind, Spaniards, Trustworthy.

(ii) *Salix purpurea*
Cultivars: Dicky meadows, Lancashire Dicks, Leicestershire Dicks.

(iii) *Salix viminalis*
Cultivar: Mealy Top.

(c) Suitable conditions

(i) Suitable soils are loams, marls and clays which must be well drained.

(ii) Sites near rivers which are capable of being irrigated.

(iii) When establishing an osier bed it is essential to lay out a system of open drains.

(d) Propagation

(i) This is done by putting in cuttings 22–38 cm (9–15 in.) long, the shorter ones being used on clays and the longer on lighter soils.
(ii) Cuttings are taken from 1-year-old rods.
(iii) Planting should be done in March and April.
(iv) In the past willows were grown at very close spacings such as 45 × 38 cm (18 × 15 in.) and 40 × 33 cm (16 × 13 in.) but as the cost of labour rose and mechanical cultivation was introduced, the spacing increased and it can now be as much as 58 × 35 cm (27 × 14 in.).

(e) After cultivation

The main task is to keep down weed growth, and although this was done by handhoeing or cutting in the past it is now usually done with a small mechanical cultivator which can be used between the rows.

(f) Harvesting

Basket willows can be cut at any time during the winter or spring before the sap begins to rise.

6. *Willow Biomass for Fuel*

(*a*) In recent years, work carried out by Long Ashton Research Station has shown that willows grown at a close spacing on a 3-year rotation, can produce 12–15 tonnes of oven-dry matter per hectare (5–6 tonnes per acre).

(*b*) When chipped, this material (generally referred to as 'willow biomass') can be used as fuel in boilers for heating glasshouses and other buildings.

(*c*) Willows are especially suitable for this purpose since they:
(i) are fast growing;
(ii) can be coppiced at frequent intervals;
(iii) are readily grown from cuttings.

(*d*) Full details may be obtained from Long Ashton Research Station, Long Ashton, Bristol BS18 9AF, which has also published a booklet entitled *Willow Biomass as a Source*.

CHAPTER VIII

Forest Management

1. *Selection of Terms used in Forest Management*

THE following are some of the commoner terms used in forest management. For a more exhaustive list reference should be made to textbooks on forest management and to *British Commonwealth Forest Terminology—Part I*, published by the Empire Forestry Association (1953):

Age class. The class or group into which the trees in a forest are divided in accordance with their age.

Basal area. The area of the cross-section of a tree which although termed 'basal', is in fact calculated at breast height, i.e. 1·3 m (4 ft 3 in.) above ground level. The basal area of a crop or stand is the total of the basal areas of the individual trees in the crop.

Compartments. A unit of area within a forest, the boundaries of which are permanent and clearly defined. The convenient size for a compartment is 6–10 hectares (15–25 acres). A sub-compartment is an area within a compartment which, owing to its age, species, etc., requires different treatment to that afforded to the rest of the compartment.

Compartment history sheet. A form of convenient design, on which are entered particulars regarding the treatment, work carried out, special damage, etc., within the compartment or sub-compartment (see Section 5 of this chapter).

Cutting section. The area to be felled under a felling series (*q.v.*) may be sub-divided into small block known as cutting sections, which are distributed over the area concerned. This distribution of felling sites may be necessary in order to disperse young regenerated areas, so as to reduce the risks of fire or insect damage, or to improve the woodlands from the point of view of game.

Cutting series—see *Felling series.*

Felling, improvement. Where the less valuable trees in a stand are removed, in order to improve the remainder, it is known as an improvement felling. This term is generally used in connection with uneven aged crops.

Felling, increment. Where a crop which is nearing maturity is heavily thinned, in order to encourage the remaining trees to put on increment, such a thinning is referred to as an increment felling.

Felling, preparatory. This is somewhat similar to an increment felling, but its object is to encourage seed production and promote conditions favourable for natural regeneration. It is carried out in the last few years of the rotation.

Felling series. Where the area covered by a working circle is too large to be worked as one unit (in so far as fellings are concerned), it may be more convenient to divide it up into sub-divisions known as felling series. If, for example, the area to be felled within the working circle is 40 hectares (100 acres) per annum, this may constitute too large an area to be dealt with in one locality. By dividing the working circle into four felling series, the area to be felled is separated into four blocks each of 10 hectares (25 acres).

Financial rotation. The rotation which produces the best financial return.

Form factor. The ratio which the bole of a tree bears to a cylinder whose mean sectional area is equal to the basal area of the tree, and whose length is equal to the height of the tree. The form factor for a tree may be calculated by the following formula:

$$\text{Form factor} = \frac{\text{Volume of tree}}{\text{Height} \times \text{basal area (at 1·3 m)}}$$

If the volume is measured under bark, then the basal area will be under bark. The mean height may be ascertained by Lorey's formula thus:

$$H = \frac{h_1 s_1 + h_2 s_2 \ldots h_n s_n}{S}$$

Where:

H = mean height of stand

S = total basal area of plot

$h_1; h_2 \ldots h_n$ = mean heights of girth groups

$s_1; s_2 \ldots s_n$ = total basal areas of girth groups.

Increment, current annual. The present rate of increment (i.e. increase in height, girth, volume, etc.) generally calculated by dividing the increment for the past few years (say, three to five) by the number of years.

Increment, mean annual. The average increment since the crop was established, or up to a given age. This equals the total yield divided by the age.

Indicating per cent. The annual increase in the value of a stand (which combines the volume increment with the increase in value per cubic metre or cubic foot) expressed as a percentage of the value at the beginning of the year.

Management plan—see *Working plan* and *Plan of operations*, and Section 4 of this chapter.

Normal forest. A forest in which all age classes are appropriately represented.

Period. The length of time adopted for the duration of the various prescriptions contained in the management plan. This is sometimes referred to more specifically as the working plan period.

Periodic block. Part of a woodland area which is marked down for treatment (such as regeneration) during a given period.

Plan of operations. An abbreviated and simplified form of management plan prescribed by the Forestry Commission for use by private woodland owners under the Woodland Grant Scheme (see Section 4 of this chapter).

Stock map. A map showing different types of woodland according to their species, age, etc.

Sub-compartment—see *Compartment.*

Sustained yield. The continuous and regular yield from a forest or woodland area.

Working circle. An area or areas controlled by the same working plan, managed on the same silvicultural system, and subject to the same prescription as to treatment.

Working plan. A written plan or programme for the management of a forest, woodland, or woodland estate, which assumes an uninterrupted sequence of control (see Section 4 of this chapter).

2. *Management tables*

The Forestry Commission first published yield tables in 1920 based upon temporary plot information and in 1953 published yield tables based on permanent sample plot data. A new and more comprehensive series of yield tables was published in 1966 entitled *Forest Management Tables* which included thinning control tables and thinning and felling forecast tables as well as normal yield tables.

In 1971 a metric edition was published, but these tables were replaced in 1981 by *Yield Models for Forest Management* (Booklet

No. 48). The yield models are very similar in form to the previous Normal Yield Tables which were included in Booklet No. 34, but cover a much wider range and are too extended to incorporate in this edition.

3. *Schneider's Formula*

(a) General

(i) If a stand of timber is measured it will be found to contain a certain number of cubic metres or cubic feet.

(ii) Each year, provided the trees are growing, the volume will be increased by a certain amount. The increase in the volume is known as the 'volume increment'.

(iii) The volume of the crop is in fact the capital, and the increment represents the interest which the capital produces.

(iv) It is possible by means of Schneider's formula to ascertain the volume increment of a single tree as a percentage of its standing volume.

(b) Schneider's formula

(i) This formula, which is given below, has two limitations, namely:

(*a*) It cannot be applied accurately to trees which are growing rapidly in height.

(*b*) The results obtained by using this formula are usually an under-estimate.

(ii) In order to ascertain the information needed for the formula, borings must be taken with a Pressler borer, which is described in Chapter IX, Section 7.

(iii) The formula:

$$p = \frac{400}{n \times d}$$

Where:

p = increment per cent, i.e. the current annual increment expressed as a percentage of standing volume;
n = number of annual rings in the outside inch of the tree;
d = the diameter at breast height under bark.

Note. The boring is taken at breast height.

4. *Working Plans*

(a) General

There are two principle types of plan in use in this cuntry:

(i) Complete working plans.
(ii) Plans of Operations.

(b) Working plans

(i) A working plan may be described as a carefully prepared programme of management for a woodland area.

(ii) Although it takes into account the past and the present, it is largely concerned with the future, and it defines the objects of management and lays down in general the procedure which must be followed and the action which must be taken in the future. It also prescribes a detailed procedure for the next few years.

(iii) A working plan should be as simple as is reasonably possible, but owing to the many factors which have to be taken into account, and to the complexity of woodland management, simplicity is not always easy to achieve.

(c) Plans of Operations

(i) Under the Dedication Scheme, the Plan of Operations for a moderately large area of woodland could be quite a substantial document. However, the Plan required for the Woodland Grant Scheme, which was introduced in 1988, has been very much abbreviated and simplfiied and now covers a period of only 5 years.

(ii) At the end of the 5 years an owner can either withdraw from the Scheme or continue for a further 5 years, under a fresh Plan of Operations.

(iii) When applying to join the Woodland Grant Scheme it is necessary to complete the Plan of Operations which forms a part of Application Form WGS1. This is divided into five sections.

(1) Management objectives.

(2) Matters which may affect or apply to the woodlands concerned and on which consultation may be needed before the application can be approved. The following are examples of these: whether any previous grants have been received; whether the woodlands are in a National Park or an Area of Outstanding Natural Beauty, or whether a tree preservation order is in operation.

(3) A summary of the work which is to be carried out under the Plan including planting, thinning, felling and natural regeneration.

(4) Information as to the way in which any matters relating to the environment and conservation are to be dealt with under the Plan.

(5) Detailed proposals, by compartments, for the ensuing 5 years as regards restocking, new planting and natural regeneration.

(iv) To assist in the completion of the Plan, the Forestry Commission has issued *Guidance Notes and Specimen Application Form* which can be obtained free of charge from the Commission.

5. *Compartment History Sheets*

(*a*) It is difficult to over-emphasize the value of properly kept forest records, which, if conscientiously maintained, can provide information of the greatest value for future reference, or for those who follow after.

(*b*) The following are examples of the information which may be entered in Compartment History Sheets:

(i) Age and origin of young trees which are planted.
(ii) Weather conditions at the time of planting.
(iii) Details of weeding and cleaning.
(iv) Information as to brashing and thinning.
(v) Items of special interest, such as damage, fire, freak weather conditions, etc.

(*c*) A suggested heading for a suitable sheet is given below:

COMPARTMENT HISTORY SHEET

Cpt. No. . . . . . .

FOREST YEAR	MONTH	SUB-CPT.	OPERATION	REMARKS

6. *Compartment Files*

(*a*) To provide a readily available record of current information in respect of each woodland area, a system of compartment files will be found very convenient.

(*b*) The covers are the usual pattern of correspondence files, with some means of firmly retaining the papers placed therein.

(*c*) One file is allotted to each compartment, and as a basis contains a tracing taken from the Ordnance Survey 25in. sheet showing the compartment area divided into sub-compartments where these occur.

(*d*) If some system of colouring the plans is adopted, whereby the silvicultural system and type of species, e.g. broadleaved or conifer, can be recognized at a glance, the value of these plans will be greatly increased.

(*e*) The value of the plan will again be enhanced if a tabular description of each compartment (by sub-compartments if applicable) is included in the file. The following is a form designed and used by the author:

.... ESTATE

....

....

Name of Wood	O.S. 1:2,500 Sheet:
Working Circle	O.S. 1:10,000 Sheet:
Compartment No.	O.S. Nos.
Sub-Comp. No.	Area
Species	Formation
Silvicultural System	Soil
Age/Date planted	Planting Distance
Details stock planted	Method of Mixing
Dates of thinnings	Crop Quality
Special damage	Site Quality
Previous Crop	Date previous crop felled

NOTES

(*f*) Other information which may be conveniently included in the file is:

(i) Copies of any application for grants.
(ii) Record of insurance cover against fire in the case of young plantations.
(iii) Record of grants received in respect of the compartment.
(iv) Copies of special correspondence dealing with the compartment, e.g. letters written to nurserymen ordering trees to be planted in the compartment.

7. *Card Index Records*

(*a*) Unless the information which has been collected and recorded is readily available, much of its value will be lost.

(*b*) A card index system will enable the details of each sub-compartment to be ascertained with the minimum amount of trouble.

(*c*) Index cards are usually about 15 cm (6 in.) long and 10 cm (4 in.) deep and consequently entries must be concise and brief. Cards with horizontal ruled lines are preferable.

(*d*) Abbreviated headings can be printed at the left-hand end of the card and the appropriate information entered on the line opposite the heading.

(*e*) The choice of headings depends on the information which is to be recorded.

(*f*) The following is an example of headings intended to provide information regarding thinnings, outturn and volume. To save space the headings are shown in two columns, although in practice they would be printed in one column on the left-hand margin of the card.

Species	Average diameter at 1·3 m (4 ft 3 in.)
Sub-cpt. No.	*Date*
Area	Average top height
Age	*Date*
Thinning dates	Yield class
Thinning condition	Total standing volume
Date	*Date*

8. *Woodland Grant Scheme*

Details of this Scheme, together with information relating to grants which can be obtained from other bodies as well as the Forestry Commission, will be found in Chapter XXIV.

CHAPTER IX

Timber Measuring

1. *Introduction*

(*a*) During recent years a number of changes have taken place in the traditional methods of measuring timber and these have been largely due to the adoption of the metric system by the Forestry Commission in 1971 and to the increased use of tariff and volume tables.

(*b*) Detailed descriptions of the new methods, and procedures which have been evolved will be found in Forestry Commission Booklet No. 39, *Forest Mensuration Handbook*, which forms a complete treatise on timber measuring. Booklet No. 49, *Timber Measurement*, which is a pocket-size summary for use in the woods, is also available.

(*c*) Although the Commission has now discarded the Hoppus system, it is still used by a number of private estates and home timber merchants, and for this reason Hoppus measure is still included in this chapter.

2. *Measurement of Standing Trees*

(*a*) *Individual trees*

This subsection deals with the calculation of the contents of an individual tree by quarter-girth measure, metric measure and with the use of Single Tree Tariff Charts.

(i) *Quarter-girth measure*

(1) This method is correctly known as 'the square of the quarter-girth measurement' and the sectional area of the tree, when this method is adopted, is equivalent to a square, one side of which is equal in length to one-quarter of the girth.

(2) It was adopted by E. Hoppus, Surveyor to the Corporation of the London Assurance, when he first drew up his timber-measuring tables in 1736. Until the introduction of metrication in 1971, quarter-girth measure was the normal method of measuring timber in this country.

(3) This system of measurement makes a large allowance for waste, the contents obtained by Hoppus being 21·5% less than the contents found by geometry.

(4) For this reason, the contents of a tree calculated by this method are known as 'Hoppus' feet and not 'cubic' feet so as to differentiate between the volume obtained by quarter-girth or Hoppus measurement and that obtained by the rules of geometry.

(5) The volume is found by multiplying the square of the quarter-girth by the length of the tree in feet. As the quarter-girth is in inches and the length of the tree in feet, the result must be divided by 144, thus:

$$\text{Volume in Hoppus feet} = \frac{(\text{mean quarter-girth in inches})^2 \times \text{length in feet}}{144}$$

Example
If the mean quarter-girth is 11¾ in. and the length 46 ft

$$\text{Volume} = \frac{11{\cdot}75^2 \times 46}{144}$$
$$= 44{\cdot}10 \text{ Hoppus feet.}$$

This figure can be converted into cubic metres by multiplying it by 0·036 and in this case the result would be 1·59 cubic metres.

(6) If, in the above formula, a divisor of 113 is used instead of 144, the volume will be in cubic feet and not Hoppus feet and, using the same quarter-girth and length, this would amount to 56·10 cubic feet or 1·59 cubic metres.

(7) In practice the volume is obtained from Hoppus's timber tables which are generally known as 'Hoppus's Measurer'. However the approximate number of Hoppus feet which a piece of round timber contains can be calculated in the following way. For certain quarter-girths the contents are obtained by dividing or multiplying the length of the butt by a given factor. These are shown in the list on p. 85.

Example
Mean quarter-girth is 21 in. and the length 20 ft. Multiply length by 3.
20 ft × 3 = 60 Hoppus feet.

6	in. quarter-girth	: divide length of butt by 4
7	„ „ „ „	: „ „ „ „ „ 3
8½	„ „ „ „	: „ „ „ „ „ 2
12	„ „ „ „	: multiply „ „ „ „ 1
16	„ „ „ „	: „ „ „ „ „ 1¾
17	„ „ „ „	: „ „ „ „ „ 2
19	„ „ „ „	: „ „ „ „ „ 2½
21	„ „ „ „	: „ „ „ „ „ 3
24	„ „ „ „	: „ „ „ „ „ 4
27	„ „ „ „	: „ „ „ „ „ 5
29½	„ „ „ „	: „ „ „ „ „ 6
32	„ „ „ „	: „ „ „ „ „ 7
34	„ „ „ „	: „ „ „ „ „ 8
36	„ „ „ „	: „ „ „ „ „ 9
38	„ „ „ „	: „ „ „ „ „ 10
40	„ „ „ „	: „ „ „ „ „ 11
41½	„ „ „ „	: „ „ „ „ „ 12
43½	„ „ „ „	: „ „ „ „ „ 13
45	„ „ „ „	: „ „ „ „ „ 14
46½	„ „ „ „	: „ „ „ „ „ 15
48	„ „ „ „	: „ „ „ „ „ 16
49½	„ „ „ „	: „ „ „ „ „ 17
51	„ „ „ „	: „ „ „ „ „ 18
52½	„ „ „ „	: „ „ „ „ „ 19
54	„ „ „ „	: „ „ „ „ „ 20

(ii) *Metric measure*

(1) This method is based on the geometrical formula for obtaining the formula of a cylinder, that is:

$$\text{Volume} = \text{sectional area} \times \text{length}$$

(2) The area of a circle is found from πr^2 where π is a constant of 3:14159 and r is the radius of the circle.

(3) However, as it is the diameter (d) of the bole of a tree or a log which is measured, and not the radius, it is simpler to replace πr^2 by $\pi(d/2)^2$ or $\pi d^2/4$.

(4) Since the diameter is measured in centimetres and the length in metres it is also necessary to use a divisor of 10,000. The formula is therefore:

$$\text{Volume in cubic metres} = \frac{[(\text{mid-dia. in cm})/2]^2 \times 3{\cdot}14159 \times \text{length in m}}{10{,}000}$$

Example
If the mean diameter is 38 cm and the length 14 m

$$\text{Volume} = \frac{(38/2)^2 \times 3{\cdot}14159 \times 14}{10{,}000}$$
$$= 1{\cdot}59 \text{ cubic metres.}$$

(5) Alternatively, Huber's formula may be used which gives the same result.

Volume in cubic metres

$$= \frac{\text{mid-dia.}^2 \times 3{\cdot}14159}{40{,}000} \times \text{length in m.}$$

(6) The contents, in cubic metres, of round timber can be readily found by means of the tables contained in Booklet No. 39. In comparison with Hoppus's Measurer, this contains:
(*a*) mid-diameters in centimetres instead of mid quarter-girth in inches;
(*b*) lengths in metres instead of in feet;
(*c*) volumes in cubic metres instead of in Hoppus feet.

(7) An estimation of the contents of a piece of timber in the round can be obtained from the following table, in which each diameter (in centimetres) together with its corresponding length (in metres) are equal to 1 cubic metre. For diameters of 36–110 cm the contents can be calculated as follows:
(*a*) The mid-diameter is measured and, on reference to the table on p. 87, the length of timber required to produce 1 cubic metre will be found opposite the diameter concerned.
(*b*) The length of the piece is then measured and this figure is divided by the length which is shown in the table opposite the diameter.
(*c*) The resulting figure will be the number of cubic metres which the piece contains.

Example

Mid-dia. of piece:		59 cm
Length of piece:		9·25 m
Length in table (opposite diameter):		3·66 m
Number of cubic metres in log	=	$\frac{9{\cdot}25}{3{\cdot}66}$
	=	2·52 cubic metres.

DIAMETERS AND LENGTHS

Dia. (cm)	*Length (m)*	*Dia. (cm)*	*Length (m)*	*Dia. (cm)*	*Length (m)*	*Dia. (cm)*	*Length (m)*	*Dia. (cm)*	*Length (m)*
36	9·80	51	4·90	66	2·92	81	1·94	96	1·37
37	9·30	52	4·70	67	2·84	82	1·90	97	1·36
38	8·80	53	4·54	68	2·75	83	1·85	98	1·33
39	8·40	54	4·36	69	2·67	84	1·80	99	1·30
40	8·00	55	4·20	70	2·60	85	1·76	100	1·28
41	7·60	56	4·05	71	2·53	86	1·72	101	1·25
42	7·20	57	3·92	72	2·46	87	1·68	102	1·23
43	6·90	58	3·80	73	2·40	88	1·64	103	1·20
44	6·60	59	3·66	74	2·32	89	1·61	104	1·17
45	6·30	60	3·54	75	2·26	90	1·57	105	1·16
46	6·00	61	3·42	76	2·20	91	1·53	106	1·13
47	5·80	62	3·32	77	2·15	92	1·50	107	1·12
48	5·55	63	3·20	78	2·10	93	1·48	108	1·10
49	5·30	64	3·10	79	2·04	94	1·43	109	1·07
50	5·10	65	3·02	80	1·99	95	1·42	110	1·05

(iii) *With single tree tariff charts*

(1) This method, which may be used for measuring individual trees or small groups, is described in detail in Booklet No. 39.

(2) Briefly the procedure is as follows:

(*a*) The diameter of the tree is measured at breast height, i.e. 1·3 m (4 ft 3 in.).

(*b*) The height of the tree is measured: conifers to the tip; broadleaved trees to timber height, i.e. 7 cm (2·8 in.) diameter or where the main bole ends.

(*c*) According to the species, select a single tree tariff chart from those contained in Booklet No. 39 and from this obtain the tariff number as instructed in the Booklet.

(*d*) Refer this number to the tariff tables in the Booklet and select the volume for the appropriate breast height diameter. This will be the over bark volume.

(*b*) *Stands of trees for sale*

(i) This method of measurement is based on the use of tariff tables and in order to calculate the volume of a stand under the tariff system three fundamental steps are necessary:

(1) all trees are counted;

(2) the trees are then classified according to their breast height diameter;

(3) the numbers of trees counted are converted into volumes.

(ii) This operation is described at length in Booklet No. 39 and in view of the very detailed procedure which has to be followed it is essential to refer to that publication. Reliable results can only be obtained by carefully following each of the steps which are laid down.

(c) Stands of trees when accuracy is not paramount

(i) This method can be used where a quick and inexpensive estimate of the volume is needed rather than a strictly accurate one, as for example when making inventories or preparing valuations.

(ii) This entails the assessment of:
  (1) the basal area per hectare;
  (2) the top height of the crop;
  (3) the net area of the stand.

(iii) Full details of the procedure to be followed, and the calculations involved, are given in Booklet No. 39, to which reference should be made for further information.

(d) Underwood and coppice

Traditionally underwood and coppice are measured in two ways, and these are still in use on many private estates.

(i) *By the acre*

The usual survey methods are adopted but since visibility is frequently difficult, the work will be greatly simplified if the area is divided up by a series of rides or rackways.

In Kent and Sussex areas of chestnut are often divided into parcels known as 'falls' or 'cants', which are felled when the crop is marketable. Measuring the area to be felled is known as 'washing out' or 'canting out'.

(ii) *By the ton*

If the underwood is a pole crop it may be sold by the ton, evidence of the weight being provided by ticket from a public weighing machine.

3. *Measurement of Felled Timber*

(a) Round timber

The method of calculating the volume of felled timber in the round is the same as that which is described for the measurement of standing trees in Section 2 of this chapter, on p. 85, under 'Individual trees—(ii) Metric measure.'

(b) Sawlogs

(i) Booklet No. 39 describes a method of measuring sawlogs which is quicker than that which is outlined in paragraph *(a)* above.

However it is only suitable for measuring conifer logs which are not more than 8·3 m in length.

(ii) In order to use the tables which are provided in Booklet No. 39 two measurements are necessary: the top diameter of the log in centimetres and its length in metres.

(iii) In constructing these tables a standard taper, of 1 cm diameter in 120 cm of length, has been adopted, although individual logs may differ from this. Consequently the tables are more accurate when a large number of logs are measured. It has also been assumed that taper only exists between the top of the log and the midpoint of its length.

(iv) Full details as to the construction of the tables and their use, are given in Booklet No. 39.

(c) Smallwood

(i) This method is intended to be used for measuring small diameter material such as garden poles, light stakes and so on.

(ii) The volumes given in the tables in Booklet No. 39 are for 100 pieces of material, the dimensions of which lie within the limits of 0·05 and 4·0 m in length and from 4 to 23 cm top diameter.

(iii) A standard taper of 1 cm diameter in 84 cm length, as between the top and a point midway along the length, has been adopted.

(iv) Full details will be found in the *Forest Mensuration Handbook*.

(d) Pitwood

(i) Booklet No. 39 provides two types of tables for the measurement of pitwood.

(ii) The first gives the volumes for pitwood in lots of 100 pieces having lengths of 0·375–4·0 m and top diameters of from 6 to 20 cm which are the dimensions required by the National Coal Board.

(iii) The second set of tables provide the volume of 100 lineal metres of material within the same dimensional limits as those given in the last paragraph.

(iv) The same degree of taper has been assumed as for smallwood, i.e. 1 in 84.

(e) Stacked produce

The system which has been evolved by the Forestry Commission for measuring stacked timber of uniform length, produced for such purposes as pulpwood, chipboard and woodwool, is described in considerable detail in Booklet No. 39. Reference should accordingly be made to that publication for information on this subject.

(f) Cordwood, firewood and faggots

(i) *General*

The measurement of stacked produce, as practised by the Forestry Commission and referred to in paragraph (*e*) above, is based on metric units of measurement. However since the traditional methods of measuring branch wood by the cord, ton or faggot are still used in many parts of the country, the following information relating to these methods is included. The equivalent metric dimensions are given where appropriate.

(ii) *Cordwood*

(1) Cordwood is the small branch wood or 'lop and top' which forms the crown of the tree and is more particularly applied to broadleaved trees.

(2) After cutting out, the material is arranged in stacks or cords, the sizes of which are in accordance with recognized dimensions as given below. The metric equivalents are also shown.

Length		*Height*		*Width*		*Contents*	
8 ft	(2·44 m)	4 ft	(1·21 m)	4 ft	(1·21 m)	128 ft^3	(3·62 m^3)
12 ft	(3·66 m)	3 ft	(0·91 m)	3 ft 6 in.	(1·06 m)	126 ft^3	(3·56 m^3)
12 ft	(3·66 m)	3 ft	(0·91 m)	4 ft	(1·21 m)	144 ft^3	(4·08 m^3)
12 ft	(3·66 m)	3 ft	(0·91 m)	3 ft 3 in.	(0·99 m)	117 ft^3	(3·31 m^3)
14 ft	(4·26 m)	3 ft	(0·91 m)	3 ft	(0·91 m)	126 ft^3	(3·56 m^3)
14 ft	(4·26 m)	2 ft 9 in.	(0·84 m)	3 ft 3 in.	(0·99 m)	125 ft^3	(3·53 m^3)

The first measurement is most frequently used.

(3) The contents shown in the above table are the product of the three measurements but the actual volume of timber in a cord of 128 cubic feet is approximately 75 cubic feet, 59 Hoppus feet or 2·13 cubic metres.

(4) The weight of a cord of wood depends on the species and the moisture content:

One cord of freshly felled wood weighs approximately 31 cwt or 1·57 tonnes.

One cord of seasoned wood weighs approximately 21 cwt or 1·07 tonnes.

These figures apply to broadleaved trees, and not to conifers which are lighter in weight.

(5) A tall well-grown oak will produce about a cord (8 × 4 × 4 ft) to every 80 Hoppus feet of timber while inferior trees will average about a cord to 46 Hoppus feet. The metric equivalent of these quantities is a cord of 2·44 × 1·21 × 1·21 m to every 2·88 or 1·66 cubic metres.

(iii) *Firewood*

(1) Firewood may be sold by the cord, as already described above, or by the ton or tonne of sawn blocks or logs.

(2) The number of blocks to a tonne or ton depends on the species and degree of dryness.

(iv) *Faggots*

(1) Large faggots are 1·22 m (4 ft) in length, with a girth of 0·91 m (3 ft) when tied in the centre.

(2) Small faggots are 22·8 cm (9 in) long with a girth of 33 cm (13 in.) when tied in the centre.

4. *Measurement by Weight*

(*a*) The Forestry Commission use weight measurements for two purposes:

(i) For selling material such as pulpwood and chipboard by the tonne.

(ii) For estimating the volume of the produce from the weight.

(*b*) Full details of the procedure and points to be taken into account are given in Booklet No. 39.

(*c*) Although the sale of produce by weight is common practice on private estates, the estimation of volume from weight would seem to have a less general application in private forestry.

5. *Bark Allowance*

(a) General

(i) When measuring a tree the tape or callipers are, of necessity, placed over the bark and consequently the volume of the tree will include the bark, unless some deduction is made for it.

(ii) For many years two methods were used for making the necessary allowance; namely, the percentage method and the one-in-twelve method. These have now been largely replaced by tables contained in Booklet No. 39.

(b) Percentage method

This varied according to the species and subsequently, under the Statutory Rules and Orders No. 2209 published in 1946, a deduction of 15% of the contents was made in respect of poplar, alder, lime and elm; 7½% for ash, beech, hornbeam, sycamore and conifers, and 10% for other species. One variation was made in the case of conifers grown in Scotland, for which the deduction was fixed at 10%.

(c) One-in-twelve method
By this method a deduction of 1 in. in the quarter-girth reading was made up to 12 in., and 2 in. for each additional 6 in. quarter-girth.

(d) Tables
(i) The procedure in making allowances for bark changed considerably when the *Forest Mensuration Handbook* (Booklet No. 39) was first published in 1975, since this contains tables for calculating bark thickness and percentages.
(ii) The first of these tables gives the double bark thickness for diameters measured over bark in respect of fourteen conifers and seven broadleaves.
(iii) A further set of tables indicate the percentage of bark contained in an overbark volume for the same species, whose height and diameter at breast height are known.
(iv) The last table sets out the amount of bark as a percentage of the underbark volume for seven species of conifer where the top diameter under bark has been measured.

6. *Taper*

(*a*) Taper may be described as the rate at which the girth decreases in proportion to the height; that is to say, the nearer to the top of the tree that the girth is measured, the smaller it tends to become.

(*b*) Until recent years the following allowances for taper were commonly made:

broadleaves: 1 in. deducted from the quarter-girth for every increase in height of 6 ft;

conifers: 1 in. deducted from the quarter-girth for every increase in height of 10 ft.

(*c*) The Forestry Commission have now adopted two 'standard tapers' as follows:

sawlogs: 1 in 120;

smallwood and pitwood: 1 in 84.

In both cases this refers to the taper between the top and the midpoint of the log. Details will be found in Booklet No. 39.

7. *Timber Measuring Equipment and Procedure*

(a) Girth measurements
(i) These measurements may be carried out either with a tape or by means of callipers.
(ii) Timber tapes are of two main kinds:
quarter-girth tapes which show the quarter-girth in inches;

metric tapes which show the diameter in centimetres, rounded down to centimetre diameter classes.

(iii) When girthing a tree the following action should be taken:

(1) The girth should be measured at breast height, that is, 1·3 m (4 ft 3 in.) above ground level.

(2) The tape should be at right angles to the bole and should not be twisted, knotted or slack.

(3) Trees growing on sloping sites should be measured from ground level on the higher side.

(4) Where a swelling or canker occurs on the bole at breast height, the girth should be taken immediately below it.

(5) Trees which are less than 7 cm ($2\frac{3}{4}$ in.) diameter are not considered to have sufficient volume to justify their measurement.

(iv) Details of the procedure followed by the Forestry Commission will be found in Booklet No. 39 and in Booklet No. 49, *Timber Measurement.*

(v) Callipers consist of a graduated rule, to which are fitted two arms; one fixed to the end of the rule and the other being movable. Both arms are fixed at right angles to the rule, the moving arm sliding along it.

(vi) In operation, the callipers are held at right angles to the axis of the stem with the fixed arm pressed against it. The sliding arm is then moved until it is against the opposite side of the bole when the reading on the rule is noted. Where the cross-section of the stem is not truly circular it is necessary to take a second reading at right angles to the first, if accurate results are to be achieved.

(b) Height measurements

(i) The height of a tree can be measured with the aid of various instruments or equipment and these include the following:

altimeter	theodolite
hypsometer	45° set square and plumb-bob
dendrometer	timber pole.

(ii) Other than using a timber pole for measuring young trees, heights are now usually obtained by means of an altimeter, of which there are several patterns such as the *Haga* and *Suunto.* Detailed instructions as to their use and method of operation are provided with the instruments, and are not therefore included in this section.

(iii) The Forestry Commission have categorized 'height' as follows:

Mean height. The mean total height of a stand.

Timber height. In the case of conifers, this is the distance from the base to a point where the diameter of the main stem is not less than 7 cm ($2\frac{3}{4}$ in.). In broadleaved trees it is usually the point at which the crown begins; that is, where the bole divides into a number of limbs or branches.

Top height. The average total height of the 100 trees which have the largest diameter at breast height, per hectare.

Total height. The distance from the base of the tree to its highest point; that is, its tip.

(iv) Further information on measuring the height of trees or stands will be found in Forestry Commission Booklet No. 39, *Forest Mensuration Handbook*.

(c) Basal area measurement

(i) The basal area of a stand can be measured by means of a *relascope* or *basal area angle gauge* which was invented by Dr W. Bitterlich, an Austrian forester, in 1948.

(ii) In its original form it consisted of a blade, 2 cm wide, fixed at the end of a rod, 1 m long. When the rod was held against the cheek and pointed at a tree at breast height (1·3 m (4 ft 3 in.) above ground level), the blade would appear to be wider than some trees and less wide than others. All trees whose diameters were wider than the blade were counted, and the number arrived at was equivalent to the basal area of the stand in square metres per hectare.

(iii) Subsequent developments resulted in the production of a relascope which operated through the medium of wedge prisms. The Spiegel Relascope, which incorporated this principle, can be used for the measurement of tree heights, tree diameters at varying heights as well as vertical angles.

(iv) Further information on the measurement of basal areas and the use of the relascope, will be found in the *Forest Mensuration Handbook*, in Booklet No. 49, *Timber Measurement*, and in Field Book No. 2, *Thinning Control*.

(d) Increment measurement

(i) Two instruments have been evolved for this purpose: Pressler's increment borer and the increment hammer. However, the latter is seldom if ever used in this country and accordingly this section is confined to Pressler's borer.

(ii) This instrument consists of three main parts:
 (1) a hollow boring spindle with a sharp cutting point and thread;
 (2) a handle which also forms a case for protecting the boring spindle;
 (3) a spill extractor.

(iii) When assembled for use, the instrument is 'T'-shaped, the handle forming the horizontal bar and the boring spindle the vertical one.

(iv) To operate, the cutting point is pressed against the bole of the tree and rotated by turning the handle. When it has penetratd to a sufficient depth, the spill extractor is inserted into the boring spindle and the borer is given half a turn in the reverse direction. This will cause the spill to break off and it can then be withdrawn.

(v) The number of annual rings and their distance apart will be seen from an examination of the spill. This will indicate the current girth increment, the increment over a period of years, the need for thinning and so on.

(vi) Schneider's formula, which may be used in connection with Pressler's borer, will be found in Section 3 of Chapter VIII.

8. *Size Assortments*

(*a*) Those who are concerned with woodland management often need information relating to the sizes of material which a stand contains, in addition to the gross volume.

(*b*) The Forestry Commission has accordingly provided information as to the 'size assortments', which may be defined as the pieces of timber of various lengths and diameters which may be obtained when cross-cutting a tree.

(*c*) The relevant information will be found in Booklet No. 39, which contains the following tables:

(i) Assortment tables in respect of individual trees; stands; volume; length.

(ii) Stand table for conifers, by means of which the proportion of the number of trees in a stand which are of a specified mean diameter at breast height, may be ascertained.

(iii) Stock table for finding what proportion of the volume of a stand is of a given diameter.

9. *Volume Tables*

The following is a brief account of the volume tables which are included in Booklet No. 39, *Forest Mensuration Handbook*.

(a) Roundwood table

This table gives the volume in cubic metres of roundwood within the length limits of 1·0–10·0 m and from 7 to 166 cm, mid-diameter.

(b) Sawlog table

This provides the volume in cubic metres of sawlogs which vary from 1·8 to 8·3 m in length and from 10 to 72 cm top diameter.

(c) Smallwood table

In this table volumes in cubic metres, per 100 pieces, are given for lengths of 0·5–4·0 m and for top diameters from 4 to 23 cm.

(d) Pitwood tables

Two tables for pitwood are provided, as follows:

(i) In the first, the volume is given in cubic metres per *100 pieces* for lengths of 0·375–4·0 m and for top diameters of 6–15 cm. The sizes which are given in the table are those which are required by the British Coal Corporation.

(ii) The second table gives the volume in cubic metres per *100 lineal metres* and covers the same size limits as the first table.

10. *Tariff Tables*

The tables in Booklet No. 39 are in respect of tariff numbers 1–60. Numbers 1–9 cover breast height diameters of 7–30 cm; numbers 10–19 cover diameters of 7–80 cm and numbers 20–60 cover diameters of 7–100 cm.

11. *Measurements and Conversion Factors*

This section contains a selection of figures and conversion factors which may be found useful in connection with timber measuring.

In the figures which are given below the following abbreviations have been used:

inch	in.	cubic foot	ft^3
foot	ft	cubic yd	yd^3
yard	yd	cubic metre	m^3
metre	m	Hoppus foot	h.ft
acre	ac	quarter-girth	q.g.
hectare	ha	diameter	dia.

(a) Metric measure

1·00 m^3	= 35·314 ft^3
	= 27·736 h.ft
	= 1·307 yd^3
0·0283 m^3	= 1 ft^3
0·0360 m^3	= 1 h.ft
0·7645 m^3	= 1 yd^3
0·0699 m^3 per ha	= 1 ft^3 per ac
0·0890 m^3 per ha	= 1 h.ft per ac
1·000 m^3 per ha	= 12·291 ft^3 per ac
1·000 m^3 per ha	= 11·224 h.ft per ac

(b) Hoppus measure

1 h.ft	=	0·036 m^3
	=	1·273 ft^3
1 h.ft per ac	=	0·089 m^3 per ha

(c) Imperial measure

1 ft^3	=	0·028 m^3
	=	0·785 h.ft
1 yd^3	=	0·764 m^3
1 ft^3 per ac	=	0·069 m^3 per ha

(d) Conversion factors

h.ft to ft^3	:	multiply	h.ft by 1·273
h.ft to m^3	:	„	h.ft by 0·036
ft^3 to h.ft	:	„	ft^3 by 0·785
ft^3 to m^3	:	„	ft^3 by 0·028
m^3 to ft^3	:	„	ft^3 by 35·315
m^3 to h.ft	:	„	m^3 by 27·736
m^3 to yd^3	:	„	m^3 by 1·308
ft^3 per ac to m^3 per ha	:	„	ft^3 by 0·070
h.ft „ „ „ m^3 „ „	:	„	h.ft by 0·090
m^3 per ha to ft_3 per ac	:	„	m^3 by 14·291
m^3 „ „ „ h.ft „ „	:	„	m^3 by 11·224
Stems per ac to stems per ha	:	„	stems per ac by 2·471
„ „ ha „ „ „ ac	:	„	„ „ ha by 0·405
dia. (in.) to girth (in.)	:	multiply	dia. by 3·142
„ (cm) to q.g. (in.)	:	„	„ „ 0·309
q.g. (in.) to dia. (cm)	:	„	q.g. „ 3·234

CHAPTER X

The Elements of Forest Surveying

1. *The Principles of Surveying*

SPACE does not permit of anything more than a very brief reference to the principles of surveying, and if more information is required reference should be made to a textbook on the subject.

(a) *General*

Broadly speaking, surveying can be divided into two classes:

(i) Chain surveys. (ii) Instrumental surveys.

(b) *Chain surveys*

(i) These are so called because the greater part of the work is carried out with an actual chain, of which there are two patterns:
Gunter's chain. This is equal to the length of a cricket pitch, i.e. 22 yd or 4 rods, and is divided into 100 links each link being 7·92 in. in length. Since 10 square chains are equal to 1 acre, this method of measurement is very convenient for calculating acreages.
The hundred-foot chain. This chain is divided into 100 links, each 1 ft in length. It is generally used in surveying building land, and not for forest or agricultural land.

(ii) The principle adopted in making a chain survey of an area of land is to set out and measure a base line. The area is then covered by subsidiary lines laid out in the form of well-conditioned triangles, and built up from the base line. This is known as triangulation.

(iii) Any features, such as hedges or buildings, which are not covered by this triangulation are plotted by means of offsets measured at right-angles from a known point on a triangulation line. If possible such offsets should not exceed 50 links.

(iv) If a metric survey is to be made the same procedure can be followed, a metre tape being used instead of a chain. A 20 m tape is almost equal to a chain, being 0·994 chains or 65·62 ft in length, while a 30 m tape is a little less than 100 ft, namely 98·43 ft.

(c) Instrumental surveys

(i) In this method a base line is again laid out and measured with the utmost accuracy.

(ii) Various points or stations are selected and their position calculated by measuring the angle between the base line and the line of sight to the station, and also by measuring the distance between stations if this is necessary.

(iii) The position of each station is then calculated by trigonometry.

(iv) The angles are measured by means of a theodolite.

(d) The application of surveying to forestry

(i) Where a large area is to be afforested and it is necessary to set out the boundaries, rides, and so on, a careful and accurate chain or instrumental survey will be necessary.

(ii) In estate forestry the afforestation of large areas is the exception rather than the rule, and normally woodland surveying in this country is confined to plotting on an existing plan areas which have been replanted, new rides, and compartment or sub-compartment boundaries.

(iii) In practice, tracings of large-scale Ordnance Survey maps, to a scale of 1 : 2,500 or 25 in. to 1 mile (1 cm to 25 m) will be found to meet the requirements of most foresters. Reproduction of these maps can only be undertaken by permission of the Ordnance Survey, as stated in Section 2 of this chapter.

(iv) Such tracings may have to be brought up to date if new areas are planted, or new rides are laid out, as stated in subparagraph (ii) above. This can usually be done by taking the necessary measurements with a chain or tape, but the presence of underwood and trees often makes visibility difficult.

(v) As soon as the planting season is over, all young plantations, felled sites, and areas of coppice which have been cut should be surveyed and plotted on a tracing of the appropriate 25 in. Ordnance Survey sheet, or the sheet itself. Failure to do this will lead to inaccurate records, and in course of time to confusion.

It will be found that the survey of such areas will be greatly facilitated if their boundaries coincide with the lines of rides or other permanent features which are already shown on the plan. If this is not possible, the boundaries of new areas should be laid out so as to avoid unnecessary or pointless changes in direction, in order to save time and to avoid possible errors.

2. *Ordnance Survey Maps*

(a) General

The following Ordnance Survey maps are the most useful in forestry.

(i) The 1 : 50,000 map
Drawn to a scale of 1 : 50,000 or 2 cm to 1 km (1¼ in. to 1 mile), this map has now replaced the former 1in. map, the scale of which was 1 in. to 1 mile or 1 : 63,360.

(ii) The 1 : 25,000 map
This map, which has a scale of 4 cm to 1 km (2½ in. to 1 mile), is intermediate between the 1 : 50,000 and 1 : 10,560 maps.

(iii) The 1 : 10,000 map
Originally published on a scale of 1 : 10,560 (6 in. to 1 mile) these maps are now being drawn to a scale of 1 : 10,000 (1 cm to 100 m).

(iv) The 1 : 2,500 map
This map is produced to a scale of 1 : 2,500 or 25 in. to 1 mile (1 cm to 25 m).

(b) The 1 : 50,000 map

(i) This map is useful for showing or identifying extensive or scattered areas of woodland.

(ii) It is also valuable for obtaining a general impression of contours, altitudes, and general topography of a district.

(iii) The map further provides a ready means of appreciating the network of roads and railways which cover an area, not only from the point of view of communications, but also as regards risk of fire and other damage.

(c) The 1 : 25,000 map

(i) The scale of this map is considerably larger than the 1 : 50,000 but smaller than the 6-in.

(ii) It shows a large amount of detail, contours being marked at 25 ft (7·6 m) vertical intervals while woodland areas, which are coloured green, are distinguished as between coniferous, non-coniferous, mixed and coppice.

(iii) The first series of this map was issued with blue covers but the second series (designated Pathfinder series) are now supplied with green ones.

(d) The 1 : 10,000 map

(i) This map has now replaced the 1 : 10,560 or 6 inch map, but in view of the very small difference in scale they can be regarded as the same for all practical purposes.

(ii) The 1 : 10,000 maps are particularly suitable when dealing with large blocks of woodlands and have been adopted by the Forestry

Commission as the basic maps in the preparation of management plans.

(e) The 1 : 2,500 map

(i) The scale of these maps is sufficiently large to show clearly the position of rides, methods of stocking, sub-compartments, etc. It also shows the areas of enclosures.

(ii) Consequently, they are very suitable for preparing working plans, compartment records, and so on.

(iii) If a system of Compartment Files is maintained (as described in Chapter VIII, Section 6), a tracing of each compartment based on the Ordnance Survey 1 : 2,500 sheet will be found most useful if it is included in the file.

Note. Before any part of an Ordnance Survey map can be reproduced, a licence must be obtained. Enquiries regarding this or any other matters relating to the Ordnance Survey should be addressed to: Information and Enquiries, Ordnance Survey, Romsey Road, Maybush, Southampton SO9 4DH.

3. *Geological Maps*

(*a*) Most geological maps are published by the Ordnance Survey for the Institute of Geological Sciences, Exhibition Road, South Kensington, London SW7 2DE. Maps can be purchased either from the Geological Museum, South Kensington or through Ordnance Survey Agents.

(*b*) Maps are issued in several scales but foresters will find that those of 1 : 63,360 or 1 : 50,000 are the most useful. Maps to these scales have been prepared for England, Wales, Scotland and Northern Ireland and information as to which are available can be obtained from the Ordnance Survey or through their Agents.

4. *Tables of Length—Metric Measure*

(a) Metric length

Kilo-metres	*Hecto-metres*	*Deca-metres*	*Metres*	*Deci-metres*	*Centi-metres*	*Milli-metres*
1	10	100	1,000	10,000	100,000	1,000,000
	1	10	100	1,000	10,000	100,000
		1	10	100	1,000	10,000
			1	10	100	1,000
				1	10	100
					1	10
						1

(b) Metric–Imperial equivalents

Metric measure	*Inch*	*Feet*	*Yard*
Millimetre	0·039	0·003	0·001
Centrimetre	0·393	0·032	0·010
Decimetre	3·937	0·328	0·109
Metre	39·370	3·280	1·093
Kilometre	39,370·1	3,280·8	1,093·6

Note. One kilometre = 0·62137 mile.

(c) Imperial–metric equivalents

Imperial measure	*Millimetres*	*Centimetres*	*Decimetres*	*Metres*	*Kilometres*
Inch	25·40	2·54	0·254	0·025	0·00002
Foot	304·80	30·48	3·048	0·304	0·00030
Yard	914·39	91·43	9·143	0·914	0·00091
Chain	20,116·43	2,011·64	201·164	20·116	0·02011
Mile	1,609,315	160,931·5	16,093·150	1,609·315	1·60931

(d) Conversion factors—metric to Imperial

Millimetres to inches	:	multiply by	0·03937
Centimetres „ „	:	„ „	0·3937
Metres „ „	:	„ „	39·370
Metres „ feet	:	„ „	3·280
Metres „ yards	:	„ „	1·093
Metres „ chains (Gunter)	:	„ „	0·049
Kilometres „ miles	:	„ „	0·6214

(e) Conversion factors—Imperial to metric

Inches to millimetres	:	multiply by	25·40
Inches to centimetres	:	„ „	2·54
Inches to metres	:	„ „	0·025
Feet to „	:	„ „	0·304
Yards to „	:	„ „	0·914
Chains (Gunter) to metres	:	„ „	20·117
Metres to kilometres	:	„ „	6·609

5. *Tables of Length—Imperial Measure*

(a) Imperial length

Miles	*Furlongs*	*Chains*	*Poles*	*Yards*	*Feet*	*Links*	*Inches*
1	8	80	320	1,760	5,280	8,000	63,360
	1	10	40	220	660	1,000	7,290
		1	4	22	66	100	792
			1	5½	16½	25	198
				1	3	4·545	36
					1	1·515	12
						1	7·92

Note *(i) Poles are also known as rods or perches.*
(ii) Chains are Gunters.

(b) Decimal equivalents of yards, feet and inches

Inches	*Decimals of a foot*	*Decimals of a yard*
1	0·083	0·027
2	0·166	0·055
3	0·250	0·083
4	0·333	0·111
5	0·416	0·138
6	0·500	0·166
7	0·583	0·194
8	0·666	0·222
9	0·750	0·250
10	0·833	0·277
11	0·916	0·305
12	1·000	0·333

6. *Tables of Area—Metric Measure*

(a) *Metric square measure*

Square kilo-metre	*Hectares*	*Acres*	*Square hecto-metres*	*Square deca-metres*	*Square metres*	*Square deci-metres*	*Square centi-metres*	*Square milli-metres*
1	100	10,000	100 00	10,000	10^6	10^8	10^{10}	10^{12}
	1	100	1	100	10,000	10^6	10^8	10^{10}
		1	0·01	1	100	10,000	10^6	10^8
			1	100	10,000	10^6	10^8	10^{10}
				1	100	10,000	10^6	10^8
					1	100	10,000	10^6
						1	100	10,000
							1	100

Note. In order to save space in the foregoing table, figures of 1,000,000 and above are shown by index notation, that is to say, the number of noughts is represented by a small indicating figure after the figure 10. For example:

$$1{,}000{,}000 = 10^6$$
$$100{,}000{,}000 = 10^8$$
$$10{,}000{,}000{,}000 = 10^{10}$$

(b) *Metric–Imperial equivalents*

Metric measure	*Square inches*	*Square feet*	*Square yards*	*Acres*
Square centimetre	0·155	—	—	—
Square decimetre	15·500	—	—	—
Square metre	—	10·763	1·196	0·0002
Acre	—	1,076·39	119·59	0·0247
Hectare	—	107,639·0	11,959·9	2·471

(c) *Imperial–metric equivalents*

Imperial measure	*Square decimetres*	*Square metres*	*Acres*	*Hectares*
Square inch	0·0645	—	—	—
Square foot	9·2899	0·0929	—	—
Square yard	83·6097	0·8360	—	—
Square pole	—	25·2919	—	—
Rood	—	—	10·1167	—
Acre	—	—	40·460	0·4047
Square mile	—	—	—	258·989

Note. A rod, pole or perch is 5½ yards in length.
A square rod is 30¼ square yards in area.
A rood is 1,210 square yards in area.

(d) Conversion factors—metric to Imperial

Square millimetres to square inches	:	multiply by 0·0015
„ centimetres „ „ „	:	„ „ 0·155
„ metres „ „ feet	:	„ „ 10·764
„ „ „ „ yards	:	„ „ 1·195
„ kilometres „ „ miles	:	„ „ 0·3861
Hectares „ acres	:	„ „ 2·471

(e) Conversion factors—Imperial to metric

Square inches to square millimetres	:	multiply by 645·16
„ „ „ „ centimetres	:	„ „ 6·451
„ feet „ „ metres	:	„ „ 0·092
„ yards „ „ „	:	„ „ 0·836
„ miles „ „ kilometres	:	„ „ 2·589
„ „ „ hectares	:	„ „ 0·404

7. *Tables of Area—Imperial Measure*

Imperial square measure

Square mile	*Acres*	*Roods*	*Square chains*	*Square rod, pole or perch*	*Square yards*	*Square feet*	*Square links*	*Square inches*
1	640	2,560	6,400	102,400	3,097,600	27,878,400	64,000,000	—
—	1	4	10	160	4,840	43,560	100,000	6,272,640
—	—	1	2·5	40	1,210	10,890	25,000	1,586,160
—	—	—	1	16	484	4,356	10,000	627,264
—	—	—	—	1	30·25	272·25	625	39,204
—	—	—	—	—	1	9	20·66	1,296
—	—	—	—	—	—	1	2·295	144
—	—	—	—	—	—	—	1	62·72

8. *Tables of Volume—Metric Measure*

(a) Metric–Imperial equivalents

1 cubic centimetre	=	0·061 cubic inches
1 „ metre	=	35·314 „ feet
1 „ „	=	27·736 Hoppus feet
1 „ „	=	1·308 cubic yards
1 „ „ per hectare	=	14·291 „ feet per acre
1 „ „ „ „	=	11·224 Hoppus „ „ „

(b) Conversion of metric to Imperial

Multiply the unit to be converted, by the British unit shown on the right, thus:

To convert cubic metres to cubic feet, multiply the number of cubic metres by 35·314.

(c) Imperial–metric equivalents

1 cubic inch	=	16·387 cubic centimetres
1 „ foot	=	0·028 „ metres
1 Hoppus „	=	0·036 „ „
1 cubic yard	=	0·764 „ „
1 „ foot per acre	=	0·069 „ „ per hectare
1 Hoppus „ „ „	=	0·089 „ „ „ „

(d) Conversion of Imperial to metric

Multiply the unit to be converted, by the metric unit shown on the right, thus:

To convert Hoppus feet to cubic metres, multiply the number of Hoppus feet by 0·036

(e) Other Imperial measure

1,728 cubic inches	=	1 cubic foot
27 „ feet	=	1 „ yard

9. *Tables of Weight*

(a) Metric–Imperial equivalents

1 gramme	=	0·035 ounces (avoirdupois)
1 kilogramme	=	2·204 pounds (lb)
1 „	=	0·078 quarters
1 „	=	0·019 hundredweights (cwt)
1 tonne	=	19·684 „
1 „	=	0·984 tons

(b) Conversion of metric to Imperial

Multiply the unit to be converted, by the British unit shown on the right, thus:

To convert kilogrammes to pounds multiply the number of kilogrammes by 2·204.

(c) Imperial–metric equivalents

1 ounce	=	28·349	grammes
1 pound	=	0·453	kilogrammes
1 quarter	=	12·700	"
1 hundredweight	=	50·802	"
1 "	=	0·0508	tonnes
1 ton	=	1·016	"

(d) Conversion of Imperial to metric

Multiply the unit to be converted, by the metric unit shown on the right thus:

To convert pounds into kilogrammes multiply the number of pounds by 0·453.

(e) Imperial avoirdupois measure

16 drams	=	1 ounce
16 ounces	=	1 pound
14 pounds	=	1 stone
28 pounds	=	1 quarter (qtr)
4 quarters	=	1 hundredweight (cwt)
112 pounds	=	1 hundredweight
2,240 pounds	=	1 ton
20 hundredweights	=	1 ton

CHAPTER XI

Forest Protection

IN this chapter certain kinds of damage to woodland areas are considered, but injuries resulting from fungi, bacteria, viruses and insects are dealt with in Chapter XII.

1. *Climatic Factors*

(a) Frost

(i) In this country the most serious damage by frost is due to:
  (1) Late spring frosts. (2) Early autumn frosts.

(ii) In some cases damage is caused by the intensity of cold in winter, but this is not common.

(iii) A very quick thaw increases the damage, and consequently south and south-east aspects suffer most, especially in the case of nurseries.

(iv) Frost crack is caused by the cambium being injured, and although the wound callouses over, the timber will generally be blemished. Frost rib occurs where repeated frosts cause a crack to open up in successive years, thin-barked trees being most susceptible.

(b) Lightning

(i) Damage by lightning may take two forms: firstly, scarring or cracking; and secondly, complete rending of the tree.

(ii) Conclusive evidence on the susceptibility of species to damage is not available, but there seems to be some foundation for the following observations:
  (1) Smooth-barked trees suffer less than rough-barked, possibly owing to less resistance being offered by a smooth surface.
  (2) Oak seems to be damaged more often than other species, followed by elm (both these trees have rough bark).
  (3) Large trees are often struck more frequently than small ones.
  (4) Old trees appear to be struck more often than young ones.

(iii) Many different species have been recorded as being struck by lightning, including, alder, ash, beech, cherry, sweet chestnut, elm, plane, poplar, sycamore, spruce, Douglas fir, larch, and Scots pine.

(c) Snow

(i) Snow can damage trees in two ways: individually by breaking leaders or side branches (especially in the case of ornamental trees, such as cedars of Lebanon); collectively by damaging groups of trees in plantations, especially where they have been under-thinned.

(ii) Damage caused by snow often results in further injury through another agent. Where branches are broken off, fungi may infect the wound. Collective damage in young pole crops may be made worse by wind-blow.

(iii) Generally speaking, evergreen trees suffer from snow more than deciduous ones, and species with a stiff horizontal branching habit more than those with drooping or flexible branches.

(d) Sun

(i) Hot sun may cause damage to trees under certain circumstances.

(ii) Young plantations

(1) Hot sun accompanied by a drying wind in April may cause serious damage to evergreen species which have a large leaf surface, e.g. Lawson cypress.

(2) Where the weeding of a young plantation has been delayed, and the small trees are suddenly exposed to hot sun, leaf scorch may occur.

(iii) Individual trees

Damage may be caused to the bark of trees if they are suddenly exposed to hot sun by a heavy thinning, or by reflected heat from roads or buildings in the case of roadside trees in towns. This is particularly the case with thin-barked species.

(iv) Nurseries

In very hot weather the soil of seed beds heat to such an extent that the stems of very young seedlings are killed at soil surface and then fall over.

(e) Water

(i) Although water can be considered as a climatic factor only indirectly, it may for convenience be included here.

(ii) An excess of water may be caused by:

(1) Poor drainage.

(2) A rise in the water table.

(iii) A shortage of water will result from:

(1) Excessive drainage.

(2) A fall in the water table.

(3) A prolonged drought.

(iv) An excess of water will cause the death of young plants, and produce 'stagheadedness' in mature or near mature trees.

(v) A deficiency in the water supply results in die-back of the leading shoots of young trees, and will also cause old trees to become 'stagheaded'.

(f) Wind

(i) Wind can cause very considerable damage to woodlands, although in many cases under-thinning is a contributory factor.

(ii) Damage by wind may take any of the following forms:
- (1) Blowing down of individual trees or groups of trees.
- (2) Blowing out of the tops of trees.
- (3) Distortion of the crown, especially near the sea coast or on exposed sites.
- (4) Excessive transpiration, resulting in stunted growth.

(iii) Although the prevailing wind for Great Britain is generally considered to be south-westerly, local prevailing winds may come from any direction.

(iv) Isolated trees, and trees on the margin of woodlands, develop strong root systems, which enables them to withstand all normal winds. If, however, trees are suddenly exposed to wind, they will frequently blow out, since their roots are not able to withstand the unaccustomed strain. Once a 'hole' has been made in an even-aged stand, the damage is likely to spread.

(v) Precautions against wind damage.
- (1) Ensure that the area is adequately drained. Wet water-logged soil provides the ideal conditions for wind-blow.
- (2) Avoid species which are susceptible to wind-blow, such as Norway spruce.
- (3) Under-thinning renders a crop very liable to damage by wind and thinning should be adequate and regular.
- (4) In certain circumstances wind damage can be reduced by planting shelter belts in suitable positions.

(vi) For details of those species which are considered wind-firm under normal conditions reference should be made to the appropriate column in Chapter I.

Note. For detailed information on climatic factors, reference should be made to *Pathology of Trees and Shrubs*, by T. R. Peace.

2. *Fire*

(a) Causes of fires

Forest fires are attributable to various causes and these include dropping unextinguished matches, throwing away burning cigarette ends (especially from cars), picnic parties and organized fires getting out of control.

(b) Danger periods

Danger from fires is probably greatest in March, before young green growth has started, and in October, after seasonal growth has finished, although a dry summer is always a dangerous time.

(c) Damage

(i) Damage varies from total destruction of young plantations to bark scorch of mature or semi-mature trees, which may ultimately cause their death.

(ii) Young broadleaved trees have considerable recuperative powers after burning, but young conifers usually succumb.

(iii) The most dangerous period for young plantations is from planting until brashing.

(iv) Thick-barked trees withstand fire better than thin-barked.

(d) Types of fires

(i) Forest fires can be divided into three main classes:
- (1) Ground fires.
- (2) Surface fires.
- (3) Crown fires: (*a*) low crown fires; (*b*) high crown fires.

(ii) *Ground fires*
- (1) These occur largely in old pine woods and on dry peats, where the top layer of soil consists of semi-decayed vegetation.
- (2) In this type of fire there are seldom any flames, but instead a steady smouldering, marked by a black spread of heat.
- (3) Ground fires are often difficult to deal with quickly, since it is difficult to locate the exact position of the fire. Furthermore, they are liable to recur unexpectedly after the area is apparently safe.

(iii) *Surface fires*
- (1) In this type of fire the ground vegetation is burnt, and most woodland fires start in this way.
- (2) Young plantations up to 10 years of age are generally wiped out, while older plantations may be badly damaged by bark scorch.
- (3) Young conifers are invariably killed, but broadleaved trees have a far greater power of recovery.
- (4) Vegetation which is particularly inflammable includes heather, *Molinia*, and dead bracken.

(iv) *Low crown fires*

Low crown fires are the next development after surface fires, in which the lower branches of large trees are set alight, while small trees are destroyed entirely.

(v) *High crown fires*
The worst and most extensive form of fire, where everything burns.

(e) *Precautions against fire*

(i) *Layout of rides*

(1) In laying out new plantations a certain number of rides should be formed at right-angles to the prevailing wind.
(2) These rides should not be less than 9 m (30 ft) wide and should be kept free of vegetation by ploughing, bulldozing and/or the application of a suitable herbicide. Details of these will be found in Forestry Commission Booklet No. 51, *The Use of Herbicides in the Forest.*

(ii) *Fire belts*

(1) In woodlands which consist chiefly of conifers, belts of hardwoods may be established at right-angles to the prevailing wind. These can often be incorporated with the rides referred to above by establishing the belt on one or both sides of the ride.
(2) The object of these belts is to provide an area which does not readily ignite; firstly, because broadleaved trees are used, and secondly, because surface vegetation will be kept down if species such as beech are used and if the area is partly coppiced. Suitable broadleaved species are: alder, beech, birch, false acacia, oak, sweet chestnut, sycamore, and white poplar.
(3) The Forestry Commission have also used Japanese larch for fire-belts.

(iii) *Distribution of regeneration areas*
If areas which it is intended to clear fell, and replant are distributed throughout the woodland area, large areas of young plantations adjacent to each other will be avoided, and the fire risk materially reduced.

(iv) *Removal of brash in fire danger areas*
Brash should be removed from areas in which there is a serious risk of fire, e.g. beside public footpaths, roads, and railways.

(v) *Erection of fire observation towers*
The expense of erecting and manning fire towers is only likely to be justified where there is a large area of young plantations. If possible, towers should be sited so that they command the most extensive view.

(vi) *Provision of fire-fighting equipment*
Fire-fighting equipment can be divided into two classes:

(1) That which is readily available in or adjacent to the plantation, e.g. fire brooms, long-handled shovels, and rakes.
(2) That which is available at centralized points in the forest area, e.g. axes, saws, mattocks, spades, and other tools, and also portable pumps, fire 'packs', and so on.

(vii) *Liaison with the local fire brigades*
Fire brigade officers are always most helpful, and will advise on fire-fighting and hazards. All estate employees should know the telephone number of the nearest brigade.

(viii) *Fire patrols*
During danger periods, patrols should be organized to watch for possible fires. This is particularly necessary at week-ends, bank holidays, and early-closing days.

(ix) *Erection of fire danger notices*
Suitable notices may be erected where footpaths and roads intersect or adjoin young plantations.

(x) *Water supplies*
Locations of suitable supplies of water for fire-fighting should be plotted on a map, a copy of which should be sent to the local Fire Officer. Members of the estate staff should be familiar with the sources.

(f) Fire-fighting

(i) The key to successful fire-fighting is prompt and immediate action, since once a fire has become established, it is much more difficult to extinguish it.
(ii) In most cases a fire should be attacked from the flanks, so as to reduce its frontage.
(iii) Ground fires can only be controlled with any certainty by digging trenches across the path of the fire sufficiently deep to reach below the layer of combustible material.
(iv) Surface fires will require organized beating, with the assistance of the fire brigade in serious cases.
(v) Crown fires; the steps to be taken will include:
   (1) Clearing a strip ahead of the fire, a bulldozer being a great asset for this task.
   (2) Assistance from one or more fire brigades.
   (3) Counter-firing or back-firing; this should only be done in extreme cases by persons who have had previous experience of it.
(vi) After a fire has been extinguished, the area should be carefully watched in case fresh outbreaks occur.

(g) Insurance of plantations

(i) Young plantations should be insured against loss by fire for a definite period after planting. This may be 10, 15, or 20 years.

(ii) Plantations should be insured for the cost of establishment, but as a plantation gains in growth and therefore in value, the insurance should be progressively increased to ensure that it is adequately covered.

Note. Further information on forest fires will be found in Forestry Commission Bulletin No. 14, *Forestry Practice*, and Leaflet No. 80, *Forest Fire Fighting with Foam.*

3. *Domestic Animals*

(*a*) All farm animals are capable of causing considerable damage to trees.

(*b*) Horses will gnaw the bark of mature trees, particularly elm and beech, and if a tree is girdled death will generally result.

(*c*) Cows, sheep, and goats may cause very serious damage through browsing young trees, if they gain entrance to a recently planted area.

(*d*) Pigs, if unringed, will root up young trees. However, they can be very useful in preparing a site in anticipation of natural regeneration, provided they are suitably restricted as, for example, by an electric fence.

(*e*) The only effective method of preventing damage by farm stock is to ensure that all woodland fences are properly maintained. Individual specimen trees must be protected by means of tree guards.

4. *Wild Animals*

(a) Rabbits

(i) Despite the outbreak of *Myxomatosis* which occurred in 1953, and subsequently spread through practically the whole of England and Wales and much of Scotland, rabbits managed to survive and have now re-established themselves.

(ii) No species of tree is immune from attack although it is commonly supposed that self-sown trees are less liable to attack than those which have been planted. In some areas Corsican pine, self-sown sycamore and lime seem to be unpalatable to rabbits.

(iii) Control methods include shooting trapping, gassing, fencing and the encouragement of the natural enemies of the rabbit, i.e. foxes, stoat, weasels, etc.

(iv) For details of rabbit fencing see Chapter XIX.

(v) Further information may be obtained from Forestry Commission Leaflet No. 67, *Rabbit Management in Woodlands* and Forest Record No. 125, *Rabbits*

(b) Hares

(i) The hare population varies very much, according to the locality.

(ii) Hares damage young trees by gnawing and barking the stem, and biting the leading shoot. They appear to prefer deciduous trees to conifers, and do not readily attack spruce or pine.

(iii) Control is mainly by shooting, and rabbit fencing cannot be considered as effective against hares.

(c) Squirrels

(i) There are two kinds of squirrel:
The red squirrel—*Sciurus vulgaris.*
The grey squirrel—*Sciurus carolinensis.*

(ii) The red squirrel is a native of this country and frequents conifer woods rather than broadleaved areas. It is gradually being driven out of the southern parts of Britain by the grey variety. Although it does little harm in comparison to the grey squirrel, it can cause considerable damage in conifer areas, by girdling the stems of trees and eating buds and seeds.

(iii) The grey squirrel causes very serious damage wherever it is found. Apart from killing young birds, destroying eggs, bulbs, and fruit, it strips the bark off hardwood trees in the late spring, often causing irreparable injuries. The species which are primarily attacked are sycamore, beech, ash, and hornbeam, although other trees are attacked. Tree seeds are also destroyed, which may adversely affect efforts at natural regeneration.

(iv) Control may be attempted by the following action:
(1) Shooting both squirrels and dreys.
(2) Trapping.
(3) Organization of squirrel clubs.

(v) The use of aluminium sectional poles for poking out dreys can give good results when shooting squirrels.

(vi) Further information on grey squirrels will be found in Forestry Commission Leaflet No. 56, *Grey Squirrel Control.*

(d) Deer

(i) Deer which are found in this country may be classified as follows: fallow, red, roe, Sika and miscellaneous such as Muntjac.

(ii) Red deer are usually confined to certain recognized districts including Exmoor, the Quantocks, the New Forest, Thetford, and the Scottish Highlands.

(iii) Fallow and roe are to be found in many woodlands but Sika are much more limited in their distribution.
(iv) Deer can cause damage by stripping bark, by rubbing, by trampling or by biting off the leaders and side shoots of young trees.
(v) Control measures comprise fencing, which is expensive, shooting, and in some cases hunting. Certain chemical deterrents have been tried but their efficacy is not always certain. Details of deer fencing can be found in Chapter XIX.
(vi) The Deer Act 1963 has done a great deal to limit the unwarranted destruction of deer, often by cruel or inhumane methods. Amongst other matters, this Act lays down close seasons and prohibits the use of certain weapons, snares and traps. Particulars of the close seasons for deer will be found in Chapter XXII.
(vii) The following Forestry Commission publications are concerned with deer. Bulletin No. 71, *The Management of Red Deer in Upland Forests*; Forest Record No. 124, *The Fallow Deer*; Leaflet No. 74, *High Seats for Deer Management*; Leaflet No. 86, *Glades for Deer Control in Upland Forests*.
(viii) Leaflet No. 73, *Chemical Repellants*, deals with the protection afforded by chemicals against browsing by deer, hares and rabbits.

(e) Mice and voles

(i) Damage may be caused by several species, including the following:
Field vole (*Microtus*) Bank vole (*Clethrionomys*)
Long-tailed field mouse (*Apodemus*)
(ii) Damage includes gnawing the bark of young trees, and eating seeds and buds.
(iii) Control may be effected by:
(1) Trapping by pitfalls or traps.
(2) Poisoning.
(3) Treatment of seeds with substances such as carbolic acid.
(4) Encouragement of predatory animals, e.g. foxes, stoats, weasels.
(5) Encouragement of predatory birds, e.g. hawks, owls, buzzards, etc.

Note. See also Forestry Commission Forest Record No. 118, *Woodland Mice*.

(f) Moles

(i) Moles can cause damage by 'lifting' young trees during their first and second years after planting.
(ii) They can also cause trouble in a nursery.

(iii) Control can be effected by trapping, or by putting poison in their runs.

Note. For detailed information on the animals referred to in this section, reference should be made to *The Handbook of British Mammals*, edited by H. N. Southern (Blackwell Scientific Publications, 1964).

5. *Birds*

(*a*) At the present time there appears to be insufficient evidence to enable all birds to be classified as either harmful or beneficial. Such a classificaton is complicated by the fact that some birds are partly harmful and partly useful.

(*b*) The damage which harmful birds cause includes:

(i) Injury to trees by eating buds or seeds, or breaking leading shoots.

(ii) Killing beneficial birds.

(*c*) Beneficial birds are useful in that they destroy insect pests, and also mice and young rabbits.

(*d*) It will be appreciated that some birds, while doing a certain amount of good, also cause a certain amount of harm. For example, a kestrel may kill mice and voles, but also small birds which do good.

(e) The following is a guide to the classification of a selection of birds from a forestry aspect:

(i) *Definitely useful*

Blackbird	Robin	Warblers
Hedge-sparrow	Thrush	Woodpecker
Night-jar	Tits	Wren
Owl		

(ii) *Definitely harmful*

Blackgame (eat pine buds)
Capercaillie (eat pine bids)
Crossbill (strip cones and eat seeds)
Jay (eat eggs and young of useful birds)
Wood-pigeon (eat seeds and buds)

(iii) *Partly useful and partly harmful*

Bullfinch (eat insects, but also buds)
Chaffinch (eat insects, but also seedlings)
Hawk (kill young rabbits, mice, and chafters, but also beneficial birds)
Lark (eat insects, but also seedlings)
Rook (eat insects, but may destroy eggs of beneficial birds)
Starlings (eat insects, but can cause serious damage by roosting habits)

(*f*) Beneficial birds can be encouraged by the provision of nesting-boxes, and to some extent by destroying their natural enemies, but great care must be exercised in this latter respect, lest the balance of nature is upset and a worse state of affairs results.

6. *Plants*

(*a*) A plant may be classed as harmful if it deprives a tree of light, air, food, or growing space, or interferes with its natural and normal development.

(*b*) The plants mentioned below may cause injury or damage to trees:

(*c*) Bracken (*Pteris aquilina*)

(i) Damage is caused by:
  (1) Suppressing and smothering young plants.
  (2) Increasing the risk of fire, when the fronds are dead and dry.

(ii) Control in woodlands is mainly by cutting, owing to practical difficulties involved in spraying, liming, etc.

(*d*) Gorse (*Ulex europaeus*)

(i) Damage results in smothering young plants, and adding to the cost of clearing a site for planting.

(ii) Control is generally by cutting in woodlands, but eradication is only likely if the roots are grubbed up. Burning tends to encourage growth rather than discourage it.

(*e*) Honeysuckle (*Lonicera periclymenum*)

(i) Damage takes the form of constriction of the stems of trees when young and in the pole stage. In addition to the stem becoming deformed, the restriction tends to produce weakness in the stem, so that windbreak may occur later on.

(ii) Control by cutting back.

(*f*) Traveller's Joy (*Clematis vitalba*)

(i) This plant, which is also known as 'Old Man's Beard', is common on limestone formations.

(ii) Damage consists of climbing up trees in the pole stage, and interfering with their growth; while young trees are often completely overwhelmed.

(iii) Control by cutting.

(*g*) Ivy (*Hedera Helix*)

(i) Damage comprises the gradual enveloping of the tree, which restricts its development.

(ii) Control by cutting at ground level.

(*h*) Poisonous trees and shrubs.

Among the commoner poisonous trees and shrubs are the following:

Yew (especially when the leaves are withered)
Rhododendron (poisonous to cattle)
Laburnum (seeds and leaves)

Daphne (the classic poison of the Ancients)
Laurel (*Laurus nobilis*).

Note. Further information on rhododendrons will be found in Forestry Commission Bulletin No. 73, *Rhododendron ponticum as a Forest Weed.*

7. *Air Pollution*

(*a*) In recent years, damage to forests by air pollution has become a very serious problem in parts of eastern North America and Europe, especially in the Black Forest in West Germany.

(*b*) There is at present a lack of evidence as to the extent to which trees in the United Kingdom are being damaged by air pollution. However, the Forestry Commission is carrying out a major research programme into the matter.

(*c*) Although air pollution is commonly referred to as 'acid rain', this is misleading since, to a certain degree, rain is naturally acid. Consequently, the term 'acid rain' should be applied only to rain which is more acid than it would normally be.

(*d*) The chemicals which can cause long-range pollution can be separated into two groups, primary and secondary.

(i) The primary group includes:

Sulphur dioxide (SO_2)	Hydrogen chloride (HCl)
Nitric oxide (NO)	Ammonia (NH)
Carbon monoxide (CO)	Hydrocarbons (HC)

(ii) In the secondary group are:
Sulphate (SO_4)
Ozone (O_3)

(*e*) The polluting agents, known as pollutants, can be deposited in either dry or wet forms. Dry deposition generally occurs near the source of the pollution while wet deposition takes place some distance away.

(*f*) In 1984 road transport was the main source of nitric oxide, carbon dioxide and hydrocarbons, while power stations produced the largest amount of sulphur dioxide.

(*g*) Further information on this subject will be found in the following Forestry Commission publications:
Bulletin No. 70, *Air Pollution and Forestry* (1987).
Pamphlet, *Acid Rain, Air Pollution and Forestry.*

CHAPTER XII

Diseases and Pests

(*a*) This chapter is divided into three sections, the first dealing with fungi and fungal diseases, the second with bacteria and viruses and the third with insects.

(*b*) In 1977 the European Economic Community (EEC) drew up a Plant Health Directive which, amongst other matters, deals with the following points:

(i) The provision of plant certificates for imported plants.

(ii) The action which should be taken to prevent the introduction of between thirty and forty pests and diseases with certain special provisions as to the United Kingdom.

(iii) Special emergency measures which should be taken to deal with unforeseen circumstances.

(*c*) The most important tree species to which the Directive applies are, as regards the United Kingdom: *Abies* (silver fir), *Larix* (larch), *Picea* (spruce), *Pinus* (pine), *Pseudotsuga* (Douglas fir), *Tsuga* (hemlock), *Castanea* (sweet chestnut), *Populus* (poplar), *Quercus* (oak) and *Ulmus* (elm).

(*d*) Further information on these matters can be found in Forestry Commission Forest Record No. 116, *The EEC Plant Health Directive and British Forestry.*

1. *Fungi*

(*a*) In this section, fungi are considered under two main headings:

(i) Those which primarily attack timber, bark, or roots.

(ii) Those which affect foliage or cause damage in forest nurseries. These are considered under one heading as it is not always easy to separate them.

In both cases fungi are listed alphabetically under their usual English names.

(*b*) A full account of the dieases of trees which are caused by fungi, bacteria and viruses will be found in *Pathology of Trees and Shrubs*, by T. R. Peace (1962), in *Diseases of Forest and Ornamental Trees* by D. H. Phillips and D. A. Burdekin (1982) and in numerous Forestry Commission publications.

A. FUNGI PRIMARILY ATTACKING TIMBER, BARK OR ROOTS

Fungus	*Description*	*Species of tree attacked*	*Damage*	*Remarks*
1. Ash canker *Nectria galligena*	Eruptions on the bark, roughly circular in shape up to about 3 in. diameter.	Ash.	Serious damage to trunk of poles, which reduces their value to that of firewood.	Ash canker can also be caused by bacterium *Pseudomonas savastanoi.*
2. Beech bark disease *Cryptococcus fagisuga* (syn. *Cryptococcus fagi*), *Nectria coccinea*	This disease is caused by the Felted Beech Scale (see Section 3D.23 of this chapter) and the fungus *Nectria coccinea*. After infection by the Beech Scale, the fungi enter mainly through the resulting wounds and patches of bark die. Subsequently, sap oozes like black slime from these areas.	Beech.	After a few years infected trees die and the main stem may break off at a height of 3–5 m (10–15 ft). This is known as 'Beech snap' and is due to other decay organisms and wood-boring beetles.	There is some evidence to suggest that outbreaks of the disease are more likely on downland sites in southern England, on slopes, in pure beech stands and after a heavy thinning. See F.C. Bulletin No. 69, *Beech Bark Disease*.
3. Beef steak fungus *Fistulina hepatica*	Fructification appears in early autumn; at first soft creamy juicy lumps, but soon becomes tongue-shaped. When mature, is deep purplish-red or brown on upper surface and creamy white below. Flesh reddish and marbled.	Chiefly oak and Spanish chestnut, but can attack some other broadleaved trees. Seldom fructifies on young trees, but is found typically on old park oaks, especially if pollarded. Does not attack conifers.	In later stages of attack produces heart rot, but little damage is done to vigorously-growing trees.	Spores enter through wounds, and spread to heartwood. Discoloration produces 'brown oak', which may enhance value of tree. Fructifications edible. See F.C. Arboricultural Leaflet No. 5.
4. Birch polyphore *Piptoporus betulinus* (syn. *Polyporus betulinus*)	A hoof-shaped fructification, the upper surface being a rather shiny greyish-white, the flesh being thick and white. It is usually found growing on birch trees several feet above ground level.	Birch.	Entering by wounds, the fungus turns the wood brown. In due course the wood is reduced to state of complete rottenness.	Very common on birch throughout the country. See F.C. Arboricultural Leaflet No. 5.
5. Bleeding canker *Phytopthora cactorum*	Invisible to the naked eye.	Horse chestnut, lime and apple.	Red, black or light brown sticky liquid seeps out of areas of dying bark. In time tree is girdled and dies.	This fungus can also cause Root Rot, as described under No. 18. See F.C.Arboricultural Leaflet No. 8.

Fungus	*Description*	*Species of tree attacked*	*Damage*	*Remarks*
6. Broadleaved tree canker *Nectria ditissima*	Fructifications: minute dull red pustules appear in spring, and are followed by white pustules in late summer and autumn. As attack develops a sunken black wound or canker occurs, which is surrounded by irregularly broken or projecting bark.	Many broadleaved trees, the following having been recorded: ash, elder, beech, cherry, hazel, hornbeam, lime, sycamore, and fruit trees generally. Probably commonest on ash. Does not attack conifers.	Where there are several cankers on a tree, the timber will be fit only for firewood. Even one large canker will greatly depreciate the value of a tree.	The only treatment is to cut out infected trees. When thinning, avoid damaging the bark of those treses which are to be left.
7. Brown cubical butt-rot or dry crumbly rot *Phaeolus schweinitzii* (syn. *Polyporus schweinitzii*)	Fructification bracket-shaped, dark rusty brown in colour, except for growing margin, which is tawny yellow. Upper surface hairy or velvety. Flesh soft and spongy, becoming fragile on drying. Fructifications invariably occur near ground level, often on roots, and half hidden by soil or leaves.	Most coniferous trees but especially Douglas fir, Sitka spruce and larch. Has also been found on oak and cherry.	Infection occurs through roots. Fungus spreads to heartwood, producing a reddish-brown rot, which tends to divide the timber into small cubes. Infected timber produces a sweet/sour resinous smell.	Fungus may grow on a tree for many years before fructification produced. May cause considerable damage. Conifers planted on old hardwood sites are especially subject to attack. See F.C. Leaflet No. 79.
8. Chestnut blight *Endothia parasitica*	Small yellow, orange, or reddish-brown pustules, about the size of a pin head, appear in very large numbers on the bark.	Sweet or Spanish chestnut (*Castanea sativa*)	The fungus kills an area of bark on the main stem of a tree or coppice pole, which very soon girdles the tree and kills that portion above the point of attack.	This fungus has caused tremendous damage to chestnut in the United States of America and Italy. If it became established in this country it is likely that the growing of chestnut would no longer be an economic proposition.
9. Conifer heart-rot or white pocket rot *Heterobasidion annosum* (syn. *Fomes annosus*)	Fructification can be flat and stalkless or bracket-shaped. The former occur on roots where they are exposed to dim light, e.g. in rabbit holes, or on upper side of large roots which are just below ground level. Brackets occur at base of trunk. Upper surface of fructification is reddish-brown with white margin. Under-side white or yellow, perforated by small brown marginal holes.	Most conifers, but more seriously Douglas fir, larch, Norway spruce, Western red cedar (*Thuya plicata*), Western hemlock (*Tsuga heterophylla*). Two of the more resistant conifers are Scots and Corsican pine. Has been known to attack broadleaved trees, but this is uncommon. Stumps of freshly felled trees should be treated with 2% solution of urea.	Infection through roots, rot spreading upwards through heartwood. Timber turns pink and rotten, and turns to tinder if dry or slime if wet. In advanced stages, trees become 'foxed' or 'pumped'. Small trees under 10 years old may be attacked and killed. Scots and Corsican pine are most susceptible to damage at this age.	Can cause serious damage. Appears more prevalent on sites which are too dry or too wet for species concerned, and in a first crop planted on arable land. May be detected by fructification, swelling at base of tree, tapping trunk with stick, use of Pressler borer, or examination of felled or wind-blown trees. See F.C. Leaflets Nos. 5 and 79.

10. Conifer red-rot *Trametes pini*	Varies in appearance from a thin shell-like bracket to a thick hoof-shaped form. At first dark rusty brown in colour, becoming almost black. Young fructifications have golden yellow margin.	Conifers.	Causes extensive rotting of the heartwood. Infection through wounds.	Although frequently found on the Continent, is uncommon in this country.
11. Coral spot *Nectra cinnabarina*	Fructification appears as bright coral red spots. Being both parasitic and saprophytic, it is found on both dead and living branches or stems.	*Parasitically* Apple, horse chestnut, lime, sycamore. *Saprophytically* Elm, hazel, lime, poplar, sycamore.	Causes death of individual branches.	Although very common, is not serious.
12. Elm disease *Ceratocystis ulmi*	Fructifications minute black bodies, about 1 mm in length. Only visible to naked eye when seen in a mass.	All species of elm grown in this country; also *Zelkova*, an uncommon ornamental tree closely related to the elm.	The disease is mainly spread by the Elm Bark Beetles (*Scolytus* spp.). After the spores have been introduced by feeding beetles into the sap stream, blockages occur, and branch affected dies. Ultimately death of whole tree occurs.	Indications that a tree is affected includes yellowing of the foliage on individual branches in midsummer. Occasional presence of brown spots if twigs cut across: the turning-down of the end of young twigs to form 'shepherds' crooks'. See F.C. Bulletin No. 60, *Research on Dutch Elm Disease in Europe*. *Note*: This fungus could also be included in the second category of fungi, i.e. those attacking foliage.
13. Elm heart-rot *Rigidoporus ulmarius* (syn. *Fomes ulmarius*)	Fructification thick and bracket-shaped. Greyish-green above, and pink below, the underside later turning reddish-brown. May appear at base of tree, or inside hollow elms.	Elms.	The fungus, which enters through wounds, attacks the heartwood, and may lead to complete destruction of the centre of the tree, leaving a thin shell.	The principal cause of heart-rot in elm. Noticeably common in parkland trees which have been damaged by deer. Infected trees should be felled. See F.C. Arboricultural Leaflet No. 5.
14. Group dying of conifers *Rhizina undulata*	Round flattened chestnut-coloured fructifications about two inches in diameter. Produced on soil surface of fire sites.	Chiefly Sitka spruce but also Norway spruce, Corsican and lodgepole pines, European and Japanese larch.	Death of groups of conifers.	Occurs on the sites of fires which have been lit in plantations. Prohibition of such fires is essential. See F.C. Bulletin No. 14.

Fungus	*Description*	*Species of tree attacked*	*Damage*	*Remarks*
15. Honey fungus *Armilaria mellea* (syn. *Armillariella mellea*)	Fructification is a brown or honey-coloured toadstool, which often appears in clumps. Upper surface flecked with darker brown scales, under surface made up of 'gills' radiating from the centre to the outer circumference. About 5 mm ($\frac{1}{5}$ in.) from top of the stalk is a ragged ring or annulus.	All conifers and most broadleaved trees. Sitka spruce especially vulnerable on old hardwood sites. Most susceptible species Corsican and Scots pine, Sitka spruce, and Western hemlock. Larch is resistant, and Douglas fir most resistant. Norway spruce is resistant when young, but less resistant when old.	Fungus spreads either by spores or by black underground growths similar to boot laces in appearance, and known as 'rhizomorphs'. These enter through roots, and form mass of felted white mycelium, which frequently kills the tree.	When deaths have occurred through this fungus, and beating up is needed, use a more resistant species. See F.C. Arboricultural Leaflet No. 2.
16. Larch canker *Lachnellula willkommii* (syn. *Trichoscyphella willkommii*)	Fructifications are very small, somewhat similar to a champagne glass in shape, the top being about 5 mm ($\frac{1}{5}$ in.) in diameter. Top concave surface yellow or orange, rim and under-surface white. In due course a canker is usually formed, the centre being depressed and resinous, and the outer edges black and broken.	European larch and Western American larch. Only in extremely rare cases have Japanese and hybrid larch been attacked.	The chief damage is caused by the presence of the cankers. In its endeavours to overcome the attack the tree increases its growth around the canker, so that contortion of the stem occurs, rendering it unfit for conversion into timber.	Considerable doubt seems to exist as to the exact cause of this disease. It appears to be closely associated with frost. There is also some evidence to show that it may enter through dead branches. See F.C. Bulletin No. 14.
17. Phomopsis disease of conifers *Phomopsis pseudotsugae*	Fructifications are small and black, and are found singly or in small groups just beneath the bark, or projecting through cracks in the bark. They are very difficult to see with the naked eye. In damp weather in winter and spring large quantities of white spores are produced.	Principally Douglas fir, but occasionally Japanese larch and other conifers.	Three kinds of damage occur: (*a*) Die-back of leading or lateral shoots. (*b*) Girdling of the stem (this spreads from the die-back of a lateral shoot). (*c*) Canker of the stem.	Die-back of leading shoots may result in serious damage in nurseries and young plantations. Girdling may kill young trees 6 to 8 years old, while canker occurs particularly on trees 15 to 20 years old.
18. Phytopthora root rot *Phytopthora spp.*	*Invisible to the naked eye.*	*Ash, beech, horse and sweet chestnut, Lawson cypress, lime Nothofagus*, yew and others.	Attacks root system which affects foliage. Leaves become small and scattered and foliage turns yellow. Bark may die at and above ground level.	See F.C. Arboricultural Leaflet No. 8.

19. Pine blister or Resin-top disease *Peridermium pini*	Fructification appears as orange-yellow tufts which break through the bark of trees in midsummer. Spores are then discharged and the fructification turns white.	Scots pine is the usual subject of attack, but any other species of pine may be affected.	The fungus develops underneath the bark, attacking the bast and cambium. If it girdles the stem, the portion of the tree above the infection will die.	Trees from 15 to 20 years seem to suffer most. Correct thinning will do much to prevent the disease. Any infected trees should be cut out and removed. See F.C. Bulletin No. 14.
20. Poplar canker *Dothichiza populea*	Dead patches occur on stem often at base of twigs or around wounds. Attacked area often 'sunk' below level of stem.	Poplars but *P. serotina* var. *erecta* and *P. gelrica* seldom attacked.	Die-back occurs particularly in poplars which have been overcrowded in the nursery or badly planted.	Avoid overcrowding in nursery and improper planting. Prune nursery stock only in summer.
21. Saddleback fungus, or Dryad's saddle *Polyporous squamosus*	Fructification a fan-shaped bracket up to 60 cm (24 in.) across. Upper surface pale fawn in colour, with dark brown scales which appear as flecks. Under-surface creamy white. Fructifications decay very quickly.	Probably it is most commonly found on elm, but most broadleaved trees are attacked. Conifers are not affected.	Infection occurs through a branch wound; in the case of elms, where a limb has fallen. The fungus penetrates to the centre of the tree, and heart-rot ensues.	Infected trees should be felled and removed. See F.C. Arboricultural Leaflet No. 5.
22. Sooty bark disease of sycamore *Cryptostroma corticale*	Fructifications appear to be minute black columns about 1 mm long, which in due course produce a large mass of blackish-brown spores having the appearance of soot—hence the common name.	Sycamore.	The fungus works beneath the bark, which ultimately causes the death of the infected branch or stem.	This disease was first noticed in Wanstead Park, London in 1945. After an interval, an exceptionally severe outbreak occurred in 1976 on sites up to 160 miles from London. See F.C. Arboricultural Leaflet No. 3.

Fungus	*Description*	*Species of tree attacked*	*Damage*	*Remarks*
23. Sulphur polyphore *Laetiporus sulphureus* (syn. *Polyporus sulphureus*)	Fructificatons are orange above and pale sulphur yellow below. Bracket-shaped with a wavy margin, the flesh is soft and soon decomposes.	Broadleaved and coniferous species are attacked. Oak and cherry are two of the commonest, but many other trees may be affected.	The fungus enters through wounds, and spreads to the heart-wood, causing butt-rot.	A very common cause of heart-rot in old oaks. See F.C. Arboricultural Leaflet No. 5.
24. White pine blister *Cronartium ribicola*	Swollen canker-like growth on branches and main stem, on which white blisters containing orange spores are produced in spring and early summer.	All five-needle pines.	Small shoots are completely girdled and cankers formed on the main stems. In many cases the tree is killed.	Alternate host on currants (*Ribes* spp.). Effect of this fungus has eliminated five-needled pines, especially Weymouth pine (*P. strobus*) in British forestry.
25. White rot *Ganoderma applanatum*	Bracket fructification, grey-brown above with whitish under-surface.	Several broadleaved species, but very common on beech.	Infection generally enters through wounds and broken branches. Extensive heart-rot occurs, which ultimately renders the tree valueless for timber.	If the whitish under-surface is marked with a knife, a red line will appear. See F.C. Arboricultural Leaflet No. 5 which also covers other species of *Ganoderma*.

B. FUNGI ATTACKING FOLIAGE AND NURSERY STOCK

Fungus	*Description*	*Species of tree attacked*	*Damage*	*Remarks*
26. Beech seedling blight *Phytopthora cactorum*	Invisible to the naked eye.	Beech seedlings.	Attacks the cotyledon and first true leaves which turn brown. Seedling frequently dies.	The spread of the disease can be controlled by spraying with a fungicide as used on potato blight. See F.C. Arboricultural Leaflet No. 8.
27. Corsican pine die back *Gremmeniella abietina* (syn. *Brunchorstia destruens*)	Black fructifications (*pycnidia*) up to 3 mm ($\frac{1}{8}$ in.) diameter on dead needles, buds and shoots, especially from November to March.	Corsican pine; occasionally Austrian, Scots and Maritime pines.	Die-back of shoots and loss of needles, thus affecting growth and increment. Symptoms may be confused with exposure.	Avoid planting Corsican pine on sites which sun does not reach, e.g. northern slopes and deep valleys or where humidity is high or shade excessive.
28. Douglas fir leaf cast *Rhabdecline pseudotsuga*	Fructifications appear as bright brown, slightly protruding patches on the underside of the needles.	Douglas fir. The Oregon or Green variety is the most resistant; the Colorado or Blue Douglas the most susceptible.	Defoliation, since the infected leaves fall at all times of year, with consequent loss of growth.	Infected nursery stock should be destroyed. Where attacks have occurred previously, spraying with soap and Bordeaux mixture from mid-April to mid-June may be successful.
29. Douglas fir leaf cast *Phaeocryptopus gaumanii*	Minute black patches appear in irregular lines on the needles.	The coastal type of Douglas is least affected.	Defoliation and loss of growth.	Little can be done other than destruction of infected trees.
30. Grey mould *Botrytis cinerea*	Grey brown 'misty' mould on needles and leaves.	All species but conifers worse than broadleaved, especially Sitka spruce, Douglas fir, Western hemlock, *Cupressus* and *Sequoia*.	This fungus can cause considerable damage in forest nurseries by killing young seedlings and weakening others through loss of needles.	Control by spraying with Bordeaux mixture or more modern counterparts.

Fungus	*Description*	*Species of tree attacked*	*Damage*	*Remarks*
31. Larch leaf cast *Meria laricis*	The fungus appears as clusters of minute white spots on the lower, but sometimes upper, surface of the needles. A more certain diagnosis can be made by staining the needle with aniline blue, which causes the spots to turn black.	European and American larch. There is no record of Japanese larch having been attacked.	The needles turn brown in early May, resembling frost damage, but the following differences should be noted: (*a*) Frost kills whole of needle at once. (*b*) *Meria* browns middle or end. (*c*) Needles killed by frost tend to remain on twig throughout the season. (*d*) Needles killed by *Meria* fall as soon as totally brown. (*e*) Needles killed by *Meria* are less shrivelled than those killed by frost.	Damp seasons favour the disease. 2-year seedlings tend to suffer worst. *Meria* plus frost may cause heavy losses. Spraying with sulphur spray consisting of amberene, sulsol, and liver of sulphur is effective. See F.C. Bulletin No. 43.
32. Oak mildew *Microsphaera alphitoides*	The fungus, consisting of minute white fructifications, appears as typical grey 'mildew'.	Pedunculate and sessile oaks, the former suffering most. Also recorded on beech and sweet chestnut.	Interference with the natural functions of the leaf, and often defoliation. Particularly bad in conjunction with attacks by oak leaf roller moth (*q.v.*). Successive attacks may prove fatal. Most serious in nurseries.	Control by spraying with sulphur spray (colloidal sulphur wash) or dry dusting with sulphur. Its natural enemies include a parasitic fungus (*Ciccinobolus* spp.) and larvae of cecidomyid fly. See F.C. Bulletin No. 43.
33. Oak seedling disease *Rosellinia quercina*	No fructification is apparent on a growing seedling. The leaves at first become pale and then wither; the upper leaves wither first, and then the lower ones. This is particularly noticeable in a wet season. On lifting an infected seedling, some small black bodies about the size of a pin-head will be found on the tap-root.	Oak seedlings 1–3 years old.	Considerable losses may be caused by this fungus, which proves fatal to young seedlings. The fungus attacks through the roots.	All infected plants should be removed and burnt, and seed beds on which oak have been grown should be used for other species.

34. Pine needle cast *Lophodermium seditiosum* (syn. *Lophodermium pinastri*)	Small black spots on needles which later turn brown and fall immaturely.	Scots pine and Corsican pine.	Defoliation through early leaf fall. Most serious amongst nursery stock.	Not a serious disease in plantations but can cause losses in nurseries. Spray with Bordeaux mixture or other suitable fungicides. See F.C. Bulletin No. 43.
35. Pine twisting rust *Melampsora pinitorqua*	Bright yellow areas of fruiting bodies like wet sawdust, produced in June on young shoots.	Scots pine with aspen poplar as alternate host. Other pines rarely attacked.	Distortion and subsequent death of current year's shoots and foliage.	Cut out all aspen near Scots pine plantations, or plant Corsican pine in aspen areas.
36. Keithia disease *Didymascella thujina* (syn. *Keithia thujina*)	Fructifications appear as minute black spots on the underside of the leaves. The fungus enters through the leaves.	All varieties of *Thuya* are liable to attack, but from a forester's point of view the most important is the Western red cedar (*Thuya plicata*).	Although the most damage is caused to seedlings, young transplants can also be attacked. Results are often fatal in the case of seedlings.	Spraying with sulphur wash, potassium permanganate or cycloheximide is recommended. Badly infected stock may have to be burnt. In some cases the cutting-back of the foliage, followed by a dressing of farmyard manure, will produce fresh healthy leaves. See F.C. Bulletin No. 14.

2. *Bacteria and Viruses*

(a) Bacteria

Probably the two most important diseases of trees which are caused by bacteria are the Watermark disease of the cricket bat willow and poplar canker. Both of these are described in the table on p. 131.

(b) Viruses

(i) Although a considerable amount of research has been carried out on the virus infection of farm crops and fruit trees, work on trees and shrubs has only started comparatively recently.

(ii) The viruses which affect plants consist of minute particles which can spread into all the tissues of the plant concerned. The symptoms of virus infection can occur in the foliage, often causing discolouration, or in the stems or branches, producing cankers, patches of dead bark or grooves.

(iii) There are in addition 'virus-like diseases', one group of which comprises into two main types:
Rickettsia-like organisms (R.L.O.s)
Mycoplasma-like organisms (M.L.O.s)

(iv) Detailed information will be found in Arboricultural Leaflet No. 4, *Virus and Virus-like Diseases of Trees*, issued by the Forestry Commission.

BACTERIAL DISEASES

Disease	*Description*	*Species of tree attacked*	*Damage*	*Remarks*
1. Watermark disease of cricket-bat willow *Erwinia salicis* (syn. *Bacterium salicis*)	This disease causes dieback of the crown, which is accompanied by a dark staining within the tree. The symptoms are briefly as follows: Leaves of infected part wither and turn reddish in April and May; this is accentuated by hot weather occurring in next few weeks. Watery liquid may be discharged from affected shoots or holes made by insects. The timber of infected trees turns dark brown or black; seen in cross section this may only affect the heartwood, or may appear as concentric circles. Watermark disease is sometimes mistaken for honey fungus (see preceding section of this chapter).	Cricket-bat willow (*Salix alba* var *coerulea*) White willow (*S. alba*) Crack willow (*S. fragilis*) Sallow (*S. cinerea*)	The timber of the tree is rendered unfit for use. In the case of bat willows this may cause a very serious financial loss to the owner. Incidental damage is the dieback of the crown.	The disease is thought to be spread by small birds, and by insects such as willow sawfly, willow gall midge, and goat moths, but there is no proof of this. The use of infected sets is a more obvious cause. Infected trees should be felled and burnt. Statutory orders have been made for the destruction of infected willows in certain countries and a list of these will be found in Chapter XXIII, Section 2, Statutory Instruments. See F.C. Leaflet No. 20.
2. Poplar canker *Pseudomonas syringae* forma *populae*	Small cracks appear in the bark of young twigs. In the spring (especially in April and May) pale brown bacterial slime exudes. The affected twigs may die, but more often a canker develops around the wound. In time the cankers may girdle and kill large branches, and disease becomes noticeable through dead branches, cankers, and discharge of slime.	Many varieties of poplar are affected, and below are given seven of the *resistant* species: *P. alba* *P. berolinensis* *P. canescens* *P. eugenei* *P. gelrica* *P. laevigata* *P. serotina*	Serious reduction in the value of the timber, and in some cases death of the tree.	Cankered trees should be felled and burnt.

3. *Insects*

(*a*) The injurious insects which are described in the following table have been divided into five classes, namely:

A. Foliage-destroying insects.
B. Excavating insects other than those which bore into timber.
C. Timber-boring insects.
D. Bark-feeding insects.
E. Root-feeding insects.
F. Gall-making insects.

(*b*) The list of insects given in the table is only a selection of the more important ones, and should not be regarded as exhaustive.

(*c*) Further information on woodland insects will be found in Forestry Commission Handbook No. 1, *Forest Insects*, while drawings of many species are included in R. Neil Chrystal's *Insects of the British Woodland*, which was first published in 1937.

(*d*) Where measurements of insects are given they refer to a fully grown specimen.

(*e*) At the end of the table will be found line drawings of eleven of the more important insects.

A. FOLIAGE-DESTROYING INSECTS

Insect	*Description*	*Species of tree attacked*	*Damage*	*Remarks*
1. Green spruce aphid *Elatobium abietinum* (syn. *Neomyzaphis abietina*)	A minute insect about 1 mm (0·03 in.) long, which exists in both winged and wingless forms. Body green with red eyes.	Various species of spruce, but Sitka spruce is particularly subject to attack.	Insects feed on the needles of the spruce, which ultimately turn brown and die.	The natural enemies of this pest include ladybirds, lace-wing flies, hover flies, tits, and tree-creepers.
2. Large larch sawfly *Pristiphora erichsonii* (syn. *Lygaeonematus erichsoni*)	*Larva*: 19 mm (¾ in.) long. Body greyish-green above, with black hairy head. *Adult*: 19 mm (¾ in.) long. Wing span 25 mm (1 in.). Wings transparent. Head black. Body black with red band around abdomen.	Larch.	The caterpillars eat the needles, which may lead to severe defoliation.	This insect caused very serious damage in Cumberland between 1906 and 1912. Since then here have not been any definite outbreaks. Adults appear from late May onwards.
3. Oak leaf roller moth *Tortrix viridana*	*Larva*: 13 mm (½ in.) long. Greyish-green above, with black or brownish-black head. *Adult*: 8 mm (⅓ in.) long. Wing span 19 mm (¾ in.). Fore wings bright green; hind wings grey; all wings have white fringes.	Pedunculate oak (*Q. robur*) and sessile oak (*Q. petraea*), the former being subject to the more serious attacks. Other broadleaved trees adjacent to oaks may also be attacked, particularly the sweet chestnut.	In serious cases, complete defoliation may result, which causes loss of increment and poor seed production. Attacks seldom, if ever, prove fatal, unless there is some additional cause, such as honey fungus (see first section of this chapter).	The natural enemies of this moth include birds such as thrushes, tits, starlings, and finches. Other enemies are ants, earwigs, and ichneuman flies. Adults appear in June and July. See drawing, p. 142.
4. Pine beauty moth *Panolis flammea*	*Larva*: 3 mm (⅛ in.) long and grey green on hatching. Later grey green with seven stripes lengthways. Finally. 38 mm (1½ in.) long with two orange stripes before pupation. *Adult*: Forewings yellowish-brown with reddish tinge and cream markings. Hind wings dark grey.	Lodgepole pine.	Heavy defoliation resulting in death of tree.	Severe outbreaks in Scotland 1976–77–78. See F.C. Forest Record No. 120.

Insect	Description	Species of tree attacked	Damage	Remarks
5. Pine looper moth *Bupalus piniaria*	*Larva*: Green with five white or cream longitudinal stripes. Head green. *Adult*: Wing span 38 mm ($1\frac{1}{2}$ in.). Male: dark brown wings with cream patches on wings near body. Antennae are bipectinate ('herring-bone'). Female: Orange-brown with darker brown markings. Antennae filiform ('threadlike').	Pines, especially Scots pine and Corsican pine.	Heavy defoliation resulting from the caterpillars feeding on the needles.	Although a serious pest on the Continent, the most serious outbreak in this country occurred at Cannock Chase in 1953. Adults appear in May and June. See F.C. Forest Record No. 119 and drawing, p. 142.
6. Large pine sawfly *Diprion pini*	*Larva*: Up to 25 mm (1 in.) long. Pale green at first, turning brownish-green. 22 legs. Feet black, but turn yellow. *Adult*: Male: 15 mm ($\frac{3}{5}$ in.) wing span. Body black, but apex reddish. White spots underside of first segment. Wings transparent. Female: 20 mm ($\frac{4}{5}$ in.) wing span. Body dull yellow; middle of abdomen black.	Pines, especially Austrian, Corsican and Scots pines.	Serious defoliation.	Adult flies normally appear from late April to early June.
7. Spruce sawfly *Gilpinia hercyniae*	*Larva*: Dull green at first, becoming bright green with white stripes. Max. length 15–20 mm ($\frac{3}{5}$–$\frac{4}{5}$ in.).	Spruces, mainly Norway and Sitka owing to their extensive use in forestry.	Serious defoliation causing a general loss of increment.	Of increasing importance on account of the large areas of spruce which have been planted. See F.C. Forest Record No. 117.
8. Vapourer moth *Orgyia antiqua*	*Larva*: 25 mm (1 in.) long. Brown to grey, with distinctive tufts of hair. Head black. *Adult*: Male: Wing span 38 mm ($1\frac{1}{2}$ in.). Wings yellowish to brown, hind pair with white crescent-shaped spot. Female: Brown and virtually wingless, grey in colour.	All kinds of trees and shrubs.	Defoliation.	Not normally serious, but sometimes becomes too numerous.

B. EXCAVATING INSECTS OTHER THAN TIMBER BORERS

Insect	*Description*	*Species of tree attacked*	*Damage*	*Remarks*
9. Ash bud moth *Prays fraxinella* (syn. *Prays curtisella*)	*Larva*: Greenish-grey with black head, 12 mm (½ in.) long. *Adult*: Wing span up to 19 mm (¾ in.). Fore wings whitish-grey with brown patch; hind wings brown.	Ash.	Destruction of the terminal buds, causing, in the case of a leading shoot, forked growth. This can be particularly serious in young plantations.	Any outbreaks in the nursery should be dealt with by cutting out infected shoots. Little can be done in plantations.
10. Douglas fir seed fly *Megastigmus spermotropus*	*Larva*: Small white legless grub. *Adult*: 6 mm (¼ in.) long. Dirty yellow in colour. Female has long sting-like projection for laying eggs. In male this is absent.	Douglas fir.	Grub feeds on seeds of Douglas fir, so that only an empty husk is left.	Control by fumigation of seeds.
11. Larch miner moth *Coleophera laricella*	*Larva*: 6 mm (¼ in.). Reddish-brown with black head. *Adult*: Wing span 10 mm (⅜ in.). Head and wings grey; distinctive marginal fringe to both fore and hind wings, the fringe being deeper on the latter.	Larch.	Damage to needles, caused by caterpillars feeding on them.	The caterpillar builds a case around itself from the remains of damaged needles. Only the head of the caterpillar projects, and when feeding it raises its body and the case in the air.
12. Larch shoot moth *Argyresthia laevigatella* (syn. *Argyresthia atmoriella*)	*Larva*: 6 mm (¼ in.) long. Greenish-yellow body, with black head. *Adult*: 5 mm (⅕ in.) long. Wing span 10 mm (⅜ in.). Fore wings grey and glossy; hind wings darker and not glossy.	European and Japanese larch.	Twigs or shoots of larch are attacked by caterpillars, which burrow into the twig so that it ultimately dies.	Very difficult to control.

Insect	Description	Species of tree attacked	Damage	Remarks
13. Common pine shoot beetle *Tomicus piniperda* (syn. *Myelophilus piniperda*)	*Larva*: Small, white, legless, having a wrinkled appearance. *Adult*: 3–5 mm (⅛ in.) long. Head and thorax black, shining but hairy. The wing covers are reddish-brown, with rows of holes running lengthways from front to rear. The second row from the centre outwards does not continue the whole length of the wing, but ends where the cover curves downwards.	Chiefly Scots pine, but other pines, and sometimes larch and spruce, are attacked.	Beetles bore into pith of young shoots, causing shoot to die or be broken off by the wind. Continuous attacks seriously affect increment, crown development is restricted, less seed is produced, and trees may be killed. Beetles also bore under the bark of suppressed or sickly trees, in order to construct breeding galleries.	Control measures include: Removing sickly trees by regular thinnings; avoid leaving felled trees in woods; trapping by leaving decoy logs which are later removed and their bark burnt. See F.C. Leaflet No. 3, and drawing, p. 145. *Note*: This insect could also be included in Section D—Bark-feeding Insects—but this is only its secondary form of damage.
14. Lesser pine shoot beetle *Tomicus minor* (syn. *Myelophilus minor*)	Similar to the pine shoot beetle (*T. piniperda*), except that the second row of holes in the wing covers continue the whole length of the wing cover. It is very slightly smaller.	Chiefly Scots pine. The beetle is chiefly found in and around Aberdeenshire, but it has also been found in the New Forest.	As for *T. piniperda*.	The breeding galleries of the species are entirely different. The main tunnel of *T. piniperda* runs vertically up the axis of the tree, while *T. minor* runs horizontally across the axis. For further details see F.C. Leaflet No. 3.
15. Pine shoot moth *Rhyacionia buoliana* (syn. *Evetria buoliana*)	*Larva*: Dark brown with black head. *Adult*: Wing span 15–23 mm (⅝–1 in.). Fore wings orange and red with silver lines; hind wings grey. All wings have a fringe of grey hairs.	Pines in the following order of susceptibility: lodgepole, Scots, Austrian, Corsican.	Destruction of the leading shoot which is subsequently replaced by a side shoot, resulting in ultimate distortion of the main stem. Such malformation is known as 'posthorn' development.	The species which were previously included under *Evetra* have been divided into four genera: *Rhyacionia*, *Blastetia*, *Petrova* and *Clavigesta*. See drawing, p. 142.

C. TIMBER-BORING INSECTS

Insect	*Description*	*Species of tree attacked*	*Damage*	*Remarks*
16. Goat moth *Cossus cossus*	*Larva*: 75 mm (3 in.) long. Upper surface of body bluish-red; remainder flesh-coloured. Head and first few segments dark brown or black. Larvae produce a strong, unpleasant smell—hence the name *goat* moth. *Adult*: Wing span 90 mm (3½) in.). Reddish-brown head: wings greyish-brown.	Broadleaved species, more particularly oak, ash, willow, and poplar.	The caterpillars bore into the trunk of the tree, causing severe damage to the timber.	Control is very difficult, especially in the case of forest trees.
17. Larch longicorn beetle *Tetropium gabrieli*	*Larva*: 20 mm (¾ in.) long. Brown head and cream body. Three pairs of legs. *Adult*: 20 mm (¾ in.) long. Dark brown or black in colour. Antennae about 90 mm (3½ in.) long.	Larch.	Boring in the sapwood of the tree, which reduces the value of the timber.	Only dying or sickly trees are normally attacked.
18. Large poplar longhorn *Saperda carcharias*	*Larva*: 30 mm (1¼ in.) long. Pale yellow and legless. *Adult*: 30 mm (1¼ in.) long. Yellow to grey in colour, with two bands of lighter yellow across the wing cases. Antennae about 20 mm (¾ in.) long.	Poplar.	Larvae tunnel under the bark, and in addition to damaging the timber may kill the tree by ringing it.	
19. Leopard moth *Zeuzera pyrina*	*Larva*: 50 mm (2 in.) long. Yellowish-white, with dark patches on the head and first and last segments. *Adult*: 75 mm (3 in.) long. Wings white, with black spots.	Broadleaved trees generally.	The timber is damaged by larvae boring, and where small branches are attacked these may subsquently break off at the point of attack.	

D. BARK-FEEDING INSECTS

Insect	*Description*	*Species of tree attacked*	*Damage*	*Remarks*
20. Ash bark beetle *Leperisinus varius* (syn. *Hylesinus fraxini*)	*Larva*: Small, white, with dark head. *Adult*: 3 mm (⅛ in.) long. Black with grey and black scales.	Ash.	Tunnels immediately beneath the bark, which is not a serious defect from the timber aspect.	
21. Black pine beetle *Hylastes ater*	*Larva*: Very small and white. *Adult*: 5 mm (⅕ in.) long. Black in colour, shining and smooth.	Conifers, especially Scots pine.	The bark and cambium layer of young conifers is attacked at ground level, while the roots are frequently damaged. When young trees are badly injured they turn brown and lose their needles. The beetle breeds in the stumps of roots of dead and dying conifers.	There are six species of hylastes of which the most important are *H. ater* (in southern districts), *H. brunneus* (in northern districts) and *H. cunicularius* (mainly on spruce). For further details see F.C. Leaflet No. 58 and drawing, p. 143.
22. Large elm bark beetle *Scolytus scolytus*	*Larva*: 13 mm (½ in.) long, white. *Adult*: 6 mm (¼ in.) long; black, shining thorax, with reddish-brown wing cases. *Note*: The adult of the small elm bark beetle (*S. multistriatus*) is similar, except in size; it is 3 mm (⅛ in.) long.	All species of elm which grow naturally in Great Britain.	This beetle and the small elm bark beetle (*Scolytus multistriatus*) are the chief agents for spreading Elm Disease (see Section 1.A.11 of this chapter). The breeding galleries, which the beetles construct under bark, form ideal locations in which the fructifications of the fungi can develop.	On emergence, beetles which have come into contact with the fungus fly to healthy trees, and feed on young twigs, thus passing on the disease. See drawing, p. 143.
23. Felted beech scale *Cryptococcus fagisuga* (syn. *Cryptococcus fagi*)	*Larva*: Minute. Yellow, with three pairs of legs and two antennae. *Adult*: 1 mm (1/25 in.) long. Lemon-coloured. Wingless and legless.	Beech.	The insect feeds on the sap and juices beneath the bark. Badly infected trees are covered with white masses of the insect, giving the bole the appearance of being white-washed.	The precise effect of this insect on the growth of the tree is uncertain. It has been suggested that only sickly trees are affected. See also Section 1.A.2 of this chapter and F.C. Bulletin No. 69.

24. Large pine weevil *Hylobius abietis*	*Larva*: 15 mm (½ in.) long. White, with brown head. Body curved and wrinkled, with row of round breathing holes. *Adult*: 15 mm (½ in.) long, brown to black in colour, the wing cases having an irregular pattern of yellow scales on them. The antennae are at the tip of the snout, and the thickest joint of each leg is notched.	Conifers of any kind, but young broadleaved trees will be attacked if there are no conifers available.	The weevil feeds on the bark of young conifers, and may completely ring a young tree, with fatal results. Less serious attacks will weaken the vigour of young trees.	Favourite breeding places are the stumps of pines, especially Scots and Corsican. Areas which have been burnt are particularly suitable as breeding sites. See F.C. Leaflet No. 58, and drawing, p. 144.
25. Banded pine weevil *Pissodes pini* *Pissodes castaneus* (syn. *Pissodes notatus*)	*Larva*: Similar to *Hylobius*, but smaller. *Adult*: 8 mm (⅓ in.) long. (*P. castaneus* is rather smaller.) Reddish-brown in colour, with two distinct bands of yellow scales. The antennae are in the middle of the snout, and the largest limbs are *not* notched.	Conifers.	The larvae damage the cambium, and may girdle the stem. Adult weevils attack all parts of a tree.	Young trees up to 10 years old are attacked, and also older trees from 35 to 40 years old. See drawing, p. 144.
26. Spruce bark beetle *Ips typographus*	*Larva*: 6 mm (¼ in.) long. Fat, white, and legless, with brown heads. *Adult*: 5 mm (⅕ in.) long. Dark brown to black. At the rear the wing cases appear to be notched when seen in profile.	Spruce.	If a heavy infestation occurs, the effect of large numbers of beetles feeding on the bark of a tree may kill it.	The spruce bark beetle is uncommon in this country, but imports of unbarked spruce logs in 1946 are thought to have resulted in the introduction of a small number of beetles. There are several other species of the genus *Ips*. See drawing, p. 146.
27. Great spruce bark beetle *Dendroctonus micans*	*Larva*: 6 mm (¼ in.) long. White with brown head. *Adult*: 6–8 mm (¼ in.) long; 3 mm (⅛ in.) wide. Brown becoming black when mature. Covered with orange-coloured hairs.	Most species of spruce and sometimes Scots pine.	Larvae feed under bark and may eventually girdle and kill the tree. This may take several years.	Signs of attack are: resin running down the trunk and clots of resin and frass at the base. See drawing, p. 146. Eggs and larvae are consumed by predator, *Rhizophagus grandis*. See F.C. Research Information Note No. 128.

E. ROOT-FEEDING INSECTS

Insect	*Description*	*Species of tree attacked*	*Damage*	*Remarks*
28. Cockchafer *Melolontha melolontha*	*Larva*: 38 mm (1½ in.) long. White and fleshy. Brown head, with powerful jaws. Three pairs of legs. *Adult*: 25 mm (1 in.) long. Head and thorax black; wing covers reddish-brown. A strong flyer.	Young trees of all species.	The larvae gnaw through or girdle the roots of young trees in the nursery. In a dry season this may have fatal results.	There are several species of chafers. Control is difficult. Cultivation in the nursery, hand picking, and encouragement of natural enemies are probably most successful. See drawing, p. 145.

F. GALL-MAKING INSECTS

Group	*Species*	*Gall on spruce*	*Alternative host*	*Appearance on alternative host*	*Remarks*
29. Spruce-larch	*Adelges viridis*	At base of shoot which it may encircle.	Larch.	White 'wool' on needles, trunk and branches of European larch. Bark exfoliation i.e. flaking off in 'plates', on Japanese and hybrid larch.	See F.C. Handbook No. 2, *Forest Insects*.
	Adelges laricis	On, or at end of, shoot.	Larch.	No 'wool'. This adelgid is more harmful to larch than spruce.	
30. Spruce-silver fir	*Adelges normannianae* (syn. *A. nusslini*)	Very rare in Britain.	Common silver fire (*Abies alba*) Caucassian fir (*A. nordmanniana*)	'Wool' which occurs at base of needles, on branches and main stem of young trees, is less conspicuous.	See F.C. Handbook No. 2.
	Adelges picae	Not found in Britain.	Most species of silver fir.	Large amount of 'wool' and many small galls are produced on stems and branches.	
31. Spruce-pine	*Pineus pini*	Only on Oriental spruce (*Picea orientalis*).	Scots pine and some other pines.	Large quantities of 'wool' are produced.	See F.C. Handbook No. 2.
	Pineus strobi	None.	Weymouth pine (*Pinus strobus*)	'Wool' on bark of branches and main stem.	
32. Spruce-Douglas fir	*Adelges cooleyi*	Up to 64 mm (2½ in.) long and enclosing the shoot. Very often on Sitka spruce.	Douglas fir, larch, pine or silver fir.	'Wool' on underside of needles, with black specks during the winter.	See F.C. Handbook No. 2.

Oak Leaf Roller Moth
Tortrix viridana × 2

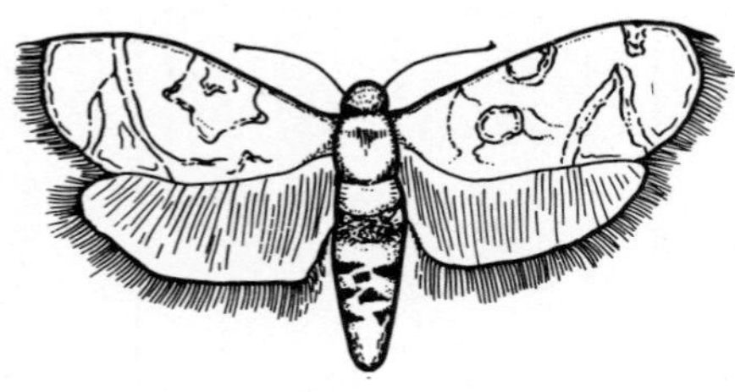

Pine Shoot Moth
Rhyacionia buoliana (syn. *Evetria buoliana*) × 2

Pine Looper Moth (Male)
Bupalus piniaria × 2½

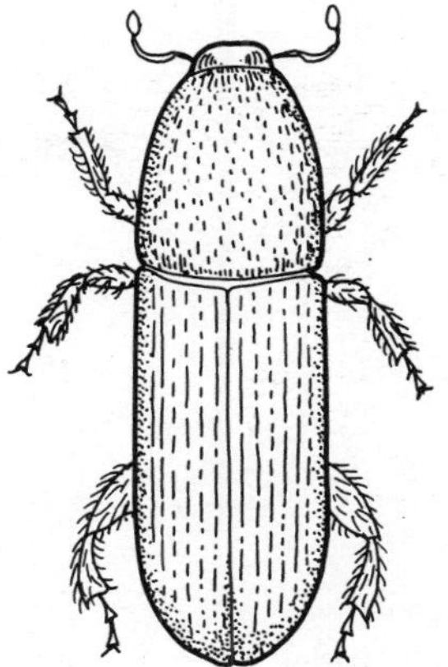

Black Pine Beetle
Hylastes ater × 10

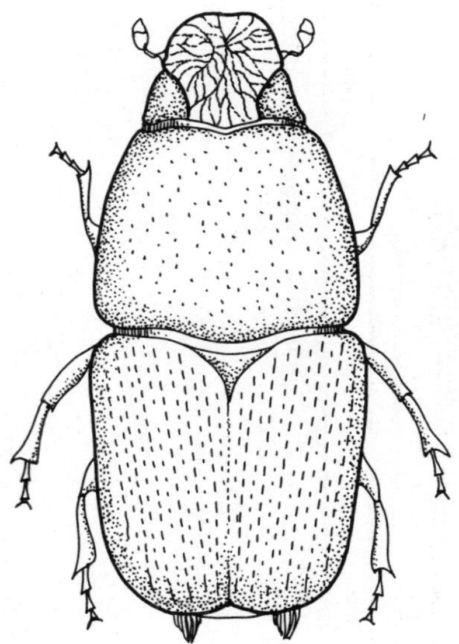

Large Elm Bark Beetle
Scolytus scolytus × 12

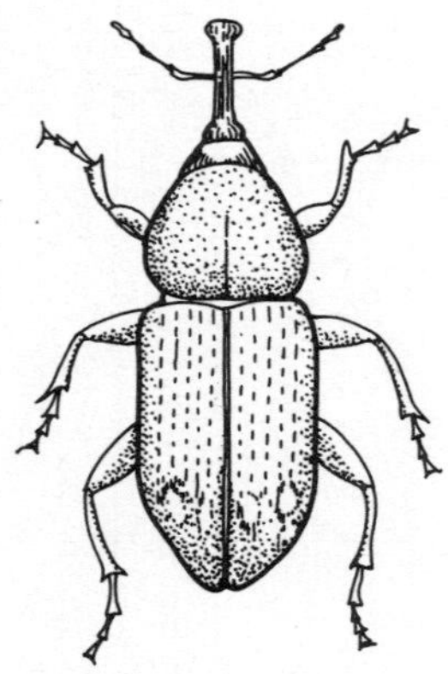

Banded Pine Weevil
Pissodes castaneus (syn. *Pissodes notatus*) × 6

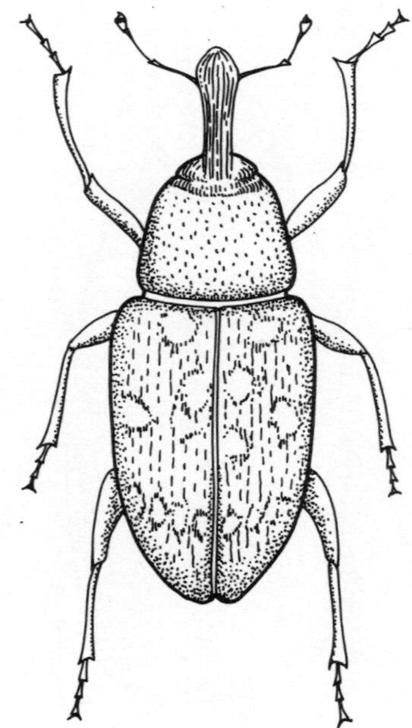

Large Pine Weevil
Hylobius abietis × 6

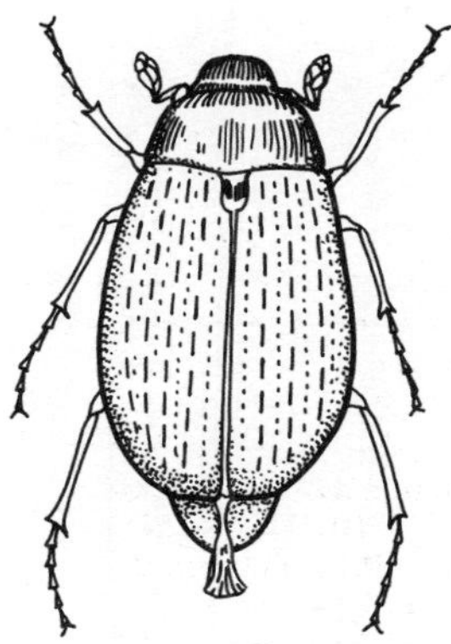

Cockchafer
Melolontha melolontha
(natural size)

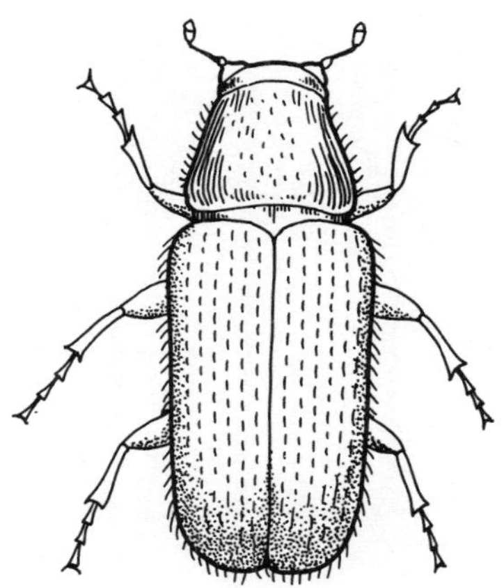

Pine Shoot Beetle
Tomicus piniperda
(syn. *Myelophilus piniperda*) × 14

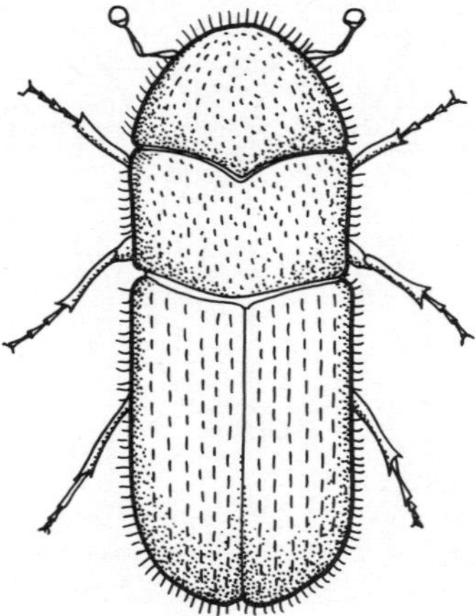

Spruce Bark Beetle
Ips typographus × 10

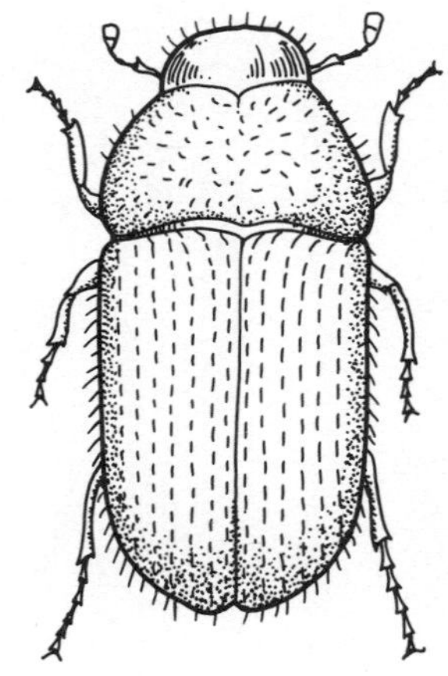

Great Spruce Bark Beetle
Dendroctonus micans × 8

CHAPTER XIII

Forest Roads and Rides

1. *Rides*

(a) The objects and uses of rides

Rides may be used for one or more of the following purposes:

(i) For the extraction of timber and other woodland produce.
(ii) For means of communication within a wood.
(iii) To facilitate the inspection and management of a woodland area.
(iv) To mark compartment boundaries.
(v) To provide fire-breaks and assist in fire prevention and control.
(vi) To improve the sporting facilities.

(b) Description

(i) Rides are unmetalled roads which normally run from a hard road into the woods.
(ii) Where conditions warrant it, a ride may be metalled at some subsequent date, when it would be then classed as a road.
(iii) Although many rides are never metalled, they are nevertheless used for extraction, and they should be planned and laid out as though they were roads.

(c) Classification of rides

(i) Rides can be divided into three types:
  (1) Main rides.
  (2) Secondary rides.
  (3) Racks or rackways.

(ii) *Main rides*
  (1) These form the framework of the system of rides within which minor rides are laid out.
  (2) They should be 6–9 m (20–30 ft) wide.
  (3) In deciding the width of the ride in a new plantation it should be borne in mind that when the young trees have grown up they will spread outwards some distance from the margin.

(4) Since a wide ride has a larger surface area, traffic over it will be less concentrated, and damage to the surface should be less.

(5) The general tendency is to make main rides too narrow, and in areas where there are serious fire hazards even 9 m (30 ft) may be considered too narrow.

(iii) *Secondary rides*

(1) These are the connecting links between main rides, or spurs running off from them.

(2) They should be 3–4·5 m (10–15 ft) in width.

(iv) *Racks or rackways*

(1) These are not rides in the proper sense, but narrow pathways cut through a woodland area to give access for inspection.

(2) In young plantations they are often formed by brashing two adjacent rows of trees so as to form a path about 1·5 m (5 ft) wide.

(d) Setting out rides

(i) The contours should be followed where reasonably possible.

(ii) The following should be avoided:
Steep gradients; sharp corners; wet, low-lying areas.

(iii) Straight rides facilitate extraction, and are favoured for hunting and shooting.

(iv) When laying out a new system of rides, or rearranging an old one, the main point or points of extraction should be settled, and rides arranged so as to converge on these. Such points of extraction may be a hard road or the sawmill.

(v) When dealing with an old woodland area it will be found that many existing rides follow the easiest route, and often have hard or semi-hard surfaces. It is consequently often cheaper, quicker, and better to improve, modify, or develop an existing system than to lay out a completely new one independent of the old.

(vi) Where old quarries or gravel pits are present in a woodland they can prove a useful source of material for making up and repairing rides.

(e) Construction of new rides

(i) The surface of the new ride should be levelled sufficiently to allow timber vehicles to move along without obstruction. This may only consist of removing projecting stumps or boulders, or it may comprise levelling the whole surface with a bulldozer or grader.

(ii) It is most important to keep a ride dry, and wet or boggy places should be drained or packed with brushwood and faggots, and culverts built over streams and large ditches.

(iii) A bulldozer should be able to cut out and grade a 3 m (10 ft) width at the rate of:
    230 m (250 yd) per day on difficult sites
    460 m (500 yd) „ „ „ easy „
  but this will depend on the size of the machine and the width of the blade.

(iv) Where necessary, ditches should be cut along the edges of the ride, but this is expensive work and should be done only where essential.

(v) The undersurface of the ride, and therefore its wearing qualities and its ability to carry vehicles in winter, depends very largely on the soil:
  (1) On gravels, limestones, and thin soils over rock it is not usually difficult to get a firm undersurface at a minimum cost.
  (2) On deep loams and heavy clays it may be found impossible to obtain a reasonably firm undersurface which will carry traffic except in periods of dry weather or hard frost.

(vi) The golden rule in ride maintenance is 'keep it dry', and this can be done by:
  (1) Digging ditches where necessary.
  (2) Cutting back overhanging branches, so that the sun and wind can dry the surface.
  (3) Keeping all ditches and watercourses clear and running.

2. *Roads*

(a) General

(i) Roads have much in common with rides, and in some cases roads begin as rides, which are subsequently metalled.

(ii) As a forest crop approaches maturity it may be worth while converting certain rides into roads.

(iii) Some of these roads may be required permanently, while others will meet the case if they last until the crop is harvested. This is, of course, more applicable to a system of clear cutting than in cases where selective felling is adopted.

(iv) Forest roads can therefore be divided into two classes:
  (1) Permanent. (2) Temporary or semi-permanent.

(b) Permanent roads

(i) These are normally water- or tar-bound macadam.

(ii) Briefly the method of construction consists of excavating the line of the road to a depth of about 25 cm (10 in.) and then placing on the bottom a layer of stones to a depth of 15–20 cm (6–8 in.). On top of these, smaller material known as 'blinding' or 'filling' is tipped and the whole rolled in. Finally a top layer of fine material is laid so as to finish the surface which may then be tarred if necessary.

(iii) For details regarding permanent road construction, reference should be made to textbooks dealing with the subject.

(c) Temporary or semi-permanent roads

(i) *Bulldozed roads*

(1) Although roads constructed by means of a bulldozer or angle-dozer are included under the heading of 'temporary' roads, on suitable sites they may well prove permanent.

(2) Bulldozers enable temporary roads to be constructed quickly and cheaply, and when fitted with a blade which can be set at an angle to the axis of advance (i.e. angle-dozers) they are particularly useful for cutting rides along hillsides.

(3) The approximate rate of progress is given under sub-paragraph 1 (*e*) of this chapter.

(ii) *Corduroy roads*

(1) In this type of road, poles are laid side by side across the track at right-angles to the movement of traffic.

(2) Every tenth pole is cut longer than the others, and stakes are driven in on either side of both projecting ends, in order to prevent the whole from 'creeping' or 'rolling'.

(3) A smoother road will be made if the wearing surface is adzed or trimmed off, or if any spaces between the poles are filled with clinker or chippings.

(4) The smaller the diameter of the poles used, compatible with strength, the smoother the road will be.

(5) This type of road has the disadvantage that, after the bark has worn off the poles, wheel-spin will occur in wet weather when rubber-tyred tractors are used.

(iii) *Slab roads*

(1) This is a development of the corduroy road, flat slabs from saw-mill waste being used instead of poles.

(2) This is generally a smoother road, but is likely to be more expensive than a corduroy road if the material has to be brought for some distance from the mill.

(iv) *Brushwood roads*

(1) Faggots of brushwood are made up and laid at right-angles to the direction of traffic.

(2) These are kept in position by driving stakes into the ground at intervals of 2·75–3·66 m (3–4 yd) to which poles or lengths of fencing wire are fixed, parallel to the wheel tracks.

(3) This type of road, although useful for crossing wet places, cannot be regarded as satisfactory for regular traffic.

(v) *Chestnut-fencing roads*

(1) This consists of laying rolls of chestnut-pale fencing on the ground, either across the whole of the track or only in each wheel rut.

(2) This type of road is cheap and easy to lay, and can often be taken up and used elsewhere.

(3) When laid, it is essential to fasten it to the ground, so as to prevent it from being picked up and wrapped around the wheels of vehicles. Chestnut fencing should always be laid on a smooth, level bed.

3. *Angles of Repose*

(*a*) In building a road it is sometimes necessary to form a cutting, or excavate the side of a slope. The steepness of the slope of the sides will depend on the natural angle of repose, and this in turn will depend on the soil.

(*b*) Below are given the various angles of repose for certain types of soil:

Firm earth (dry)	50°	Vegetable earth	28°
Clay (well drained)	45°	Sand (wet)	22°
Sand (dry)	38°	Clay (wet)	16°

4. *Gradients*

(*a*) The term 'gradient' denotes the rate of slope of a surface.

(*b*) Gradients are generally expressed as fractions; thus $\frac{1}{4}$ represents a rise or fall of 1 in 4, $\frac{1}{10}$ that of 1 in 10, and so on.

(*c*) At the same time a given gradient forms an angle with the horizontal, and in the case of an inclination of 1 in 10 this angle is 5° 43′.

(*d*) Again, gradient can be expressed as a given rise of metres per kilometre or feet per mile.

(*e*) The following table gives the equivalent of these various forms by which gradient can be expressed.

Gradient	*Angle*	*Rise in metres per kilometre*	*Rise in feet per mile*	*Gradient*	*Angle*	*Rise in metres per kilometre*	*Rise in feet per mile*
1 in 10	5° 43′	100·0	528	1 in 18	3° 11′	55·5	293
1 in 11	5° 11′	90·9	480	1 in 19	3° 0′	52·6	277
1 in 12	4° 46′	83·3	440	1 in 20	2° 52′	50·0	264
1 in 13	4° 24′	76·9	406	1 in 24	2° 23′	41·6	220
1 in 14	4° 5′	71·4	377	1 in 25	2° 18′	40·0	211
1 in 15	3° 49′	63·3	352	1 in 26	2° 15′	38·3	203
1 in 16	3° 35′	62·5	330	1 in 30	1° 55′	33·3	176
1 in 17	3° 22′	58·8	310	1 in 40	1° 25′	25·0	132

5. *Weight of Spoil*

The following table gives the approximate number of cubic metres and cubic feet of rock or soil which will weigh 1 tonne or 1 ton.

Spoil	No. of m^3 *to 1 tonne*	*No. of ft^3 to 1 ton*
Sandstone rock	0·402 to 0·460	14 to 16
Sand (wet)	0·488 to 0·546	17 to 19
Clay (not compacted)	0·518 to 0·575	18 to 20
Gravel	0·546 to 0·575	19 to 20
Sand (dry)	0·661 to 0·719	23 to 25
Earth (loose)	0·719 to 0·805	25 to 28
Peat (wet)	0·949 to 1·035	33 to 36
Peat (dry)	1·726 to 2·071	60 to 72

CHAPTER XIV

Felling, Extraction and Transport

1. *Felling*

(a) Methods
Trees may be felled by hand or by power saw.

(b) Felling by hand
(i) To all intents and purposes, manual felling has been replaced by the chain saw although small thinnings are still sometimes felled by hand. In such cases a light axe or bowsaw of the 'Bushman' pattern is generally used.
(ii) The snedding or trimming of poles is also occasionally carried out with an axe.

(c) Felling by power saw
(i) Although the first chain saw was produced by Andreas Stihl in Germany in 1927, subsequent developments were delayed by the Second World War. However, by 1960 power saws were in general use in this country and since then they have become an essential factor in timber felling.

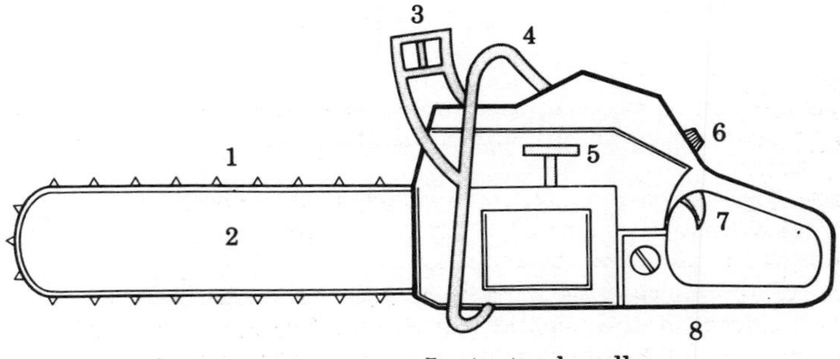

1 chain	5 starter handle
2 guide bar	6 on/off switch
3 front hand guard and chain brake	7 throttle
4 handle	8 chain breakage guard

(ii) The principal external parts of a chain saw are shown in the figure on page 153 but further information will be found in Forestry Safety Council Guide No. 10—*The Chain Saw*.

(iii) The procedure which is adopted, when felling a tree with a chain saw, varies according to the size of the tree.

(1) *Small trees*

(*a*) These are trees with a basal diameter which is less than the length of the guide bar.

(*b*) A 'V'-shaped cut, variously known as a 'mouth', 'throat', 'gullet', 'beak' or 'sink', is made at the base of the tree on the side on which it is intended that the tree shall fall.

(*c*) Sawing is then started on the opposite side of the tree at a slightly higher level, and is continued until the tree falls.

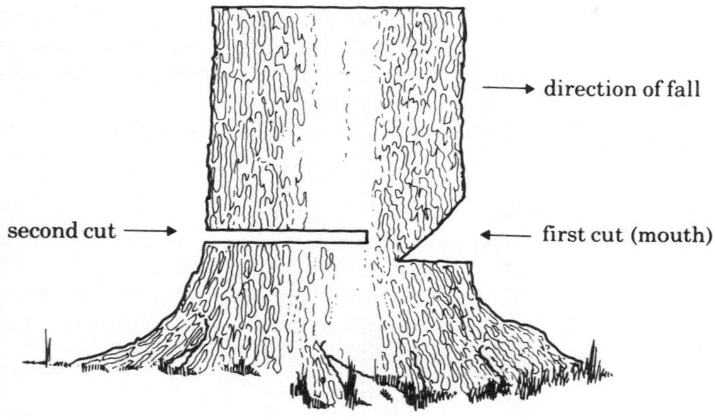

(2) *Medium-sized trees*

(*a*) These have a basal diameter equal to 1–1½ times the length of the guide bar.

(*b*) After the mouth has been made, the main cutting operation is begun by using the end of the saw and then working round in a clockwise direction, as if following the spokes of a wheel.

(*c*) The sequence of action is shown by the numbers and arrows in the top diagram on p. 155, a 'hinge' being left next to the mouth.

(3) *Large trees*

(*a*) Large trees are those which have a basal diameter equal to 1½–2½ times the guide bar length.

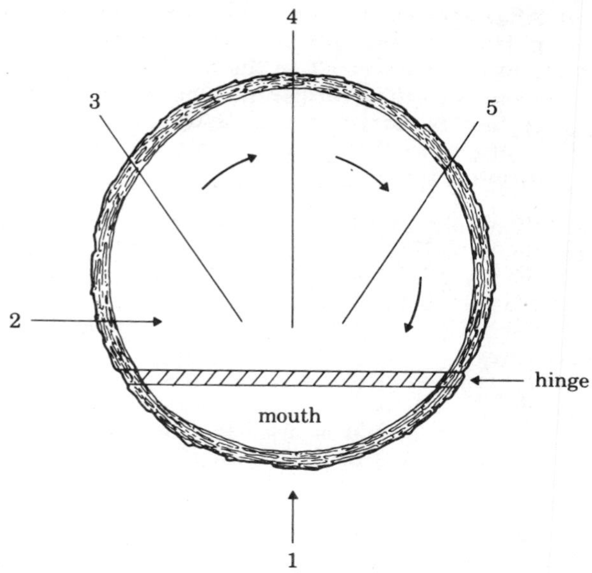

Felling medium-sized trees by power saw

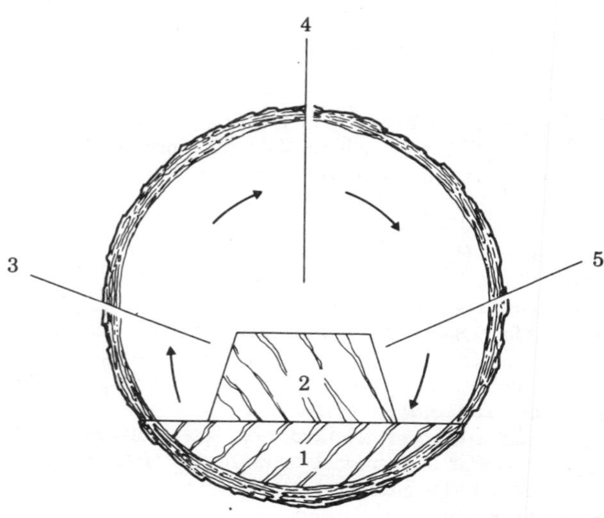

Felling large trees by power saw

(*b*) After making the 'mouth' ('1' in the bottom diagram on p. 155), it is enlarged by cutting a further area into the centre of the tree ('2' in the diagram).

(*c*) The saw is then withdrawn and, starting at one side, cutting is carried out in a clockwise direction. The sequence is shown in the diagram by numbers and arrows.

(iv) This section only provides a brief summary of the procedures which should be followed when felling trees with a chain saw. For further detailed information, reference should be made to Forestry Safety Council Guide No. 11, *Felling by Chain Saw* and Forestry Commission Leaflet No. 75, *Harvesting of Windthrown Trees*.

(d) Equipment

The equipment which should be used in order to ensure safe and efficient work when using a chain saw, may be divided into two categories:

(i) *Personal equipment*

This should include:

Safety helmet	Safety gloves
Visor for eye protection	Safety boots
Ear protectors	Snag-proof clothing
First aid kit.	

For further information regarding safety see Chapter XXXII—Safety in Forestry.

(ii) *Technical equipment*

In addition to the saw, which should be provided with a guard, the following items are amongst those which are normally required:

Wedges	Cant-hook
Hammer	Breaking bar
Felling tongs	Fuel and oil cans

A light hand-operated winch, such as the Tirfor, can also be of considerable assistance when dealing with trees which are hung-up.

(e) Chain saw maintenance

(i) Chain saws are carefully designed and accurately constructed machines and it is essential to maintain them properly if they are to start easily, cut efficiently and operate reliably.

(ii) Full instructions are issued by the manufacturers of the numerous chain saws which are on the market, and these instructions should be carefully studied.

(iii) An excellent manual which deals exclusively with the maintenance of chain saws has been published by the Oregon Saw Chain Division of Messrs Omark U.K. Ltd. Single copies can be obtained free of charge from this firm at 6, Station Drive, Bredon, Tewkesbury, Glos. GL20 7HQ.

(f) Felling precautions

(i) *Trees growing on slopes*
Trees on steep slopes should not be felled up-hill as there is a considerable risk that the butt may 'jump back' and injure the faller. On moderate gradients trees may be felled 'across the slope'.

(ii) *Hung-up trees*
These are trees which, as they are being felled, fall against a standing tree and become lodged in it. They can be released with a cant-hook, lever, felling tongs or winch. Attempts should never be made to dislodge a hung-up tree by jumping on the bole, by felling the tree in which it has become jammed, or cutting off part of the butt or by felling another tree across it. Further information will be found in Forestry Safety Council Guide No. 14, *Takedown of Hung-up Trees.*

(iii) *Felling large trees*
Special precautions should be taken when dealing with large trees, particularly heavily crowned broadleaves standing on open sites. Felling should not be undertaken in a high wind as this may cause a change in the direction of fall. Where overhead electric or telephone wires are close to a tree, the authority concerned should be contacted beforehand. Large trees should always be examined for signs of butt rot before beginning work. See also Forestry Safety Council Guide No. 17, *Felling Large Hardwoods.*

(iv) *Felling across obstacles*
Trees should not be felled across banks, walls or other trees since there is considerable risk that they will be broken or damaged by such action.

(g) Other chain saw operations

(i) In addition to felling trees, chain saws can be used for many other purposes and these include snedding, cross-cutting logs and poles and clearing wind-blow.

(ii) Each of these operations requires a specialised technique and detailed instructions will be found in the following guides issued by the Forestry Safety Council.

No. 12, *Chainsaw Snedding.*
No. 13, *Cross-cutting and Stacking.*
No. 15, *Chainsaw Clearance of Windblow.*

2. *Extraction*

(*a*) Extraction is the process of removing timber, thinnings or firewood from the growing site in the wood to a point where the material is either loaded on to vehicles or is piled or stacked prior to removal or conversion.

(*b*) Material can be removed from the growing site by:

Skidders	Cablecranes
Forwarders	Helicopters

and brief descriptions of these machines and the methods employed are given below.

(*c*) For more detailed information on the various aspects of machinery and equipment used in the extraction of timber and thinnings, reference should be made to Forestry Commission Bulletin No. 14, *Forestry Practice.*

(d) Skidders

(i) This general term is used to describe tractors which extract timber or thinnings by raising one end of the log or poles and allowing the other end to trail along the ground.

(ii) Tractors in this category may be:

(1) Farm tractors with two-wheel drive which have been modified for timber work and fitted with a single- or double-drum winch.

(2) More powerful tractors which have four-wheel drive and have also been modified for forestry work and equipped with a double-drum winch. A grab is sometimes fitted for loading or stacking.

(3) Tractors which have been specially designed for work in the woods. They are generally fitted with a high-powered winch and a hydraulic grab.

(iii) During extraction operations poles are attached to the winch rope by means of detachable slings known as chokers which are fitted with choker hooks. Chokers are frequently made of chains but some users prefer those of polypropylene rope. When small poles are being extracted about six chokers can be attached to the winch rope.

(iv) The safety precautions which should be taken during skidding operations are described in Forestry Safety Council Guide No. 22, *Extraction by Skidder.*

(e) Forwarders

(i) Forwarders are made up of three basic parts: firstly, a tractor or tractor unit; secondly, a trailer which is either a separate component or one which forms an integral part of the tractor unit; and thirdly, a loading crane.

(ii) Whereas in the case of skidding, material is dragged along the ground, in forwarding it is lifted off the ground and placed on the trailer or trailer unit.

(iii) There are two main types of forwarders.

(1) Two- or four-wheel drive farm tractors which have been appropriately modified for forestry work and fitted with a loading crane, together with a detachable trailer. The trailer may or may not have power-driven wheels.

(2) Specially designed machines with frame-steering, in which the engine and cab are built over the front axle and all wheels, including those of the trailer, are power-driven.

(iv) Forwarders are normally equipped with a single-drum winch so that material lying beyond the scope of the crane can be winched in.

(v) The safety aspects of forwarder operations are set out in Guide No. 23. *Extraction by Forwarder*, issued by the Forestry Safety Council.

(f) Cablecranes

(i) The term 'cablecrane' is somewhat confusing since it is used in two senses. First, it can refer to the system of overhead ropeways by means of which timber and thinnings can be extracted. Secondly, it may be used with reference to the actual machinery which provides the operating power.

(ii) The material is generally transported clear of the ground although in some cases the lower end of the load may drag along it.

(iii) In this country, two types of cablecranes are generally used: the high lead and the skyline.

(iv) *The high lead cablecrane*

(1) This consists of three component parts: a tractor, a steel tower about 6–7 m (20–23 ft) in height and a double-drum winch.

(2) Two lines are rigged from the top of the tower to a spar tree, one being known as the 'main line' and the other the 'haul-back line'.

(3) The load is borne by a small carriage or block which runs on the haul-back line and to which the main line is attached.

(4) When operating, one drum winds in the main line (and the load) while the other drum operates the haul-back line.

(5) High lead cranes are usually more satisfactory than skylines for operating over short distances of about 120 m (130 yd) their limit being about 180 m (200 yd).

(v) *The skyline cablecrane*

(1) The equipment and operation are similar to the high lead *except* that the block which carries the load runs on a separate fixed ropeway known as a skyline, instead of on the haul-back line.

(2) The skyline can be attached to supports which are fixed to selected trees spaced at suitable intervals. Consequently a much longer operating distance is possible with lengths of up to 600 m (655 yd).

(vi) More information on cablecrane operations will be found in Forestry Commission Bulletin No. 14, *Forestry Practice* and Forestry Safety Council Guide No. 25, *Extraction by Cablecrane*.

(g) Helicopters

(i) Although extraction by air has not been practised to any great extent in this country, sufficient use has already been made of helicopters, to indicate their potentialities. These are particularly evident where material has to be removed from sites to which access is difficult or where the usual methods of extraction are presented with special problems.

(ii) Several companies which operate helicopter services have experience in timber extraction, fertilizer application and other operations applicable to forestry.

(iii) A very informative account by Lieutenant Colonel J. D. Stephenson, describing extraction by helicopter, will be found in *Timber Grower* No. 57 (1975), under the title of 'Extraction by Helicopter in South Wales'.

3. *Transport*

(*a*) Although, in the past, various means have been used for transporting timber from the forest, road haulage has now virtually replaced all other methods.

(*b*) Timber of large dimensions is usually transported on timber carriages which are also known as 'drugs' or 'pole waggons' and hauled by a self-contained detachable power unit.

(*c*) The front axle of the carriage is fixed to a 'pole' or central member running the length of the vehicle and carries the front bunk or bed on which the butt end of the trees rest, when loaded.

(*d*) The rear axle or pair of axles can be moved along the pole either forwards or backwards, so that trees of different lengths can be carried. A rear bunk or bed is fitted over, and parallel to, the rear axle.

(*e*) A normal load for a four-wheeled carriage is from 9·0 to 12·6 cubic metres (250 to 300 Hoppus feet). It is essential that a timber carriage is fitted with an efficient and reliable brake system.

(*f*) In certain cases, large logs are cross-cut to the required lengths to enable them to be loaded on to platform lorries of conventional design.

(*g*) Platform lorries are also used for the conveyance of smaller material which has been cut to sizes, such as pitwood, stakes and pulpwood.

4. *Loading*

(a) Timber, poles and smaller produce can be loaded on to vehicles by the methods which are outlined below, the procedure adopted depending largely on the size and weight of the material.

(b) Hydraulic cranes and grapples
These are mainly used for loading poles, stakes and so on but some types are able to deal with heavy saw logs.

(c) Front-end loaders
With these machines large logs, as well as thinnings, can be loaded very quickly but both their initial and operating costs are high. Some makes are specially designed for working on rough forest sites.

(d) Parbuckling or cross-hauling

(i) To a large extent this method of loading has been replaced by hydraulic cranes and front-end loaders. However, parbuckling is still used where very large logs have to be loaded or on small woodland estates where heavy capital investment in machinery is not justified.

(ii) By this method a log is rolled up a ramp, formed by two baulks of timber, on to a timber carriage. Two wire ropes are first passed under the log and their ends taken back, over the carriage, and attached to the winch rope of a tractor, standing on the far side. As the rope is winched in, the load is rolled up on to the carriage.

CHAPTER XV

Sawmills and Conversion

1. *Estate Sawmills*

(a) Advantages of estate conversion

(i) Estate conversion enables an owner to sell his timber in a greater range of markets than if sold unconverted.

(ii) Second- and third-grade timber which is difficult to sell in the round can be converted into produce which can be disposed of more readily, such as dunnage, rough boarding, fencing material and so on.

(iii) Transport costs are reduced, since unprofitable waste is removed at the mill and freight charges are consequently confined to marketable produce.

(iv) Difficulties which may be caused by delays in felling and extraction, when timber is sold standing, can be avoided or substantially reduced.

(v) When the price of round timber is low, estate conversion can be particularly advantageous.

(b) Disadvantages of estate conversion

(i) It is essential to have a team of men in the mill who know their jobs, and such a team may not be easily recruited.

(ii) Good organization in the mill coupled with skilled supervision are essential, and this means the employment of a first-class manager. Such a person may be difficult to find.

(iii) Efficient and economical plant must be installed if production costs are to be kept to a minimum, and this may call for a heavy capital expenditure.

(iv) If the estate undertakes its own timber haulage, further expenditure will be involved in the provision of vehicles and equipment and in their running costs.

(v) Assuming that it is intended to run the mill at full production, an adequate supply of timber will be needed and it may be necessary to buy timber if the estate woodlands cannot supply it.

(vi) In an endeavour to keep the mill in production there may be a tendency to over-cut the timber on the estate, thus reducing the capital value of the woods.

(c) Points to consider before setting up a mill

(i) Are there adequate markets for sawn timber in the vicinity or within an economic operating distance of the proposed mill?
(ii) Are there any mills which are already in production in the district and which may subsequently be in competition.
(iii) Are the estate woodlands able to provide a sufficient and regular supply of timber (within the limits of the working plan or plan of operations) to keep the mill in production? If not, from what sources are supplies to be obtained?
(iv) What power is to be used for driving the mill?
(v) Is the necessary labour force available and will housing have to be provided?
(vi) How is the proposed mill located in relationship to the estate woodlands?
(vii) Has the site adequate access by roads which are able to carry the anticipated weight and volume of traffic?

(d) Power

The following sources of power can be used in estate sawmills.

(i) *Electricity*

(1) This provides instant starting and is clean and safe in operation.
(2) If run off a mains supply it is an expensive form of energy which may be subject to power cuts and line breakdowns.

(ii) *Diesel*

(1) This source of power is normally used to generate a supply of electricity which in turn operates the various machines in the mill. It is quick-starting and provides a considerable power output.
(2) However the ever-increasing cost of fuel oil, together with the prospect of diminishing supplies, may raise doubts as to the advisability of adopting it under such circumstances.

(iii) *Steam*

(1) Steam produces a regular and flexible supply of power of which it has an ample reserve. Although it was originally used to drive machinery through shafts and belting, it is equally adaptable for generating electricity as in the case of diesel power.
(2) Provided that a suitable firebox is fitted, sawdust and wood waste can be used as fuel.
(3) The two main disadvantages of steam power are: firstly the time taken to raise steam before starting, and secondly the

need for proper attention when running it in order to ensure correct stoking and boiler pressure.

(4) Although in recent years there has been an increasing tendency to regard steam as an obsolete form of power, there is now much to be said for a new appraisal of the situation in view of the continually rising costs of oil and electricity.

(iv) *Water*

(1) Before 1950 water-driven sawmills were to be found on some estates and examples could be seen at Yettington near Budleigh Salterton, Devon; at Colesbourne near Cheltenham, Gloucestershire and at Long Handborough near Woodstock, Oxfordshire.

(2) While water can provide a cheap form of power, its value will be greatly diminished unless an adequate and regular supply is available at all times of the year. The actual power can be obtained either through a water wheel or turbine.

(e) Sawmill machinery and equipment

(i) *Circular rack benches*

(1) These benches are usually fitted with a saw which is 1·52–1·83 m (60–72 in.) in diameter and an automatic or hand-operated table about 6·0 m (20 ft) in length.

(2) Circular rack benches are easy to operate while the sharpening of the saws does not call for any high degree of skill. This is particularly so where saws of the inserted tooth type are used.

(3) Owing to the need for rigidity and strength, the larger diameter saws tend to be thick in section. Consequently a considerable amount of wood is removed as sawdust and this may be as much as 6 mm (¼ in.) thick.

(4) To a large extent circular rack benches have now been replaced by band-mills.

(ii) *Band rack benches and band-mills*

(1) These may be of the vertical or horizontal type, the table usually being operated automatically.

(2) The advantages of bandsaws as compared with circular saws are:

faster cutting, better quality sawing and less waste in sawdust while the size of the log to be converted is not limited by the diameter of the saw.

(3) The disadvantages are:

band saws are considerably more expensive and need skilled attention in maintenance, especially in sharpening and tensioning the saw blade—this requires the services of a 'saw doctor' who has been specially trained in such work.

(iii) *Circular push benches*

(1) The diameters of saws which are usually fitted to push benches are 0·45, 0·61, 0·76, 0·91 and 1·06 m (18, 24, 30, 36 and 42 in.).

(2) Push benches vary considerably in design from light firewood benches to massive joinery benches fitted with rise-and-fall tables.

(iv) *Multiple frame saws*

These consist of several saw blades set parallel to each other in a vertical frame which moves up and down. By this means a complete log can be converted into a number of smaller pieces in one operation.

(v) *Other equipment*

In addition to the above, other items of equipment may be included in a mill, such as mortising and planing machines, but the choice of these will largely depend on type of markets which the mill supplies.

(f) Terms used in describing saw teeth

The following is a list of terms which are used in connection with the teeth of a saw, some of which are shown in the diagram.

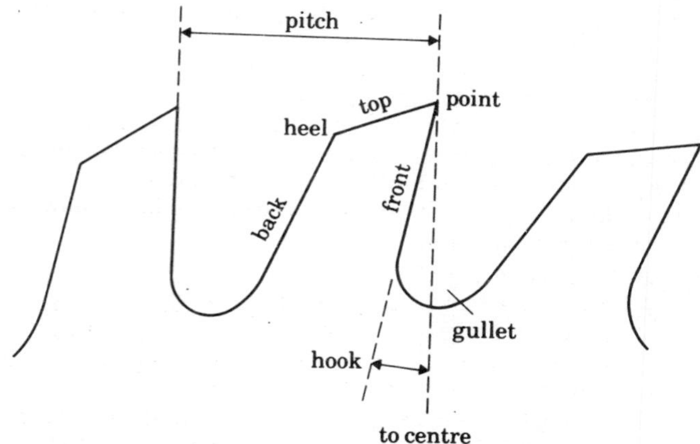

Point: the tip of the saw tooth.
Gullet: the lowest point between two teeth.
Pitch: the distance between the points of any two adjacent teeth.

Set: the amount which any tooth is displaced from the vertical as seen from behind the saw when it is in the running position.

Kerf or saw gate: the width of the saw cut. The kerf is equal to the gauge plus twice the set.

Hook: the angle which the front of a tooth makes with a line drawn from the point to the centre of the saw. Normal hook occurs when the front of a tooth inclines forward. Where the front inclines to the rear, it is termed 'negative hook'.

Heel: the angle formed between the back and the top.

Back: the side of the tooth furthest from the point.

Front: that part of the tooth which is behind the gullet.

Top: that part of the tooth between the heel and the point.

(g) Circular saw details

(i) *Depth of cut*

the approximate depth of cut of a circular saw on a push bench can be found by the formula:

$$\text{Depth} = \left(\frac{\text{diameter of saw in inches}}{2}\right) - 2\text{ in.}$$

In metric measure this becomes:

$$\text{Depth} = \left(\frac{\text{diameter of saw in metres}}{2}\right) - 0{\cdot}051\text{ m}$$

In the case of a rack bench 3 in. or 0·076 m should be deducted.

(ii) *Saw teeth*

(1) Saw teeth may be solid or inserted. Solid teeth are part of the saw blade so that any damage to the tooth means damage to the whole saw. Inserted teeth are removable and if damaged can be replaced in a few moments.

(2) Inserted teeth have the following advantages:
broken teeth can be replaced immediately;
the teeth are made of harder steel than the rest of the saw and so remain sharp for longer periods;
the saw always retains its diameter since there is no reduction in size through sharpening—this prevents any loss of rim speed and efficiency is maintained.

(1) The chief disadvantage of an inserted tooth saw is the higher initial cost.

(iii) *Saw fence*

(1) This is a rectangular plate which is attached to the saw

table, in order to keep the timber, which is being sawn, at a fixed distance from the saw blade. This regulates the thickness of the cut.

(2) The fence can be moved closer to, or further away from the face of the saw so that varying thicknesses can be cut.

(h) Bark peeling machines

(i) Peeling machines may be used elsewhere than in the vicinity of the sawmill as for example in the woods or on site where fencing material is being prepared.

(ii) A major consideration when operating them is the disposal of the peeled bark and shavings. One method of dealing with this problem is to use one or more farm trailers fitted with high sides and tops, similar to those employed in harvesting silage. When full the vehicles can be taken to another site for disposal of the contents.

(iii) In order to ensure that work continues safely and efficiently, it is essential that the layout of the working area is properly organized. The siting of both the unpeeled and peeled material, in relation to the machine, is of major importance.

(i) Safety regulations, appliances and precautions

(i) Safety regulations in respect of sawmills are laid down under the Factories Act 1961 and the Woodworking Machinery Regulations, 1974. Mobile sawbenches which are used in the woods and in other comparable locations are covered by Statutory Instruments 1959 No. 427—The Agricultural (Circular Saw) Regulations 1959.

(ii) At least one box containing first-aid kit, which conforms with Health and Safety (First Aid) Regulations 1981, should be provided in a small sawmill but in large ones several boxes should be available at easily accessible points. To assist in locating these boxes, the wall behind and surrounding them should be painted in a distinctive colour, over an area of about 1 square yard or square metre.

(iii) A riving knife, which is a thin curved blade of steel, should be fitted behind each circular saw. Its purpose is to prevent the timber which is being sawn from binding together as it clears the saw blade.

(iv) All circular saws should be fitted with a top guard over the saw which is usually segment-shaped and not unlike a foreshortened bicycle mudguard. It can be adjusted for height or completely removed when sawing oversize pieces. An alternative form consists of a hinged frame which protects the top of the saw but which can be raised when sawing large material.

(v) Full protection must be given to the under-parts of a saw so as to protect employees from touching the lower part of the saw when it is running. This can best be done by boxing in the saw table in the case of a push bench, but provision must be made for clearing sawdust when the saw is stationary. Rack benches are usually protected by the foundations.

(vi) Since sawmills are generally surrounded by stacks of sawn and round timber, they should always be regarded as a major fire hazard and the necessary steps taken accordingly. These should include an adequate number of regularly serviced fire extinguishers and, in the larger mills, a system of hydrants and hoses. Close contact should be maintained with officers of the local fire brigade and sawmill staff should be given instruction and practice in the use of firefighting equipment.

(vii) For further information on safety precautions reference should be made to the following Forestry Safety Council Guides:
No. 30, *Mobile Saw Bench*
No. 31, *Mobile Peeling Machine.*

2. *The Principles of Conversion*

(a) Methods of converting timber

There are four main methods of converting timber: (1) plain sawing, (2) quarter sawing, (3) rotary cutting, (4) cleaving; these are dealt with briefly below. All these methods have variations and modifications.

(b) Plain sawing

(i) This is also known as 'through and through cutting', 'slash cutting', 'bastard cutting', 'flat sawing', 'back sawing', and 'planking'.

(ii) In this method of conversion a 'flitch' or 'slab' is removed from the outside of the log, and successive parallel cuts are made until conversion is complete.

(iii) Where a butt is defective, as, for example, where the centre has been damaged by heart rot, some modification of this method may be necessary. When sawing is arranged so as to avoid a rotten core it is known as 'boxing the heart'.

(iv) The term 'bastard cutting' as applied to plain sawing should not be confused with 'bastard quarter sawn' referred to below.

(c) Quarter sawing

(i) This method is also known as 'quartering', 'rift cutting', 'cutting on the quarter', and 'bastard quarter sawing'.

(ii) Under this system the majority of the saw cuts are made more or less parallel to the radius of the log.

(iii) Strictly speaking, 'quartering' is a term applied to the initial cutting of a baulk preparatory to converting it into boards by quarter sawing.

(iv) Bastard quarter sawing is a modified method which produces less waste than the normal quartering.

(v) The advantages of quarter sawing over plain sawing are:
  (1) Distortion during seasoning reduced to a minimum.
  (2) Greater strength.
  (3) Better decorative effect in the grain of certain timber, especially oak.

(vi) The disadvantages of quarter sawing are:
  (1) Slower rate of cutting, and therefore more expensive.
  (2) Produces narrower planks.
  (3) Results in more waste.

(d) Rotary cutting

(i) This method is used in cutting veneers, the logs being set up on a large lathe and rotated against a sharp knife, so that a thin layer or veneer is removed.

(ii) Logs are softened before cutting, either by soaking them in water or treating them with steam.

(iii) The sheets may be used for furniture veneers, or for the manufacture of plywood.

(e) Cleaving

(i) Cleaving can be done by hand, using a 'froe' or 'dull-axe'. This consists of a cutting blade fixed at right-angles to a short handle, and driven through the material to be riven by hitting it with a wooden beetle.

(ii) Larger material can be cleft by using an axe, timber wedges, and beetle.

(iii) Box boards may be produced by machine cleaving, the timber having first been soaked or steamed. One type of machine consists of a pair of blades each set at opposite ends of a weighted arm which is pivoted in the centre, the operative motion being that of a see-saw.

3. *Terms Used in Conversion*

(a) Cross-cutting

A general term to denote cutting across the grain.

(b) Ripping

(i) Cutting with the grain.

(ii) The teeth of a ripping saw are set at a forward angle, while those of a cross-cut saw are almost vertical.

(c) Wain

The rough edge of a board formed by the outside of the tree, which occurs in the initial stages of breaking down a log.

(d) Cant

A square baulk formed by cutting a slab off four sides of a round log, the process being known as 'cutting a cant'.

(e) Flitch or slab

The first cut off a log. One side of a flitch is covered with bark; the other is a straight-sided saw cut.

(f) Re-sawing

The sawing of timber which has been partly converted. The initial stages of conversion are known as 'breaking down'.

CHAPTER XVI

Utilization

ALTHOUGH in recent years several substitutes have been found for wood, the demand for timber has steadily increased so that, by the beginning of the 21st century, a world shortage is considered to be very probable.

In course of time changes may occur regarding the extent to which timber is used for a particular purpose. This may be due to the introduction of other kinds of materials, such as plastics, or may be accounted for by the fact that the article which is made from timber, is no longer in demand. However, such changes tend to take place gradually over a prolonged period.

1. *The Characteristics and Uses of Home-grown Timber*

A. BROADLEAVED SPECIES

Because of the changes which have occurred during recent years as regards the uses to which broadleaved species have been put, these are shown under two subheadings; namely, traditional uses and current uses. Those which are noted under the latter heading only comprise a selection and should not be regarded as a complete record.

1. *Alder*

(*a*) *Characteristics*: comparatively light and soft; moderate strength and ease of working; will last almost indefinitely under water.

(*b*) *Traditional uses*: clog soles, brush backs, textile rollers and in the manufacture of gunpowder.

(*c*) *Current uses*: general turnery, toys, artificial limbs, hat blocks, piles and underwater structures, pulpwood.

2. *Ash*

(*a*) *Characteristics*: strong and tough; flexible; easy to work; of medium weight; not very durable.

(*b*) *Traditional uses*: cart shafts, wheel felloes, agricultural implements, bodywork framing for vans and motor vehicles.

(*c*) *Current uses*: sports goods, e.g. hockey sticks, tennis rackets, billiard cues, etc., turnery, tool handles, furniture, pulpwood.

3. *Beech*

(*a*) *Characteristics*: strong; cleaves easily; easy to work; stains and polishes well; not durable except under water; can be bent after treatment.

(*b*) *Traditional uses*: brush backs, shoe heels and lasts.

(*c*) *Current uses*: furniture, turnery, pattern-making, toys, kitchenware, tool handles, pulpwood, veneers.

4. *Birch*

(*a*) *Characteristics*: works fairly easily; not durable; takes stain and polish well; tough and moderately strong; does not splinter.

(*b*) *Traditional uses*: bobbins, spindles, boxes, brush backs, handles, general turnery.

(*c*) *Current uses*: furniture, toys, plywood, pulpwood.

5. *Chestnut, Horse*

(*a*) *Characteristics*: very white in colour; works easily when dry; soft and lacks strength; not durable.

(*b*) *Traditional uses*: bobbins, turnery, dairy and kitchen utensils.

(*c*) *Current uses*: toys; fruit storage racks (wood will absorb moisture); pulpwood.

6. *Chestnut, Sweet or Spanish*

(*a*) *Characteristics*: strong but inferior to oak; cleaves easily; works, polishes and stains well; very durable.

(*b*) *Traditional uses*: furniture, coffin boards, gates.

(*c*) *Current uses*: the traditional uses given above and also pulpwood. Owing to its somewhat similar appearance to oak it is sometimes used in place of it.

7. *Cherry*

(*a*) *Characteristics*: works well; very tough and strong; stains and polishes well.

(*b*) *Traditional uses*: furniture and cabinet making.

(*c*) *Current uses*: furniture and cabinet making, turnery and pulpwood. Although seldom grown as a timber crop, cherry can be used for most estate purposes.

8. *Elm, Common*

(*a*) *Characteristics*: strong, tough and very difficult to split; works fairly well but is liable to warp when seasoned naturally; does not splinter; very durable if entirely submerged in water.

(*b*) *Traditional uses*: cart bottoms, wheelbarrows, beetle and maul heads, brush backs, boxes for the tinplate industry.
(*c*) *Current uses*: coffin boards, turnery, weather-boarding, piles for underwater work, pulpwood.

9. *Elm, Wych or Scotch*
(*a*) *Characteristics*: stronger than the common elm; almost as tough as ash; difficult to split; easy to work.
(*b*) *Traditional uses*: boat-building, turnery.
(*c*) *Current uses*: steamed bent wood, general estate work, pulpwood.

10. *Hornbeam*
(*a*) *Characteristics*: moderately heavy, hard and strong; not durable for external use in its untreated state; hard to work; takes stain and polish well.
(*b Traditional uses*: wooden cogwheels, wood screws, tool handles and pulleys.
(*c*) *Current uses*: mallet heads, skittles, butchers' blocks, small articles where hard-wearing qualities are required.

11. *Lime*
(*a*) *Characteristics*: soft with a fine close texture; easy to work when seasoned; takes stain and polish well; white in colour; not durable except for internal use.
(*b*) *Traditional uses*: the most suitable timber for carving which was frequently used by Grinling Gibbons (1648–1721); also used in furniture making, turnery work and beehives.
(*c*) *Current uses*: as for traditional uses and also pulpwood.

12. *Oak*
(*a*) *Characteristics*: hard, strong and rather heavy; very durable except the sap wood; coarse textured; cleaves well; produces chemical reaction on metals.
(*b*) *Traditional uses*: wheelwright's work, shipbuilding, railway wagon construction, cooperage.
(*c*) *Current uses*: furniture, floors, panelling, coffin boards, beams for constructional work, gates, fencing, estate use, pulpwood, veneers, chipboard.

13. *Poplar*
(*a*) *Characteristics*: light, soft and easily worked; dents rather than splinters; moderately strong yet splitting easily; polishes well but staining may be patchy; holds nails well; does not ignite easily.
(*b*) *Traditional uses*: colliery tramway waggons, floors of lorries and other load-carrying vehicles, brake blocks, matches and matchboxes, chip baskets, toys.

(*c*) *Current uses*: plywood, pulpwood, box boards. Since the manufacturers decided, during the 1970s, to terminate the purchase of home-grown poplar for matchmaking and to discontinue the production of chip baskets, the uses for poplar have been seriously curtailed.

14. *Sycamore*

(*a*) *Characteristics*: strong, moderately heavy; not durable unless treated; white in colour; works well and will take stain and polish.

(*b*) *Traditional uses*: large textile rollers, brush backs, bobbins, bread boards, rolling pins.

(*c*) *Current uses*: turnery work, toys, kitchen and dairy utensils, furniture and cabinet making, pulpwood.

15. *Walnut*

(*a*) *Characteristics*: moderately hard and tough; easy to work and gives a fine smooth finish; does not split easily.

(*b*) *Traditional uses*: furniture and cabinet making, veneers, gunstocks, domestic items such as bowls and plates.

(*c*) *Current uses*: as for traditional uses.

16. *Willow*

(*a*) *Characteristics*: light, soft but fairly tough; not durable; easy to work.

(*b*) *Traditional uses*: cricket bats, toys, chip baskets.

(*c*) *Current uses*: cricket bats, toys, artificial limbs, pulpwood.

B. CONIFERS

1. *Cedar, Western red* (Thuya plicata)

(*a*) *Characteristics*: resistant to decay and insect attack; not particularly strong; easy to work; reddish-brown in colour but turning grey when exposed to external conditions; may stain unevenly.

(*b*) *Uses*: weather-boarding, roof shingles, internal decorative panelling, fencing.

2. *Cypress, Lawson*

(*a*) *Characteristics*: strong scented; white to yellow in colour; durable; not very strong; easy to work; gives a good finish and polishes and stains well.

(*b*) *Uses*: joinery, wardrobes and clothes chests, fencing.

3. *Douglas fir*

(*a*) *Characteristics*: moderately light but strong; reasonably easy to work; pinkish-brown in colour.

(*b*) *Uses*: constructional timbers, general building purposes, boarding, estate work, pitprops, fencing, chipboard, packing cases.

4. *Silver fir*

(*a*) *Characteristics*: white or yellowish white in colour; soft and light in weight; odourless; easy to work; takes stain well.

(*b*) *Uses*: joinery, boxes, packing cases, toys, general building purposes, wood pulp.

5. *Larch*

(*a*) *Characteristics*: one of the hardest and strongest of the conifers; durable; works well and takes stain satisfactorily.

(*b*) *Uses*: building work, gates, fencing, boatbuilding, piles (Venice is largely built on larch piles), chipboard, garden furniture.

6. *Scots pine*

(*a*) *Characteristics*: moderately light in weight; reasonably durable; can be nailed easily; takes polish well.

(*b*) *Uses*: building construction generally; gates, fencing, boxes, overhead service line poles, pitprops. Sometimes referred to in the building trade as red deal.

7. *Corsican pine*

(*a*) *Characteristics*: of medium weight and strength; on the whole is similar to Scots pine; will take preservatives without difficulty.

(*b*) *Uses*: as for Scots pine, and also woodwool, fibreboard.

8. *Common or Norway spruce*

(*a*) *Characteristics*: light in weight and of medium strength; finishes and works well; holds nails well and takes stain and polish.

(*b*) *Uses*: boxes, joinery, pulpwood, general building work, pitprops, kitchen furniture, chipboard. In the building trade it is often referred to as white deal, or whitewood.

9. *Sitka spruce*

(*a*) *Characteristics*: as for Norway spruce but lighter in weight.

(*b*) *Uses*: similar to Norway spruce.

2. *Utilization of Thinnings*

The disposal of thinnings, especially those from broadleaved stands, can be difficult and much depends on their age, size, straightness and quality. The following are some of the outlets which may be available.

(a) Broadleaved species
Fencing, hurdle and gate material, wire stakes, firewood and pulpwood.

(b) Conifers
Poles for overhead service lines, rustic poles for gardens, fencing and gate material, pulpwood, chipboard, pitprops and firewood (selected species).

3. *Specialized Woodland Produce*

(a) Coppice and underwood
Several changes have taken place during the past few years in some of the traditional uses of coppice material. The mechanical hedge-cutter has almost entirely replaced the art of cutting and laying hedges, for which large quantities of hedge stakes and binders, or hetherings, were needed. In the potteries, the use of hazel for the construction of crates has been brought to an end by the introduction of plastic packing cases.

The following are some of the purposes for which coppice and underwood are still used.

(i) *Hazel.* Pea and bean sticks; flower and tomato stakes; wattle hurdles; thatching spars; fascines for river banks.
(ii) *Sweet chestnut.* Wirework poles for hop gardens; cheft pale fencing; fencing stakes and spiles; flower and tomato stakes.
(iii) *Ash.* Sheep hurdles; fencing rails; tool handles.
(iv) *Sycamore.* Turnery work; fencing posts if impregnated.
(v) *Birch.* Turnery; besoms (brooms); material for making up jumps for steeplechasing, shows and horse trials.

Note. See also Chapter VII—Coppice and Underwood.

(b) Bark
(i) Bark is used in the process of tanning leather and for this purpose oak bark is considered to be the best. However tannin is also found in the bark of other species including alder, birch, willow, Sitka spruce and larch.
(ii) Oak bark can be stripped when the sap begins to 'run', usually in April or May, and after drying it is sold to the tanneries by the ton or tonne.

(c) Foliage
(i) A market sometimes exists, in the vicinity of large towns, for the foliage of certain species although the demand often tends to be irregular.
(ii) The material which may be of interest to florists includes sprays of foliage of Lawson cypress, Western red cedar, Douglas fir and box and also sallow or 'willow palm', spindle, rowan and, at Christmas-time, holly and mistletoe.

(iii) Some florists are prepared to send their own employees to cut foliage in order to obtain their precise requirements.

(d) Christmas trees

(i) Although the Norway spruce is the recognized Christmas tree in this country, other subsidiary species such as Douglas fir, silver fir and Scots pine sometimes appear on the market, although generally at lower prices.

(ii) Trees are sold according to their height and those of 0·6–1·2 m (2–4 ft) are usually in the greatest demand, the price being calculated according to the height.

(iii) Trees may be offered for sale with the roots attached, with the roots cut off, or as the tops of larger trees.

(iv) In 1960 the British Christmas Tree Growers Association was formed in order to promote the sales of Christmas trees and generally to assist members of the Association. Details of the Association will be found in Chapter XXVII.

(e) Firewood

(i) During the past few years wood has become increasingly popular as a fuel for domestic heating, for two main reasons. Firstly the substantial rise in the cost of other forms of heating and secondly the introduction of modern wood-burning stoves.

(ii) Firewood is sold in two ways:

(1) Cordwood, consisting of pieces of round wood usually cut into lengths of 1·21 m (4 ft). Further information on cordwood will be found in Chapter IX, section 3(*f*).

(2) Logs which are sold wholesale by the ton or tonne and retailed by local measure such as the load or bag.

(iii) In assessing the firewood qualities of a given species of tree the following points should be taken into account:

(1) Amount of heat given out whilst burning.

(2) Speed of combustion: species which burn too quickly are uneconomical.

(3) Degree of dryness needed for satisfactory ignition: ash will burn whether green or dry; elm must be well seasoned.

(4) Liability to spark: larch is a serious offender in this respect.

(5) Scent emitted during burning: apple wood produces a very pleasing smell.

(iv) The following is a guide to the firewood qualities of the species listed below.

First-quality firewood:

Apple	Hazel	Pear
Ash	Holly	Plane
Beech	Hornbeam	Sycamore
Birch	Oak	Yew
Hawthorn		

Second-quality firewood:

Cedar of Lebanon	Maple
Cherry	Willow
Elm	

Third-quality firewood:

Alder	Larch	Scots pine
Chestnut (sweet and horse)	Lime	Spruce
Corsican pine	Poplar	Walnut

Notes

(1) When burning larch in an open grate, a fire-guard should be used owing to its tendency to produce sparks.

(2) To get the best results, elm should be thoroughly dry.

(v) Further information on firewood will be found in a pamphlet published by the Forestry Commission—*Wood as Fuel.*

(f) Charcoal

(i) Charcoal burning provides a useful outlet for material which might otherwise be difficult to sell except for firewood.

(ii) The following types of kiln are in use at the present time:

(1) The traditional earth-covered kilns, drawings of which are to be seen in the second edition of *Sylva* by John Evelyn, published in 1670.

(2) Batch kilns, which may be either of the portable or the fixed type. The former consists of a circular iron drum not less than 2·1 m (7 ft) in diameter which is fitted with a detachable lid and chimney. These kilns can be dismantled and removed to another site when necessary. The fixed type is similar in operation but, as the name implies, it cannot be moved so that the wood has to be brought to the kiln instead of the kiln to the wood.

(3) Continuous kilns which consist basically of an upright 'tube' about 30 m (100 ft) in height, into the top of which wood is tipped. By the time this has reached the bottom of the tube, it has been converted into charcoal.

(iii) Forest Record No. 121 (see below) states that the most suitable species for the production of charcoal are—in order of preference—beech, birch, hornbeam, oak, ash, elm and conifers.

(iv) Points to note in the production of charcoal are:

(1) Good quality charcoal is black with a slightly blue metallic tinge; a brown colour indicates faulty production. Slow burning produces a better-qality charcoal than fast burning.

(2) Charcoal should be comparatively clean to handle and if a sample is dropped gently, it should give a metallic ring. It should always be stored under dry conditions, since it readily absorbs moisture.

(v) The following figures relate to the average production of charcoal:

1 bushel of charcoal weighs, on average, 18½ lb or 8·4 kg.
1 ton of wood yields not less than 40 bushels, 680 lb or 308 kg of charcoal.
1 cord of wood yields about 30 bushels, 555 lb or 250 kg of charcoal.
100 ft^3 (2·83 m^3) of hardwoods produce about 37 bushels, 685 lb or 310 kg of charcoal.
100 ft^3 (2·83 m^3) of conifers produce about 53 bushels, 980 lb or 445 kg of charcoal.

Note. Further information on charcoal burning will be found in Forest Record No. 121, *The Production of Wood Charcoal in Great Britain* (Forestry Commission, 1980).

4. *Weights of Home-grown Timbers*

(*a*) The weight of a piece of timber largely depends on its moisture content, and the more moisture it contains the heavier it will be.

(*b*) Freshly felled or 'green' timber contains a large amount of water, and consequently the weight of newly felled trees is far greater than when seasoned.

(*c*) In the table on p. 180 are given the weight of various timbers when the moisture content is 15%.

WEIGHTS OF TIMBER

Species	*Average weight in kg per m³ (15% moisture content)*	*Average weight in lb per ft³ (15% moisture content)*
(i) *Broadleaved species*		
Oak	736·8	46
Beech	720·8	45
Ash	704·8	44
Hornbeam	688·7	43
Wych elm	688·7	43
Birch	672·7	42
Walnut	656·7	41
Cherry	640·7	40
Sycamore	640·7	40
Sweet chestnut	560·6	35
Common elm	560·6	35
Lime	560·6	35
Alder	528·6	33
Horse chestnut	496·5	31
Poplar	448·5	28
Willow	448·5	28
(ii) *Conifers*		
European pine	592·6	37
Scots pine	528·6	33
Corsican pine	512·5	32
Douglas fir	496·5	31
Japanese larch	496·5	31
Silver fir	480·5	30
Western hemlock	480·5	30
Lawson cypress	448·5	28
Norway spruce	432·4	27
Redwood (*Sequoia*)	416·4	26
Sitka spruce	400·4	25
Western red cedar	400·4	25

CHAPTER XVII

Timber Seasoning and Preservation

1. *The Seasoning of Timber*

(a) The need for seasoning

Green timber contains a large amount of water, and it is necessary to remove this by seasoning, in order that the timber may:

(i) Become stable.
(ii) Increases in strength.
(iii) Be reduced in weight.
(iv) Have increased resistance to decay.
(v) Be treated more successfully with preservatives, stains, and polish.

(b) Defects occurring during seasoning

(i) When the moisture content of a piece of timber is reduced, shrinkage, followed by a change in shape, i.e. warping, frequently occurs.
(ii) The greatest shrinkage takes place in a direction tangential to the annual rings.
(iii) Where the outside portion of a piece of timber becomes seasoned while the inside does not, the timber is said to be 'case hardened'.
(iv) Some of the other defects which occur in seasoning are:
  (1) Heart shake or checking.
  (2) End splitting of sawn pieces.
  (3) Surface checking.
  (4) Loosening of knots.
  (5) Corrugation or 'washboarding' of planks.

(c) Air-seasoning

(i) This is also known as 'natural' seasoning, as opposed to kiln seasoning, which is sometimes known as 'artificial' seasoning.
(ii) In air-seasoning, timber is stacked so as to allow the free circulation of air, and in course of time the moisture content is reduced to reasonable limits.
(iii) Poles and fencing material may be stacked so that each successive layer in a heap is at right-angles to the one below

it. It takes about 6 months for a pole 15·2 cm (6 in.) in diameter to dry by this method but the time taken depends on the season of the year. During the winter months little or no drying takes place but in a hot summer less than 6 months may produce the desired results.

(iv) Before stacking sawn timber the site should be levelled and, if possible, covered with ashes. The timber which is to be seasoned should be raised about 30 cm (12 in.) above the ground by providing wooden bearers or old rails laid on top of a series of brick on concrete piers, the top of the bearer or rail being 30 cm (12 in.) above ground level.

(v) Timber may be stacked in two ways:
   (1) Piling in log form. This applies to the through-and-through method of converting a butt. After sawing, the planks are stacked so that the original outline of the log is retained. This procedure is used where it is desired to leave the edges of planks untrimmed, so that advantage can be taken of the natural curves of the wood, as is often necessary in the furniture trade. Each plank is separated from its neighbour by sticks (see below).
   (2) Stack piling. This method is used for piling square-edged sawn timber, and consists of building up a stack of timber, taking the necessary steps to ensure air circulation by inserting sticks.

(vi) The maximum width of a stack should be 1·8 m (6 ft) while the height depends on the space available and the stability of the stack.

(vii) There should be a space of 2·5 cm (1 in.) between the planks and this is achieved by inserting 'sticks' between each layer. The 'sticks' are sawn battens, usually 2·5 × 2·5 cm (1 × 1 in.) or 1·3 × 1·9 cm ($\frac{1}{2}$ × $\frac{3}{4}$ in.) section.

(viii) Sticks should not be placed more than 0·6 m (24 in.) apart and not closer than 0·2 m (9 in.), and they should be so arranged that each stick is immediately above the one below it.

(ix) The stack should be made on level ground and the top of it protected against rain.

(d) Time taken to effect air-seasoning

(i) The popular rule regarding the time needed for a piece of timber to season is: 'A year for each inch of thickness.'

(ii) This rule, however, takes no account of the following considerations:
   (1) Whether the timber is a hardwood or softwood.
   (2) The natural ability of the species to dry out.
   (3) The weather during the time the timber was piled, i.e. excessively wet summer, etc.

(iii) The following figures have been suggested as a general guide to drying rates for air seasoning (R. G. Bateson, *Timber Drying*, 2nd edition, 1946).

(1) *Conifers*. 2·5 cm (1 in.) thick: if stacked in spring, should dry to 20% moisture content in 2–3 months. 5 cm (2 in.) thick: if stacked in spring, should dry to 20% moisture content in 3–4 months.

(2) *Broadleaves*. 2·5 cm (1 in.) thick: if stacked in autumn should dry to 20% moisture content in 10 months. 5 cm (2 in.) thick: if stacked in autumn, should dry to 20% moisture content in 12 months.

(e) Kiln-seasoning

(i) Kiln-seasoning depends on the use of artificial heat and the controlled moisture content of the air, which ensures controlled air conditions and air circulation. Kiln-seasoning gives quicker and more uniform results.

(ii) There are two basic types of kiln:
(1) The progressive kiln. (2) The compartment kiln.

(iii) *The progressive kiln*
In this type the timber to be seasoned travels progressively from one end to the other, and as it proceeds it gets drier.

(iv) *The compartment kiln*
The timber remains stationary in this type, and the air temperature is varied as the moisture content falls. Compartment kilns may be operated on the principle of natural draught or forced draught.

(v) Kiln-drying is now used throughout the timber industry, owing to its ease of control and economy of time.

(f) Time taken to effect kiln-seasoning

(i) The time which is required to season timber in a kiln depends on a number of factors including the species and dimensions of the timber to be seasoned, the type of kiln used and the method of treatment.
(ii) A compartment kiln using forced draught can deal with green conifer timber 5 cm (2 in.) thick in 1–2 weeks.
(iii) Green timber from broadleaved species needs considerably longer, the period being 3–12 weeks.
(iv) Compartment kilns using natural draught usually take up to half as long again.

2. *The Preservation of Timber*

(a) The facility of treatment

(i) The ease with which timber can be treated with presrevative depends on various factors, including:
(1) The species of timber.
(2) The proportion of heartwood and sapwood.
(3) The size of the piece to be treated.
(4) The moisture content.

(ii) *Species which absorb preservative very readily*

Alder	Chestnut, horse	Pine, Corsican
Ash	Hornbeam	Pine, Scots
Beech	Lime	Sycamore
Birch		

(iii) *Species which absorb preservative moderately well*

Cypress, Lawson	Spruce, Norway
Elm	Spruce, Sitka
Fir, silver	

(iv) *Species which do not absorb preservative readily*

Chestnut, sweet	Larch	Wellingtonia
Cedar, western red (*Thuya*)	Oak (heartwood)	Willow
Fir, Douglas	Poplar	Yew

(b) The preparation of timber before treatment

(i) *Removal of bark*
This is essential.

(ii) *Seasoning*
(1) For the best result, timber should be allowed to season before treatment.
(2) Not only is the moisture content reduced, but it allows any splitting or cracking to take place before treatment.

(iii) *Incising*
(1) This consists of passing timber to be treated through two vertical and two horizontal rollers covered with sharp teeth, which make indentations in the timber and assist penetration.
(2) Incising is very seldom practised on estates, and is usually confined to large depots dealing with telephone poles, overhead service line poles, and sleepers.

(iv) *Pre-framing*
Where joinery, gates, doors, and so on are to be impregnated,

the best results will be obtained by treating the timber after it has been prepared (i.e. sawn to sizes, planed, mortised, etc.), and then reassembled after treatment.

(c) Types of preservatives

Excluding paints and varnishes, wood preservatives can be divided into three main classes:

(i) *Tar oil type*

(1) Creosote and tar are the best known examples of this type of preservative. Tar, in some cases thinned by the addition of creosote, is applied by hand and has been widely used in certain districts, e.g. Kent.

(2) Creosote has been used as a preservative for many years with considerable success but more recently water soluble preservatives (see below) have replaced it in many cases.

(3) The disadvantages of creosote may be summarized as follows:

(*a*) It is not possible to paint creosoted timber.

(*b*) Timber so treated tends to 'weep' for a considerable time after application.

(*c*) Freshly creosoted timber is dirty to handle.

(*d*) Creosote increases the inflammability of timber.

(*e*) Creosoted timber is not suitable for internal uses in houses on account of some of the points mentioned above.

(4) Nevertheless creosote provides good protection to timber and its colour is still held by some to be an essential for satisfactory preservation. It is still used to a large extent for treating railway sleepers, electricity and telephone poles.

(ii) *Water solution type*

(1) Water-soluble salts are now widely used in timber preservation.

(2) The advantages of water-soluble salts are

(*a*) Timber can be painted after impregnation.

(*b*) Treated timber does not 'weep'.

(*c*) After treatment the timber dries quickly and is then clean and pleasant to handle.

(*d*) Water-soluble salts do not increase the inflammability of the timber.

(*e*) Timber so treated has a very wide range of uses.

(iii) *Organic solvent type*

(1) This type of preservative is not so widely used as the two types already described, for bulk preservation.

(2) While they enjoy several of the advantages of the water solution type preservative, they are often highly inflammable, have a strong smell and tend to be expensive.

(d) Methods of applying preservatives

(i) The four methods of applying preservatives which are described below relate only to creosote and/or water-soluble salts. They are:
  (1) Brush application (or spraying).
  (2) Cold steeping.
  (3) Hot-and-cold steeping.
  (4) Pressure.

(ii) *Brush application*
  (1) The application of creosote with a brush or by spraying is unsuitable for external work which is in contact with the ground, since it only gives a skin-deep protection.
  (2) Where creosote has to be applied by this method it should be heated and several coats given.
  (3) In the case of water-soluble salts brush application should only be used on cut ends of pressure-impregnated timber, which have been exposed after treatment. In such cases salts should be mixed at double or greater strength.

(iii) *Cold steeping*
  (1) Timber is placed in a tank of cold creosote and allowed to remain in it for 2–3 weeks.
  (2) This method is very slow, absorption is only skin deep, and there is little to recommend it.
  (3) Cold steeping is not suitable for water-soluble salts.

(iv) *Hot-and-cold steeping*
  (1) A tank, varying from a 409–litre (90-gallon) oil drum to a 5,460-litre (1,200-gallon) tank may be used, but the process is the same in both cases.
  (2) The timber is immersed in creosote which is then heated to about 93°C (200°F).
  (3) This temperature is maintained for about 1 hour, during which time the air in the wood cells expands, and a certain amount may be expelled.
  (4) The fire is then drawn, and the creosote in the tank is allowed to cool. As this takes place, the air which is left in the wood cells contracts and forms a partial vacuum, so that the creosote is forced into the wood by pressure of the atmosphere. Absorption thus takes place during cooling.
  (5) The timber is usually left in the tank until the creosote is cold, but it is possible to save time by transferring the timber from the hot tank to a cold one, or by draining off the hot creosote and replacing it by cold, although the results will not probably be quite so good.
  (6) Creosote tanks should be drained from time to time, and any deposit cleaned out. A grid or grating should be

provided in the bottom of the tank, so as to ensure that the timber is not in direct contact with the tank.

(7) A very simple type of hot-and-cold tank can be made by cutting out the top of a 409-litre (90 gallon) oil drum and setting it over a rough brick fireplace. A length of drainpipe can be provided as a chimney, to improve the draught. This plant can be used successfully for creosoting fencing and gate posts at a minimum of cost.

(8) This method is not suitable for water-soluble salts.

(v) *Pressure treatment*

(1) There are two main systems of pressure treatment:
 (a) The full-cell or Bethell process.
 (*b*) The empty-cell process.
 (i) The Rueping method. (ii) The Lowry method.

(2) The chief differences in these systems are concerned with the initial stages. In the full-cell or Bethell process the first stage is the creation of a vacuum, after which the preservative is introduced. This is the usual method adopted for treatment by soluble salts. If creosote is used this should be heated to a temperature of between 60°C and 93°C (140°F and 200°F).

(3) In the Rueping method, air is first pumped in under a pressure of 25 to 100 lb per square inch, and the preservative is pumped in afterwards. If creosote is used, this should be heated as described above.

(4) In the Lowry method, no preliminary vacuum or build-up of pressure is produced: instead, the preservative is pumped in, and pressure is applied afterwards.

(e) Preservation by charring

Fence posts and gate posts can be made proof against insect and fungus attack by charring the ends of the posts to a height of about 15 cm (6 in.) above ground level. This is carried out by burning the bottom of the posts, but care must be taken to ensure that the burning is controlled, so that a layer of charred wood is produced without materially reducing the strength of the post. Some authorities doubt the effectiveness of this method.

CHAPTER XVIII

The Valuation and Sale of Timber

1. *Points to Consider in Valuing Timber*

(*a*) If timber is growing near a hard road it is easier to extract than if it is remote from a road. Timber near a road normally has a good 'get out', and this may add to its value considerably.

(*b*) Extraction is a matter which should always be borne in mind. Difficult extraction reduces the value of the timber.

(*c*) In valuing timber the following are some further points which should be taken into account:

(i) Barbed wire nailed to the trees.
(ii) Damage caused by lightning.
(iii) The presence of fungus growing on the tree.
(iv) Woodpecker holes in a tree.
(v) Whether large limbs have been broken off by the wind, or other causes, which may give rise to rot and decay.

2. *Methods of Offering Timber for Sale*

(a) There are three methods of offering timber for sale:
(i) By private treaty. (ii) By tender. (iii) By auction.

(b) Private treaty

(i) In this method the vendor must either know what the timber is worth or obtain a reliable valuation.
(ii) In private treaty no competition exists between prospective purchasers.
(iii) From the vendor's point of view this is the least expensive method of selling timber.

(c) Tender

(i) Sales by tender may either be 'public', i.e. particulars are published in the local press, or 'private', i.e. particular are circulated privately to possible purchasers.
(ii) Offers are made in writing before a given date.

(iii) This method is not expensive, and some elements of competition is present.
(iv) Not a popular method with timber merchants because:
   (1) The reserve is not known, and the tender may be a waste of the merchants' time.
   (2) The highest tender is not necessarily accepted.
   (3) Some intending vendors may use the highest tender as a free valuation.

(d) Auction
(i) This method is usually justified only if a large amount of valuable timber is to be sold.
(ii) Success from the vendor's point of view depends to no small extent on the auctioneer's ability.
(iii) Higher prices are often obtained in the heat of the moment.
(iv) Expenses of a sale by auction are usually high owing to:
   (1) The auctioneer's commission.
   (2) The advertising costs.
   (3) The general expenses, such as the hire of sale rooms, advertising, printing of catalogues, etc.

3. *Methods of Selling Timber*

Quite apart from the three ways in which timber may be offered for sale, as described in the previous section, timber or thinnings may be sold either standing or felled but there are several variations in the way in which this can be done. These are set out below:

(i) *Standing timber*

Procedure A
(1) The price is agreed for the timber as it stands. This is a lump sum and is calculated on the estimated volume and estimated value per cubic foot of the standing timber.
(2) Prospective purchasers will safeguard themselves in the case of trees which they think are of doubtful quality and soundness.
(3) Felling is carried out by the purchaser.
(4) This method is one which has been commonly used in the past and will doubtless be used in the future. When it is adopted for the sale of hardwoods which are often variable in size, this method can lead to inaccuracies. The sale of conifers by this method is referred to below.

Procedure B
(1) This is a variation of Procedure A and is commonly adopted by the Forestry Commission when dealing with standing thinnings.

(2) Thinnings which are to be sold are often offered for sale by tender. In such cases the Commission states the estimated volume and the intending purchaser then calculates the value based on the stated volume and tenders such an amount as he thinks fit.
(3) Felling is carried out by the purchaser.

Procedure C

(1) The trees are sold standing, the purchaser being responsible for felling.
(2) The price per cubic foot is agreed before felling but the volume is agreed after felling.
(3) This is, in effect, the same as selling the timber felled, except that the onus of felling is placed on the purchaser. This fact should be taken into account when agreeing the price.
(4) This procedure is one which is sometimes adopted by estates which have a large thinning programme to carry out, but those permanent labour force is insufficient to undertake the work.

(ii) *Felled timber*

Procedure D

(1) The trees are felled by the vendor and are then offered for sale.
(2) The volume and price are consequently fixed after felling.
(3) This method enables the timber to be graded in the round before selling.
(4) Some species, notably beech, will deteriorate unless converted reasonably soon after felling. In such cases it is essential to sell the felled butts without delay.

4. *Agreements for the Sale of Timber*

As will be seen from the preceding section, there are basically two ways of dealing with timber for sale, i.e. to sell it standing or felled. The agreement to be used in these two cases will differ in certain respects but many of the clauses are equally applicable to both.

Below is given a form of agreement for the sale of timber and attention is drawn to the following notes on its use:

(*a*) The agreement as printed is for use in selling *standing* timber.

(*b*) However the agreement is equally applicable to the sale of *felled* timber, i.e. where the vendor has felled and trimmed out the trees before offering them for sale, subject to the following amendments:

(i) That the words in italics in the following clauses are omitted: Clauses 1, 7, 19, 27, 30, 31.
(ii) That the whole of the following clauses are omitted: Clauses 4, 5, 6, 9, 10, 12, 14, 15, 16.

(*c*) The following notes, as to the completion of the agreement, may be found helpful:

Paragraph 1. The name and address of the vendor and the purchaser should be inserted.

Paragraph 2. The purchase price may be stated as a lump sum, as a price per cubic metre or cubic foot or in any other way which is applicable.

Clause 5. If this clause is retained, clause 6 should be deleted. Trees may be marked by blazing, paint or scribing and the method adopted stated in the agreement.

Clause 6. If this clause is adopted clause 5 should be deleted. Where areas are to be clear felled a plan of the area should be included and the fact stated in this clause.

Clause 7. If sub-clauses (i), (ii) or (iii) are not applicable, the sub-clause concerned should be deleted.

Clause 8. An appropriate figure should be inserted in sub-clause (*a*). Either sub-clause (*a*) or (*b*) should be deleted.

Clause 11. Sub-clause (*a*) or (*b*) should be deleted, and if (*b*) is retained the necessary figure should be inserted.

Clause 29. The method of payment should be inserted. The purchase money can be paid in several ways of which the following are examples:

(*a*) On signing the agreement.
(*b*) A proportion of the whole on signing the agreement and the balance:
  (i) within a stated time of signing the agreement, *or*
  (ii) before any timber is removed, *or*
  (iii) before any trees are felled.

Third Schedule. Loading areas should be marked on the plan attached and preferably coloured.

Note.
Although readers are welcome to make use of this agreement, the author and publisher cannot accept any legal responsibility for it or for any action which may arise out of its use.

AN AGREEMENT made the .... day of .... 19 ....
BETWEEN ....
as Agent for ....
in the County of .... (hereinafter called 'the Vendor')
of the one part and ....
of .... (hereinafter
called 'the Purchaser') of the other part.

WHEREBY IT IS AGREED that the Vendor will sell and the Purchaser will buy subject to the following terms and conditions set out below all those trees which are more particularly described in the First Schedule hereto and that the purchase price shall be ....

CONDITION OF SALE

ACCESS

Access to area

1. Subject to these Conditions of Sale, the purchaser, his servants or agents shall have free access to the *felling and* loading areas for the purpose of *felling, trimming or* removing the trees.

Access routes

2. The purchaser shall use only those routes described in the Second Schedule and coloured yellow on the plan attached hereto; for the purpose of gaining access to the site on which the trees are growing and for their extraction and removal, unless otherwise agreed in writing between the parties.

Removal and reinstatement of fences and gates

3. The purchaser may at his own expense remove those gates, posts, walls, fencing or hedging which are set out in the Fourth Schedule hereto:

(*a*) Subject to their reinstatement to the satisfaction of the owner and the occupier of the land before the date set out in the Schedule, and

(*b*) Subject to the permission of the occupier of the land being obtained not less than 24 hours before the work is carried out, and

(*c*) Subject to the purchaser at his own expense erecting suitable stockproof fences of a temporary character at all necessary times.

FELLING

Method

4. The purchaser shall fell the trees in a workmanlike manner, severing them as close to the ground as is practicable and to the reasonable satisfaction of the vendor or his agent.

Marking trees

5. Except where the area is to be clear felled the vendor shall mark all trees to be felled in the following manner:

Partial clear felling

6. Where part of a stand of timber is to be clear felled the

boundary of the area to be felled shall be indicated in the following manner:

Felling and removal

7. (*a*) The following restrictions shall apply as to felling and entry on the site:

(i) No *felling of the trees or* entry on the site shall be permitted before the .... day of .... 19 ......

(ii) No *felling of trees or* entry on the site shall be permitted between the .... day of .... 19 ... and the .... 19 ...

(iii) The *felling and* removal of the trees shall be completed before the .... day of .... 19 ......

(iv) No *felling of trees or* entry on the site shall be permitted during the hours of darkness without the written consent of the vendor, such consent not to be unreasonably withheld.

(*b*) Provided always that the above dates shall be subject to variations by agreement in writing between the vendor and the purchaser.

(*c*) The vendor reserves the right after notice in writing to the purchaser or his agent to stop all extraction *and/or burning* if, in the opinion of the vendor, weather and other conditions make these operations hazardous, or if, in the opinion of the vendor, ground conditions are unsuitable for these operations. If such a stoppage takes place the date of completion of the operations shall be suitably extended.

Non-removal of trees within contract period

8. If the purchaser shall fail to remove the trees or any part of them within the time specified for their removal in this Agreement or such extended period as may have been agreed in writing then:

(*a*) The purchaser shall pay to the vendor the sum of £
for each week beyond the time specified for every acre
that is occupied by the purchaser's timber.

OR

(*b*) The vendor may at any time after the expiration of such time or extended period serve a notice on the purchaser requiring the removal within six weeks of any trees or parts thereof remaining upon the site, and any trees or parts thereof which remain upon the site after the expiration of the time specified in the notice shall be forfeited and become the property of the vendor, who shall not be liable to make any allowance, payment, compensation or satisfaction therefor, and the purchaser shall be liable to reimburse the vendor for any reasonable expense incurred by the vendor in removing such trees or parts thereof.

Prohibition of felling

9. If the purchaser is prohibited by Her Majesty's Government or any Local or Statutory Authority from felling the timber or any part thereof which is the subject of this Agreement then the purchase money or an agreed proportion of it shall be repaid by the vendor to the purchaser.

Felling of timber not in sale

10. If the purchaser, his servants or agents fell any trees not included in this Agreement, or without written consent of the vendor, the purchaser shall be liable to pay to the vendor twice the value of such tree or trees and in the event of disagreement the value shall be determined in accordance with Clause 36 of these Conditions of Sale.

Cordwood, lop and top

11. (*a*) The cordwood, lop and top shall remain the property of the vendor.

OR

(*b*) The purchaser shall, whether or not any conversion takes place on the site, remove all the firewood and cordwood from the site and remove or burn within .... weeks after the date fixed for the removal of the timber, and without damage to the vendor's property, all lop and top not used as cordwood together with all bark and sawdust arising from the use of saw benches.

12. No cordwood shall be stacked against trees not included in the sale.

Obstruction to felling and extraction

13. The purchaser shall be responsible for the removal and reinstatement or safeguarding of any electricity supply lines, telephone lines, ropeways or other obstructions, whether in public or private ownership, and shall give all notices and meet all expenses connected therewith.

Obstruction of rides

14. The purchaser shall, within seven days of felling any tree remove from the surface of any ride any timber, cordwood, brash branches and tops from trees which have been felled by him across such rides.

Defective timber

15. Except where the sale is in felled measure, the timber which is the subject of this Agreement shall be accepted by the purchaser with all its defects or deficiency in quantity, quality, number or description without any allowance or abatement whatever.

Treatment of stumps

16. The purchaser shall treat the stumps of any conifers which are felled by him, immediately after felling, with such antiseptic dressing as the vendor may require in order or to prevent the dissemination of fungal diseases; all brushes and containers which are required, being provided by the vendor but the purchaser shall replace any which are lost by him or his employees.

EXTRACTION

Extraction works

17. The purchaser shall not erect or construct any road, tramway, timber chute or overhead ropeway on the vendor's property without the written consent of the vendor.

Roping

18. The purchaser shall not attach any ropes, chains or other equipment to trees which are not included in the sale.

Obstruction of watercourse

19. The purchaser shall on receiving seven days' notice in writing from the vendor or his agent, remove any obstruction placed by him in any ditch, drain or watercourse or *any timber, cordwood, brash, branches or tops of any tree which has been felled by him and* which in the opinion of the vendor is causing an obstruction in any ditch, drain or watercourse.

Loading areas

20. The purchaser shall only use the area described in the Third Schedule and coloured on the plan attached hereto for loading or stacking timber in addition to the area on which the trees are growing.

CONVERSION ON THE SITE

Consent

21. The purchaser shall not convert any trees on the site other than for the preparation of firewood or pitwood or pulpwood without the written consent of the vendor.

Erection of buildings

22. When the consent is obtained under Clause 21 the purchaser

shall be entirely responsible for the erection of all buildings and machinery, and for obtaining all necessary consents from local and planning authorities prior to the erection of such buildings, and shall be responsible for the payment of any rates levied on such buildings or plant.

Reinstatement of site

23. The buildings and plant shall be dismantled, all timber, sawdust and wood waste removed, and the site reinstated within four weeks after the date fixed for the removal of timber, as stated in Clause 7(*a*).

DAMAGE

Purchaser's responsibility

24. The purchaser shall be responsible for any damage or injury (other than damage or injury of a type necessarily resulting from the prudent exercise by the purchaser of the rights hereby granted) arising out of any act or omission or by any licensee, employee, agent or other person working for him.

Liability for late completion

25. The purchaser shall be liable for all loss or damage occasioned to the vendor by reason of the purchaser failing to comply with the terms of the Agreement or any of them within the time limited by this Agreement.

Fires

26. The purchaser shall take all necessary precautions to prevent damage by fire, and shall immediately discontinue all burning upon the receipt of a written notice from the vendor given in pursuance of Clause 7(*c*) of the Conditions of Sale, and the purchaser shall thereupon be given an adequate extension of time in respect of Clause 7(*a*).

Indemnity against claims

27. The purchaser shall indemnify the vendor and/or his tenants against any reasonable claims arising from any damage or neglect caused through or arising out of any act or omission in connection with the *felling, cording, burning or* removal of the trees so purchased, and shall meet all reasonable claims by any third party in respect of damage or injury occasioned by or resulting from any act or omission by or on behalf of the purchaser, his servants or agents under or in respect of this Agreement.

Insurances

28. Before commencing any work on the site, the purchaser shall

if required to do so by the vendor insure against all claims which may be made against the vendor arising out of this Agreement, and for all damage which may be caused to the vendor's property during the period for which this Agreement remains in force.

PAYMENT

Payment of purchase money

29. The purchase money shall be payable in the following manner:

Default of payment

30. In the event of the purchase price herein agreed or any part thereof not being paid to the vendor within the period or at the time stated in the Conditions of Sale, the vendor shall be entitled on giving seven days' notice in writing to the purchaser, his servants or agents to prevent the *felling and/or* removal by the purchaser, or by anyone acting on his behalf or under his instructions, or claiming through him any of the said trees or timber which shall remain on the vendor's land until all due payment shall have been made.

MISCELLANEOUS

Re-selling and sub-contract

31. (*a*) The purchaser shall not re-sell the timber purchased under this Agreement *while the timber is standing, or part with possession of felled timber while still on the land*, to a third party, or *sub-let contracts for cording of lop and top and the burning of brushwood*, without the written consent of the vendor, such consent not to be unreasonably withheld.

(*b*) The purchaser shall remain bound by the terms of the Agreement in the event of any re-sale or sub-contract, and shall take all necessary steps to ensure that any sub-purchasers or sub-contractors shall be bound by and subject to the terms of this Agreement (save by Clause 29 of these Conditions) in the same manner and to the same extent and as if they were the purchasers in this Agreement, and the purchaser shall be responsible for any acts or omissions or any non-compliance with the terms of this Agreement by any sub-purchasers or sub-contractors their servants or agents, as if they were the purchaser in this Agreement.

Caravans

32. (*a*) The purchaser and his servants or agents shall not bring any caravans on to the site or erect huts on the site without the written consent of the vendor, such consent not to be unreasonably withheld.

(*b*) In the event of such permission being given by the vendor, the purchaser shall be responsible for obtaining any necessary consents from the local and planning authorities, and shall be responsible for the payment of rates levied on any such caravans or huts.

Objection to purchaser's employees

33. The purchaser shall discontinue the employment on the vendor's property of any workmen reasonably objected to by the vendor.

Dogs, guns and traps

34. No dogs, guns, snares or traps shall be taken on to the vendor's property by the purchaser, his servants, agents or sub-contractors or their servants or agents.

Disposal of interest in land

35. If during the period when this Agreement is in operation the vendor disposes of his interest in the land, he shall reserve to the purchaser all the purchaser's rights and title under this Agreement.

Arbitration

36. In the event of any disagreement arising out of the terms of this agreement, including the Conditions of Sale and the Schedules, the vendor and purchaser shall refer such disagreements to an arbitrator to be mutually agreed upon, or in default of agreement to two arbitrators, one to be appointed by the vendor and the other by the purchaser. Such arbitrators shall previous to entering upon arbitration appoint an umpire whose decisions shall be final and binding on all parties. Should either party fail to appoint his arbitrator within 14 days after being requested to do so in writing by the other party, then the arbitrator of the defaulting party shall be appointed as follows:

(*a*) The vendor's arbitrator by the President or failing him by a Vice-President of the Royal Institution of Chartered Surveyors.

(*b*) The purchaser's arbitrator by the President or failing him by the Vice-President of the British Timber Merchants Association (England and Wales).

Such arbitration shall be subject to the Arbitration Act, 1950 or any statutory modification thereof for the time being in force.

AS WITNESS the hands of the said parties the day and year first before written.

SIGNED BY THE above named }

In the presence of:

SCHEDULES

First Schedule

Description of Timber

Second Schedule

Access and Extraction Routes

The following access and extraction routes are laid down in accordance with the Conditions of Sale:

Third Schedule

Loading Areas

The following loading areas are laid down in accordance with the Conditions of Sale:

Fourth Schedule

Removal and reinstatement of Gates, Fences, etc.

In accordance with and subject to the provisions of Clause 3 of this Agreement and also subject to their reinstatement by the date stated below, the following gates, posts, walls, fencing or hedges may be removed by the purchaser:

Description	Situation	Date for resinstatement

CHAPTER XIX

Gates and Fencing

1. *Gates*

(a) Types of gates

(i) The following are the types of gates which may be found on an estate:

(1) Common field gates.
(2) Extra wide field gates.
(3) Heave gates.
(4) Hunting gates.
(5) Footpath gates.

(ii) *Common field gates*

(1) Usually 2·74–3·53 m (9–11 ft) wide although 3·20 m (10 ft 6 in.) is preferable as a maximum width.
(2) They may be constructed of timber or metal.
(3) Two patterns in general use are the diamond-braced and the half-braced, but some counties have evolved their own particular type such as the Devon gate and the Sussex heave-gate.
(4) Metal gates may be built of angle iron or tubular bars.
(5) Field gates may be 1·21–1·37 m (4 ft–4 ft 6 in.) high, the measurement referring to the heel post (see sub-section (*b*) below).

(iii) *Extra-wide field gates*

The need for wider gateways has been met by providing various types of gates, including:

(1) Two small-size field gates shutting onto a small centre stop or stump, or shutting against themselves.
(2) Single gates with tall heel and long brace.
(3) Two 'halved' or double-leafed tubular metal gates.

(iv) *Heave gates*

(1) These gates are not hinged, but hang on 'U'-shaped brackets, or slide into 'D'-shaped irons.
(2) Heave gates are useful for providing access to plantations which, although necessary on occasions, are seldom used.

(b) Parts of a gate

There are many local names for the parts of a gate, according to the district or county concerned. The following names are those which probably have the widest use:

(i) *Heel*

(1) The vertical member to which the end of the bars are fixed. When the gate is hung the heel is next to the hanging post.

(2) For a gate 3·04 m (10 ft) wide, the heel would measure about 127 mm × 76 mm × 1·37 m (5 in. × 3 in. × 4 ft 6 in.) high.

(ii) *Head*

(1) The vertical member at the opposite end of the gate to the heel, to which the other ends of the bars are fastened. The gate fastening is generally attached to the head.

(2) The dimensions of the head of a gate 3·04 m (10 ft) wide are usually 76 mm × 63 mm × 1·37 m (3 in. × 2½ in. × 4 ft 6 in.).

(iii) *Top rail*

The top horizontal member joining the head and the heel. It is deeper at the end nearest the heel and tapers from 127 × 76 mm (5 × 3 in.) to 76 × 76 mm (3 × 3 in.).

(iv) *Bars*

(1) Secondary horizontal members below the top rail which join the head and the heel.

(2) Suitable dimensions are 101 × 25 mm (4 × 1 in.) tapering to 76 × 25 mm (3 × 1 in.) at the head.

(v) *Braces*

(1) Braces are used to strengthen the gate, and their size and arrangement depend on the particular pattern in question. In a diamond-braced gate four braces are used, two extending from the bottom corners to the centre of the top rail, and two from the top corners to the centre of the bottom bar.

(2) In patterns other than the diamond, some of the braces may be fixed in a vertical position between the top rail and the bottom bar; while others are fixed at an angle to the bars.

(3) Braces are commonly 76 × 25 mm (3 × 1 in.).

(c) General observations on gates

(i) If the various members of a wooden gate are bolted together, the individual parts can be readily removed if broken and replaced with a minimum of trouble.

(ii) When fixing the top rail it should be mortised through the head and the heel. The bottom bar but one should be mortised through the head, but all other ends of rails should only be partly mortised, and the rails should not pass right through.
(iii) If a gate is to have a long life it must be kept so that it is able to swing. A gate which is allowed to drag will soon be broken.
(iv) Iron gates if damaged or bent will generally have to be removed and sent for repair. Timber gates can be repaired on the spot.

2. *Gate Ironwork*

(a) General
(i) Gate ironwork varies considerably in design, but basically consists of two gate hooks, which are fixed to the gate post, and two hinges fixed to the gate, which fit on to the hooks.
(ii) In addition, the gate latch fixed to the head is frequently made of iron, although some types are wooden.

(b) Points in ironwork
(i) There should be some means of adjusting the gate so that any drag can be taken up.
(ii) The adjustment can be contained in the top hinge, whereby the top of the gate is pulled in towards the post through the medium of an adjustable nut.
(iii) Alternatively, the adjustment can be effected in the bottom hinge, whereby the bottom of the gate is pushed out away from the post.

(c) Gate hanging
(i) All gates should be hung so that they are self-closing.
(ii) This can be done if the two hooks are not set in the same vertical line, i.e. the top hook in line above the bottom, and also by ensuring that the bottom hook is set out further from the gate than the top hook.
(iii) The centre of the top hook should be fixed 25–31 mm (1–1¼ in.) closer to the edge of the post which is nearest to the heel, than the centre of the lower hook. At the same time the bottom hook should stand out from the post 13 mm (½ in.) more than the top hook.

3. *Miscellaneous Information*

(a) Gates
(i) a field gate 3·04 m (10 ft) wide contains about 0·08 m^3 (3 ft^3) of timber.

(ii) A field gate 3·04 m (10 ft) wide, complete with ironwork weighs about 50·8–76 kg (1–1½ cwt) according to the species of timber and type of ironwork used.

(b) Gate posts

Type	*Size*	*Volume*	*Approx. weight*	
			Oak	*Larch*
Hanging post				
Field gate	203 mm × 203 mm × 2·43 m	0·10 m³	72·5 kg	59·0 kg
	8 in. × 8 in. × 8 ft	3·55 ft³	160 lb	130 lb
Hunting gate	152 mm × 152 mm × 2·13 m	0·05 m³	36·3 kg	29·5 kg
	6 in. × 6 in. × 7 ft	1·75 ft³	80 lb	65 lb
Shutting post				
Field gate	177 mm × 177 mm × 2·13 m	0·06 m³	50·0 kg	40·8 kg
	7 in. × 7 in. × 7 ft	2·38 ft³	110 lb	90 lb
Hunting gate	127 mm × 127 mm × 1·98 m	0·03 m³	22·6 kg	18·1 kg
	5 in. × 5 in. × 6 ft 6 in.	1·12 ft³	50 lb	40 lb

Note. Further information on gates will be found in the following publications.

(a) *Fencing*, a handbook published by the British Trust for Conservation Volunteers obtainable from the Trust, 36 St Mary's Street, Wallingford, Oxfordshire OX10 0EU.

(b) British Standard Specification B.S. 3470, *Field Gates and Posts*, published by the British Standards Institution, 2 Park Street, London W1A 2BS.

4. *Fencing*

(a) General

(i) During recent years the cost of fencing has increased substantially and efforts have been made to find ways of reducing expenditure. One of the most successful developments has been the use of new types of high tensile wire in place of the traditional mild steel wire.

(ii) There are now three kinds of wire which may be used in fencing; namely, mild steel wire, high tensile wire and spring steel wire. These are referred to below and in the descriptions of wire fences, mild steel and spring steel are shown separately.

(iii) Mild steel wire is the traditional type of wire which, despite the introduction of other forms, is still used to a large extent.

(iv) High tensile wire is somewhat similar to spring steel and has been approved by the Ministry of Agriculture for use on farms but the Forestry Commission do not consider it satisfactory for forestry fencing. One reason for this is the fact that it tends to develop weak spots which result in the wire becoming brittle and breaking, especially if it is subjected to fire.

(v) Spring steel wire, which is described in detail in Forestry Commission Forest Record No. 87—*Forest Fencing*, has several advantages which may be summarized as follows:
   (1) It is very much stronger than mild steel wire.
   (2) It retains its tension and does not become slack.
   (3) Consequently the distance between straining posts and between stakes can be considerably increased. This means a reduction in the number of posts and stakes.

(vi) The disadvantages are:
   (1) Spring steel wire is more difficult to handle and a certain number of specialized tools are required.
   (2) Great care is necessary in the erection of this kind of fencing.

(b) Rabbit fence (mild steel wire)

Straining posts: 152 mm top dia. × 1·83 m (6 in. dia. × 6 ft) placed at intervals of about 90 m (100 yd), at corners and at definite changes in direction.

Struts to straining posts: 100 m × 1·83 m (4 in. × 6 ft).

Stakes: 50–75 mm top dia. × 1·52 m (2–3 in. top dia. × 5 ft) placed every 3·65 m (12 ft).

Wire netting: 1·06 m (42 in.) wide, 31 mm (1¼ in.) mesh, 18 gauge.

Top wire: 4 mm (No. 8 gauge) mild steel wire, 10 m per kg (563 yd per cwt).

Erection:

(i) the bottom 152 mm (6 in.) of the netting may either be turned outwards at an angle of 45° with the vertical and buried in a shallow trench or turned out at 90° with sods of earth placed on the netting to keep it in position;

(ii) the top edge of the netting is attached to the top wire by netting clips or tying wire.

(c) Rabbit fence (spring steel wire)

Straining posts: 130 mm top dia. × 2·13 m (5 in. × 7 ft) placed at a maximum interval of 1000 m (1100 yd), at corners and at definite changes in direction.

Struts to straining posts: 100 mm × 2·0 m (4 in. × 6 ft 6 in.).

Wire netting: 1·06 m (42 in.) wide, 31 mm (1¼ in.) mesh, 18 gauge.

Top wire: spring steel 12 gauge, 23 m per kg (1,265 yd per cwt).

Erection: the wire netting is fixed as described for a mild steel wire rabbit fence.

(d) Deer fence (mild steel wire)
Straining posts: 178 mm top dia. × 2·75 m (7 in. top dia. × 9 ft) placed at corners and major changes of direction.
Struts to straining posts: 130 mm × 2·43 m (5 in. × 8 ft).
Stakes: 152 mm top dia. × 2·75 m (6 in. top dia. × 9 ft) placed 6 m (20 ft) apart. Height of fence when erected is 1·82 m (6 ft).
Wires: three No. 6 gauge wires are fixed to the top, middle and bottom respectively, of each post. Between these, netting of the woven hinge joint stock fencing type is fixed. Examples of such netting are pattern numbers C6/90/30 and C8/80 15 as manufactured by Messrs. Johnson and Nephew (Manchester) Ltd.

(e) Deer fence (spring steel wire)
Straining posts: 130 mm top dia. × 2·8 m (5 in. top dia. × 9 ft 3 in.) placed at corners and at major changes of direction.
Struts to straining posts: 100 mm × 2·5 m (4 in. × 8 ft 3 in.).
Stakes: 50–80 mm top dia. × 2·5 m (2–3 in. top dia. × 8 ft 3 in.) placed 10–14 m (11–15 yd) apart.
Wires: three No. 10 gauge spring steel wires are fixed to the top, middle and bottom respectively of each post. Between these are attached woven hinge joint stock fencing as described under section (*d*).

Note. This fence is designed for protection against roe deer but by substituting smaller mesh in the lower half, protection can also be obtained against rabbits. For red, fallow and Sika deer a stronger fence is needed, as described in Leaflet No. 87, *Forest Fencing*.

(f) Stock fence (mild steel wire)
Straining posts: 127 mm top dia. × 2·43 m (5 in. top dia. × 8 ft) placed at intervals of 90 m (100 yd) at corners and at definite changes in direction.
Struts to straining posts: 101 mm × 1·98 m (4 in. × 6 ft 6 in.).
Stakes: 76 mm × 1·67 m (3 in. × 5 ft 6 in.) placed 2·74 m (9 ft) apart.
Wire: six strands of wire of gauges 6 or 7. The top wire and the third from the top may be replaced by barb wire.
Erection: the height of the fence when erected is about 1·14 m (3 ft 9 in.).

(g) Stock fence (spring steel wire)
Straining posts: 130 mm top dia. × 2·3 m (5 in. top dia. × 7 ft 6 in.).
Struts to straining posts: 10 mm × 2 m (4 in. × 6 ft 6 in.).
Stakes: 76 mm top dia. × 1·8 m (3 in. top dia. × 6 ft) placed between 10 m and 14 m (11 yd and 15 yd) apart.
Wire: four strands of spring steel wire (gauge 10) are fixed as follows. One strand as a top wire; one strand as a bottom wire fixed about 100 mm (4 in.) above ground level; the two remaining wires at

intervals of 0·5 m (1 ft 8 in.) above the bottom wire. To these two wires and to the bottom wire are fixed woven hinge joint stock fencing as described under *(d) Deer fence.*

(h) Sawn post and rail stock fence
Posts: 127 mm × 101 mm × 2 m (5 in. × 4 in. × 6 ft 6 in.) placed 2·75 m (9 ft) apart.
Stakes: 89 mm × 63 mm × 1·67 m (3½ in. × 2½ in. × 5 ft 6 in.).
Rails: 89 mm × 38 mm × 2·9 m (3½ in. × 1½ in. × 9 ft 6 in.).

(i) Details of fencing wire
(i) *Mild steel wire*
The following table provides details of mild steel wire in Standard Wire Gauge and metric sizes.

Standard Wire Gauge (nearest to metric sizes)	6	7	8	10	12	14	16
No. of metres per 100 kg	683	813	983	1536	2328	3936	5152
No. of yards per 100 kg	748	890	1075	1682	2547	4306	6729
No. of metres per cwt	347	413	499	780	1182	1998	3123
No. of yards per cwt	380	452	546	854	1293	2186	3416
Standard metric size (dia. in mm)	5·00	4·50	4·00	3·15	2·50	2·00	1·60
No. of metre per 100 kg	651	804	1018	1641	2605	4070	6359
No. of yards per 100 kg	711	880	1109	1792	2872	4529	6958
No. of metres per cwt	330	408	514	832	1333	2101	3228
No. of yards per cwt	361	447	563	910	1458	2299	3532

(ii) *Spring steel wire*
The table below gives particulars of gauges numbers 10 and 12.

Gauge	10	12
Dia. in mm	3·1	2·6
No. of metres per 100 kg	1641	2324
No. of yards per 100 kg	1795	2541
No. of metres per cwt	833	1180
No. of yards per cwt	911	1290

(iii) *Barbed wire*

Information is given in the following table of two sizes of wire, namely, 2·50 mm and 1·70 mm.

Dia. of wire in mm	*2·50*	*1·70*
Weight:		
Per kilometre	110 kg (235 lb)	55 kg (121 lb)
Per mile	176 kg (376 lb)	88 kg (194 lb)
Per 200 m reel	22 kg (48 lb)	11 kg (24 lb)
Per 400 m reel	—	22 kg (48 lb)
Length:		
Metres per 100 kg	920	1,800
Yards per 100 kg	1,050	1,970
Metres per cwt	480	930
Yards per cwt	525	1,020
Per reel	200 m (218 yd)	200 m (218 yd)
	—	400 m (436 yd)

(j) *Netting*

(i) *Hinged joint fencing*

This is obtainable in rolls of 50m (54·7 yd) and in widths or heights varying from 500 to 1,250 mm (20–45 in.). The height of style number C6/90/30 is 900 mm (approximately 36 in.) and that of number C8/80/15, 800 mm (31 in.).

(ii) *Wire netting*

Often referred to as rabbit netting, this can be obtained in rolls of 25 and 50 m (27·3 and 54·7 yd) of varying widths. Those which are probably the most useful to foresters are 750, 900 and 1,200 mm (29, 36 and 48 in. approximately).

Note. More detailed information on fencing will be found in the following:

(a) Forestry Commission Leaflet No. 87, *Forest Fencing.*

(b) The British Trust for Conservation Volunteers' handbook, *Fencing*, which can be obtained from the Trust at 36 St Mary's Street, Wallingford, Oxfordshire OX10 0EU.

Note. Information regarding individual tree guards and shelters will be found in Chapter XXI, Section 5.

CHAPTER XX

Hedges and Shelter Belts

1. *Hedges*

(a) Species

(i) Many different species are found growing in hedges, but in planting a new hedge the following are probably the best from which to make a selection:

Hawthorn or quick	Beech
Blackthorn or sloe	Hornbeam
Myrobalan or cherry plum	Holly

(ii) The choice will depend on the soil, and the purpose for which the hedge is required.

(iii) *Hawthorn*
A fast growing, hardy species, which will grow on most soils, except at high elevations. It stands cutting and trimming very well, and provides a strong stock-proof fence. It is the best species for farm hedges.

(iv) *Blackthorn*
A slower growing species than blackthorn, which will grow on light or heavy soils, and also near the sea. It stands exposure well and, when established, forms a thick, strong, stock-proof hedge. Produces many suckers.

(v) *Myrobalan (Prunus cerasifera)*
Grows well and quickly, even on the poorer soils. Will thrive on exposed sites.

(vi) *Beech*
A suitable hedge for planting around forest nurseries or gardens, because of its habit of retaining its dead leaves during the winter. Although it grows well on chalks and limestones, it will thrive on practically any well-drained soil. It should not, however, be planted on peat or heavy clay.

(vii) *Hornbeam*
Hornbeam grows well on the stronger soils, such as clays and

heavy loams, and forms a hedge similar to beech. It withstands frost more readily than beech, and also retains its leaves during winter.

(viii) *Holly*
A slow growing species, but one which forms an excellent hedge, which is not only stock-proof but provides considerable shelter. It will grow on practically any soil or site, except one which is waterlogged.

(ix) *Cotoneaster simonsii*
This is a useful species for forming hedges in or around forest nurseries. It grows well on most soils and takes clipping well. If kept trimmed it retains many of its leaves during the winter.

(x) *Privet*
An evergeeen garden hedge, which will grow and survive in towns. It is easily trimmed, and develops quickly on almost all soils and sites.

(xi) *Lawson cypress*
This species grows quickly, and produces a thick evergreen hedge, which provides considerable shelter in gardens and nurseries. It is sometimes affected by smoke in industrial towns, but is unaffected by frost, insect, or fungus pests.

(xii) *Western red cedar (Thuya plicata)*
A hedge very similar in appearance to Lawson cypress is produced by this species, but when young it is subject to damage by frost and by the fungus *Keithia thujina*, and for this reason it should not be used for hedges in estate nurseries.

(xiii) *Yew*
Owing to the poisonous properties of its foliage it should never be planted where farm animals can reach it. In gardens it produces an excellent hedge, which can be grown to a considerable height. It will thrive on most soils, and is at home on chalk.

(b) Planting methods
Hedges may be established in three ways:
(i) On a level site. (ii) On a bank. (iii) On the side of a bank.
The first method is to be preferred.

(c) Number of plants required
(i) A hedge may be planted in a single or double row, and the number of plants required for a single row are shown in the following table. In the case of a double row the numbers should be doubled:

Distance between plants in the row in metres	*Number of plants per*				*Distance between plants in the row in inches*
	Metre (approx.)	*Kilo-metre*	*Mile*	*Yard (approx.)*	
0·10	10	10,000	18,240	9	4
0·15	6	6,666	10,560	6	6
0·20	5	5,000	7,920	5	8
0·22	4	4,545	7,038	4	9
0·35	3	2,857	5,280	3	12
0·45	2	2,222	3,519	2	18
0·61	1	1,639	2,640	1	24
0·76	1	1,315	2,112	1	30
0·91	1	1,098	1,760	1	36

(ii) The distance apart depends on the species and size of the plants used, young hawthorn 0·45 m (18 in.) high being planted about 0·22 m (9 in.) apart. If a double row is needed, the distance between the rows should be about 0·22–0·35 m (9–12 in.), the distance again depending on the size of the plants used. When planting double rows, the plants should be staggered, i.e. a plant in one row should be opposite the space between two plants in the other row.

(d) Tending and maintenance

(i) *Weeding*

Until the young hedge is fully established it will probably be necessary to help it by keeping down weed growth. The amount of weeding will depend on the species and rate of growth.

(ii) *Trimming*

Nursery and garden hedges, and farm hedges which are not 'cut-and-laid' (see below), should be trimmed every year. Although commonly done by hand, the increased use of mechanical hedge-cutters is to a large extent replacing hand-trimming or brushing.

(iii) *Cutting-and-laying*

As an alternative to trimming, farm hedges can be cut-and-laid. This is skilled work, and consists of partially severing each individual growth in a hedge and laying it down at an angle of about 30° with the ground. The angle depends on the particular system adopted, which in turn varies from county to county. Stakes are driven in to keep the layers in position, and 'hethers' or 'binders' are woven along the tops of the stakes. However since mechanical hedge trimmers came into general use, comparatively few hedges are now cut-and-laid.

(iv) *Ditching*
Hedge-side ditches should be kept clear, and should be thoroughly cleaned out from time to time. Where hedges are cut-and-laid, the ditch is normally cleaned out after the hedge has been laid.

Note. A great deal of information on many aspects of hedges and their upkeep will be found in *Hedging*, a handbook published by the British Trust for Conservation Volunteers. The address of the Trust is 36 St Mary's Street, Wallingford, Oxfordshire OX10 0EU.

2. *Shelter Belts*

(a) *Types of shelter provided by trees*

Three main types of shelter are provided:
(i) Belts of trees planted to give protection from the wind.
(ii) Rows of trees planted as tall 'hedges' or screens, such as those found around hop gardens.
(iii) Clumps of trees, small plantations or spinneys, which give protection against the elements to buildings or farm stock.

(b) *Species suitable for planting in shelter belts*

(i) *General conditions*

Hardwoods:

Beech	Rowan
Sycamore	

Conifers:

Austrian pine	Mountain pine
Corsican pine	Scots pine
Japanese larch	Sitka spruce
Lodgepole pine	

(ii) *Sea-coast areas*

Hardwoods:

Sycamore	Whitebeam

Conifers:

Maritime pine (*P. pinaster*)	Corsican pine
Monterey cypress (*C. macrocarpa*)	Austrian pine
Monterey pine (*P. radiata*)	

(c) *General*

(i) If possible a shelter belt should not be less than 20 m (22 yd) in width if it is to be really effective and it can well be wider.
(ii) The wider belts will produce more thinnings and therefore more material and where this is an important factor, the belt may be up to 45 m (50 yd) wide.

(iii) Trees should be planted 1·52–2·0 m (5–6½ ft) apart except for four rows on the exposed side which should be planted at about 2·28 m (7½ ft) so as to allow more space for the development of both the roots and the side branches.

(iv) As the trees in a shelter belt grow, it may become open at the bottom but the introduction of undergrowth will help to counteract this tendency. Species which will provide this 'bottom' include thorn, privet, elder, laurel and rhododendron according to the type of soil.

Note. Further information on shelter belts will be found in *Shelter Belts and Windbreaks* by J. M. Caborn (Faber & Faber, 1965).

CHAPTER XXI

Amenity Planting

1. *Amenity Woods*

(a) Definition

(i) Amenity woods are woods whose management is primarily based on considerations other than those of timber production, although in fact they may produce timber.

(ii) Such woods include the following:
  (1) Woods planted near the mansion house for beauty, privacy, or shelter.
  (2) Shelter belts.
  (3) Parkland planting for landscape effect.

(b) Management of amenity woods

(i) The main object in the management of these woods is to maintain a permanent cover of trees.

(ii) Clear felling must be avoided at all costs.

(iii) To ensure permanency there must be an adequate series of age classes; that is to say, there must be trees of all ages or groups of ages on the area so that shelter is continually maintained.

(iv) To achieve these objects, amenity woods should be managed on one of the following silvicultural systems:
  Selection system. Group system. Strip system.
For information regarding these, reference should be made to Chapter VI—Silviculture.

(v) Ornamental trees, flowering shrubs, and exotics may be introduced along the margins of amenity woods if it is thought desirable.

2. *Park Timber*

(a) General

(i) Since trees planted in parks are often allowed to develop as individuals or widely-spaced groups they frequently tend to develop girth and crown at the expense of height.

(ii) Consequently, branch development in many cases is much greater, and in maturity and decline the presence of large branches often results in serious damage by wind, snow, frozen rain, and so on.
(iii) In the management of park trees, the greatest attention should be paid to pruning, lopping, the treatment of wounds, and attacks by insects and fungi.
(vi) Several methods can be adopted for planting park trees, of which the following are the more usual:

(1) Single trees	(4) Groves
(2) Groups	(5) Belts
(3) Clumps	

(b) Single trees
(i) These should not be too numerous.
(ii) It is essential that single trees should be shapely and symmetrical.
(iii) Suitable species for this purpose include:

Beech	Atlas cedar
Horse chestnut	Cedar of Lebanon
Lime	Deodar
Pedunculate oak	Scots pine
Plane	

(iv) Particular care is needed in the pruning and lopping of single trees, or they will become badly balanced and misshapen.

(c) Groups
(i) Groups may be defined as clusters of three to five trees, the crowns of which unite in a compact mass of foliage.
(ii) The result is to produce a more solid effect than single trees.
(iii) Although more than one species can be planted in a group, it is generally more effective to restrict the numbers to one.

(d) Clumps
(i) The objects of a clump are:
(1) To provide a background where it is needed.
(2) To obscure or break up a bare skyline.
(3) To give depth and variety to the scenery.
(ii) Clumps may consist of one or more species, but a mixture will often prevent too formal an appearance.
(iii) Clumps should, if possible, be irregular in shape, so as to avoid too rigid an outline.

(e) Groves
(i) These are used where it is desired to divide up an area into several smaller parts, and can be adopted for separating the more formal part of a park from the remainder.

(ii) Groves may occupy such situations as:
  (1) Long ridges.
  (2) High or broken ground.
  (3) On level ground, so as to form short rides or avenues.
(iii) The shape and size vary, but irregular areas which vary in width are probably best, especially if the margins are broken.
(iv) Any of the species commonly used for woodland planting may be used for groves, subject to site restrictions.

(f) Belts
(i) Belts may be planted for shelter, screening, or in connection with shooting.
(ii) For details, reference should be made to Chapter XX—Hedges and Shelter Belts, and to Chapter XXII—Forestry and Shooting.

3. *Avenues*

(a) Length
(i) If an avenue leads from one definite point to another, e.g. from a house to a monument, its length is automatically defined.
(ii) In other cases, the length should be decided in the light of certain guiding factors, including the following:
  (1) If too long, an avenue tends to become monotonous.
  (2) If very long, care must be taken to ensure that it is not too narrow, in which case it will tend to shrink to vanishing point before the end of it is seen.
  (3) If a very long avenue is made too wide, in order to avoid the last pitfall, the trees of which it is composed will appear to be dwarfed.
  (4) Avenues should not normally be more than one-half to three-quarters of a mile in length if the above points are to be avoided.

(b) Width
(i) The width between the two flanking rows of trees may vary considerably, according to:
  (1) The habit of the species planted: large-crowned trees need more space than those with narrow crowns.
  (2) The length of the avenue: long avenues should be rather wider than those of shorter length.
  (3) The number of rows of trees of which the avenue is composed: an avenue of two single rows should be rather narrower than one of two double rows.
(ii) Consequently, it is difficult to lay down the exact width of an avenue, and the following should be regarded only as a guide:

Length of avenue		*Width of avenue*	
Metres	*Yards*	*Metres*	*Feet*
90	100	9.0	30
90–180	100–200	12·0	40
180–365	200–400	15·2	50
365–550	400–600	18·3	60
550–640	600–700	21·3	70
640–730	700–800	24·3	80

(c) Distance between trees in the rows

(i) Avenues may be of two types:
 (1) Close planted: adjacent trees merge into each other.
 (2) Wide planted: adjacent trees are far enough apart to develop as individuals.

(ii) *Close planting*
 (1) If unthinned, a close-planted avenue eventually becomes almost a hedge on a large scale.
 (2) It may be adopted for trees which have an irregular outline.
 (3) The distance between trees is from 4·5 to 7·6 metres (15 to 25 ft).
 (4) By removing alternate trees in due course, a close-planted avenue can assume the appearance of a wide-planted one.

(iii) *Wide planting*
 (1) By this method each tree in the avenue is allowed to develop as an individual.
 (2) It is best suited to trees which are symmetrical in appearance, and consequently it is often used for conifers.
 (3) The distance between trees is 9·1–18·2 m (30–40 ft).

(d) Species

(i) A species suitable for planting in an avenue should:
 (1) Attain a reasonable height.
 (2) Have a shapely outline.
 (3) Develop symmetrically.

(ii) Species which form ragged or irregular crowns should be avoided.

(iii) The following species are among those suitable for planting in avenues:
 (1) *Broadleaved*

Beech	Oak
Chestnut, horse	Plane

Chestnut, sweet
Lime
Norway maple
Poplar
Sycamore

(2) *Conifers*
Cedars: Atlas, Deodar, Lebanon, and the Incense cedar (*Calocedrus decurrens*)
Douglas fir
Larch
Lawson cypress
Pines, especially Scots, Corsican, and the Monterey pine (*P. radiata*)
Redwood (*S. sempervirens*)
Silver firs
Wellingtonia
Western red cedar (*Thuya plicata*)

4. *Roadside Trees*

(a) General

(i) The planting of trees on the sides of roads, as opposed to the natural growth of trees in roadside hedges, is a comparatively recent practice in this country. In contrast poplars have been planted as roadside trees on the Continent, especially in France, for many years.

(ii) The increase in roadside planting in the United Kingdom has been due to the construction of many new roads, at first as arterial and by-pass roads and later as motorways.

(b) The objects in planting roadside trees

Roadside trees may be planted for one or more of the following reasons:

(i) For their general appearance and in some cases, for their flowering capacity.

(ii) To emphasize the features of a road, e.g. by planting Lombardy poplars to draw attention to road intersections, or by planting silver birches on bends or islands where their white bark will show up at night.

(c) Siting trees on roadsides

Trees may be planted in the following positions:

(i) On the outer margins of the roadside verges which are well away from the edge of the road.

(ii) On the sides of cuttings: this chiefly applies to motorways.

(iii) On traffic islands and on waste land which has been acquired for the construction or widening of the road, but has subsequently been found surplus to requirements.

(d) Considerations in roadside planting

(i) Trees should not be planted so as to obstruct the view of road users.

(ii) Trees should be planted sufficiently far from the edge of the road to reduce the risk of vehicles hitting them when taking emergency action.

(iii) In the interests of amenity it is better to plant trees which blend with those which are growing naturally in the particular district through which the road is passing. In the suburbs of towns 'garden' trees and flowering shrubs may be acceptable, but they are out of place in the open country.

(iv) In the past, amenity appears to have been the main consideration, but there are many open spaces adjoining roads which could well be planted with timber trees and used for timber production. The example set by France is one which should always be borne in mind.

5. *Tree Guards*

(*a*) Tree guards in one form or another are normally necessary in the case of amenity trees.

(*b*) These may be of various patterns, of which the following are examples:

(i) *Stakes and wire netting sleeve*
The simplest and cheapest, which only gives limited protection, mainly against rabbits, sheep, and goats.

(ii) *Welded wire mesh guards*

(1) Although these are more rigid than wire netting or plastic mesh, a stake is still required and should extend for the total height of the guard.

(2) Full details will be found in Arboricultural Leaflet No. 10, *Individual Tree Protection*, issued by the Forestry Commission.

(iii) *Plastic mesh guards*

(1) These consist of a sleeve of plastic mesh and, except for the material, are very similar to those made of wire netting.

(2) These are described in Leaflet No. 10, *Individual Tree Protection*.

(iv) *Iron guards*
These are generally used in towns and parks. Their chief disadvantage is the effect produced by failure to remove them as the tree grows, so that the guard eventually becomes embedded in the tree.

(v) *Narrow wooden guards*

(1) There are many different patterns but the most satisfactory provide some means of gaining access to the tree after the guard has been placed in position. This can be by a hinged 'door' or a removable panel in the side of the guard.

(2) Large trees can be protected from horses, which can kill an old tree by gnawing the bark; by placing a 'collar' of close-spaced chestnut-pale fencing around the bole.

(3) Guards should be sufficiently high to prevent cattle from browsing the higher branches.

(vi) *Wide wooden guards*

These are in effect railings around the tree and cover a large enough area so as to prevent cattle leaning over and damaging the tree.

(vii) *Tree shelters*

(1) As the cost of wire netting and labour increased in the early 1980s, steps were taken to produce a plastic tube which could be placed over a young tree so as to provide it with adequate protection at a lower cost.

(2) At first referred to as 'tree tubes', these are now known as tree shelters and as well as giving protection, create conditions inside the shelter which encourage faster growth.

(3) Each shelter must be attached to a stake so as to ensure its stability, and this is done with a tying wire or specially designed plastic clip, depending on the manufacturer. Shelters which are round in cross-section, incorporate a recess into which the stake fits.

(4) Shelters can be obtained in the following variations:
Heights: 0·6 m (2 ft) to 1·8 m (5 ft 10 in.)
Colours: brown, green, white or translucent.
Cross-sections: square, triangular, hexagonal and round.

6. *Trees and Shrubs for Sea Coast Planting*

(a) Trees

The following trees are suitable for planting near the sea:

Holm oak (*Quercus ilex*)
Monterey cypress (*Cupressus macrocarpa*)
Mountain ash (*Sorbus aucuparia*)
Pines:
  Austrian (*P. nigra* var. *nigra*)
  lodgepole (*P. contorta*)
  maritime (*P. pinaster*)
  Monterey (*P. radiata*)

Poplars:
white (*P. alba*)
grey (*P. canescens*)
Sycamore (*Acer pseudoplatanus*)
White beam (*Sorbus aria*)

(b) Shrubs
Berberis stenophylla
Bupleurum fruticosum
Cornelian cherry (*Cornus mas*)
Evergreen spindle tree (*Euonymus japonicus*)
Gorse (*Ulex europaeus*)
Sallow (*Salix caprea*)
Sea buckthorn (*Hippophae rhamnoides*)
Tamarisk (*Tamarix gallica* and *tetrandra*)

CHAPTER XXII

Forestry and Shooting

1. *The Keeper's Requirements*

(a) What the keeper wants

(i) Areas of woodland which will prove attractive to birds, e.g.:

(1) Low cover, distributed at intervals throughout the woods, which will provide shelter, protection, and warmth in wet, cold, and windy weather.

(2) Suitable trees in which birds can roost.

(3) Trees and shrubs which provide food for pheasants, i.e. beech mast, acorns, and the fruit of covert plants.

(ii) Sufficiently dense growth of trees on the edge of woods to provide shelter from the wind, i.e. marginal cover.

(iii) Flushing points, i.e. areas of low-growing cover situated at the end of a beat which are dense enough to hold birds, but not so thick that they cannot be driven out.

(iv) In some cases, lines, blocks, or clumps of tall trees may be sited beyond the flushing point, in order to encourage pheasants to rise over the guns.

(b) What the keeper does not want

(i) A large area of dense, even-aged covert.

(ii) Areas of tall, mature or semi-mature trees with little or no ground covert beneath them.

(iii) Woodland areas out of which it is impossible to drive game owing to the density, extent, layout, or composition, e.g. dense plantations of Sitka spruce, or areas of overgrown rhododendrons.

2. *The Forester's Requirements*

(a) What the forester wants

Well-managed woods which aim at the following:

(i) An even distribution of age classes throughout the area.

(ii) Protection for young plantations from the prevailing wind.

(iii) Avoidance of large areas of young plantations, so as to reduce risks of damage by fire. Where large areas of devastated woodlands are being replanted this is not possible.
(iv) Division of the woods into compartments, i.e. clearly defined areas of up to 8 hectares (20 acres).

(b) What the forester does not want
(i) Rabbits, grey squirrels or too many deer.
(ii) Indiscriminate cutting of underwood.
(iii) Delayed weeding of young plantations in the summer months.
(iv) The balance of nature upset.

3. *The Compromise between Forestry and Shooting*

(*a*) Since the needs of the keeper and the forester in fact have much in common, it is possible in many cases to compromise.

(*b*) Low cover can be provided, either by young plantations themselves, by the introduction of special covert plants (see below), or by allowing a certain amount of weed growth to develop under a crop, e.g. brambles or elder (if cut back).

(*c*) Roosting places may be provided:
(i) By mature stands of timber, and by conifer plantations in the pole stage.
(ii) By leaving half a dozen trees standing at the intersection of rides, or in definite belts along the edges of rides in cases where the surrounding trees have been felled. Probably the best species are Douglas fir or Norway spruce, or larch surrounded by Douglas fir. Evergreen trees are best, since they are warm and obscure roosting birds from the sight of poachers.

(*d*) Flushing points can be planted at suitable points where it is intended the drives should end. Shrubs which can be used for this purpose are given below, in Section 4.

(*e*) Trees to encourage birds to rise may be:
(i) Specially planted.
(ii) Left unfelled from a previous crop.
(iii) Provided by an adjoining stand.

(*f*) If trees are to be specially planted, the following points should be borne in mind:
(i) Rapid growth (poplars, willows).
(ii) Denseness (evergreen species better than deciduous).
(iii) Height which is ultimately attained.

4. *Covert Plants*

Below are given a list of shrubs which may be planted in order to improve the holding capacity of an area. The planting of these shrubs may achieve this object, by providing physical cover from the rain or wind, by converting a bare forest floor into an area covered or partly covered with undergrowth, or by providing food in the form of berries.

(a) Shrubs primarily of value for cover

Butchers broom (*Ruscus aculeatus*)
Cherry laurel (*Prunus laurocerasus*)
Lonicera nitida
Portugal laurel (*Prunus lusitanica*)
Rhododendron ponticum
Rose of Sharon (*Hypericum calycinum*)

Note. Rhododendron and cherry laurel must be kept strictly under control.

(b) Shrubs of value for food and cover

Cotoneaster simonsii
C. frigida
C. microphylla
Dogwood (*Cornus alba*)
Elder (*Sambucus nigra*)
Flowering nutmeg (*Leycesteria formosa*)
Oregon grape (*Mahonia aquifolium*)
Privet (*Lingustrum vulgare*)
Ramanas rose (*Rosa rugosa*)
Raspberry (*Rubus idaeus*)
Shallon (*Gaultheria shallon*)
Snowberry (*Symphoricarpus albus*)

5. *Seasons and Close Seasons*

(a) Deer

(i) *Close Seasons*

The following are the statutory close seasons, all dates being inclusive.

Red deer		
England and Wales	Stags	1 May to 31 July
	Hinds	1 March to 31 October
Scotland	Stags	21 October to 30 June
	Hinds	16 February to 20 October
Fallow deer		
England and Wales	Bucks	1 May to 31 July
	Does	1 March to 31 October
Scotland	Bucks	1 May to 31 July
	Does	16 February to 20 October

Sika deer

England and Wales	Bucks	1 May to 31 July
	Does	1 March to 31 October
Scotland	Bucks	21 October to 30 June
	Does	16 February to 20 October

Roe

England and Wales	Bucks	1 November to 31 March
	Does	1 March to 31 October
Scotland	Bucks	21 October to 31 March
	Does	1 April to 20 October

There is no close season for deer in Northern Ireland.

(ii) *Hunting*

The seasons for hunting deer are:

Staghunting	1 August to 12 October (approx.)
Spring staghunting	25 March (approx.) to 30 April
Hindhunting	1 November to 28 February.

(b) Fox

The hunting season is usually considered to be:

Cubhunting	Mid-August to 30 October
Foxhunting	1 November to 31 March (approx.).

(c) Hare

Hare hunting generally takes place between 1 October and 15 March but in some districts these dates are slightly amended.

(d) Game and other birds

The seasons for these are as follows:

Blackgame	20 August to 10 December
Capercaillie	1 October to 31 January
Grouse	12 August to 10 December
Partridge	1 September to 1 February
Pheasant	1 October to 1 February
Ptarmigan	12 August to 10 December
Snipe	12 August to 31 January
Woodcock	
England & Wales	1 October to 31 January
Scotland	1 September to 31 January
Wildfowl (Duck and geese)	
Inland	1 September to 1 February
Foreshore	1 September to 20 February.

Note. (i) The close seasons in the case of certain species were altered by the provisions of the *The Wildlife and Countryside Act*, 1981, to which reference should be made for fuller information.

(ii) *The Gun Code*, published by the British Field Sports Society, contains an admirable summary of the various species of birds which may and may not be shot, together with the shooting season in England, Scotland, Wales and Northern Ireland. The address of the Society is 59 Kennington Road, London, SE1 7PZ.

(e) Fishing

The following are the approximate seasons for fishing but in the case of salmon and trout these vary in different parts of the country, according to the rivers.

Salmon	1 February to 30 September
Trout	Mid-April to 30 September
Other fish	June to March

6. *The Killing of Ground Game*

(*a*) Under the Ground Game Act, 1880, tenants have the right to kill ground game (hares and rabbits) on their farms.

(*b*) For this purpose a tenant can:

(i) Use a gun himself.

(ii) Authorize any one other person to use a gun.

(iii) Authorize:

(1) any resident members of his household.

(2) any one other person *bona fide* employed for reward, to kill ground game by any lawful means *other* than using a gun.

(*c*) In putting this into effect, two important points should be noted:

(i) Only one person besides the tenant can use a gun.

(ii) Everyone (except the tenant himself) who kills ground game by any means must carry the written authority of the tenant while he is engaged in killing hares or rabbits, and he must produce it if asked to do so.

(*d*) Where the shooting is reserved, the landlord has the right to kill ground game on the land he lets to a tenant, or to let this right to any third party. However, this does not prevent the tenant from exercising his rights as set out above.

(*e*) Where the shooting in the woods is let to a third party the landlord should make it clear in the agreement for letting the shooting that he reserves the right to kill rabbits, hares, grey squirrels, or any animal which causes injury to trees.

7. *The Firearms Acts 1968 and 1988*

(*a*) Under the Firearms Act 1968 anyone wishing to purchase, acquire or have in their possession a shotgun, must obtain a Shotgun Certificate from the police.

(*b*) The term 'shotgun' refers to smooth bore guns with a barrel length of not less than 24 in. (60·96 cm); it does not include air guns.

(*c*) A shotgun with barrels of less than 24 in. requires a Firearms Certificate and an application for this must be made to the local Chief Police Officer.

(*d*) Certain exemptions in respect of shotgun certificates are granted by the Act; details of these can be obtained from the Police.

(*e*) *The Firearms (Amendment) Act*, 1988 is concerned with shotguns and rifles including self-loading patterns, the sale of ammunition and firearms and shotgun certificates. It also provides for the establishment of a Firearms Consultative Committee.

CHAPTER XXIII

Trees and the Law

1. *Acts of Parliament*

This section contains short notes on the principal Acts of Parliament which deal with forestry and also several Acts which contain provisions relating to trees.

(a) Forestry Act 1967

(i) This Act repealed all the earlier Forestry Acts which are given below unless otherwise stated:
  - Forestry Act 1919 (except parts of S.3(2))
  - Forestry (Transfer of Woods) Act 1923
  - Forestry Acts of 1927, 1945, 1947, 1951
  - Forestry (Sale of Land) (Scotland) Act 1963

(ii) The Act covers a number of matters including the constitution, administration and powers of the Commission; the control of felling and issue of felling licences; the acquisition and disposal of land by the Commission and the constitution of the Home Grown Timber Advisory Committee and the Regional Advisory Committees.

(b) Forestry Act 1979

By this Act parts of S.9 and S.43 of the 1967 Act were amended by the substitution of metric for Imperial measure. It also reaffirmed the powers of the Commissioners to make grants and loans.

(c) Forestry Act 1981

This Act deals with the disposal of property belonging to the Forestry Commission, the transfer of sums from the Forestry Fund to the Consolidated Fund and increases the maximum number of Forestry Commissioners from 9 to 10, excluding the chairman.

(d) Trees Act 1970

Under this Act a tree preservation order can only be made in respect of land which has been dedicated, or in respect of which a planting grant has been paid, if there is no management plan in operation and if the Forestry Commission agree to such an order.

(e) New Forest Acts 1949, 1964, 1970

(i) The 1949 Act is chiefly concerned with the election of verderers, the enclosure and regeneration of the ancient and ornamental woods and roads through the Forest.

(ii) The 1964 Act altered the perambulation, i.e. the boundary, of the Forest and made certain amendments to the New Forest Acts 1877–1949.

(iii) Under the 1970 Act, provision was made for the enclosure of open waste lands by the Forestry Commissioners and for the fencing of the road between Cadnam and Lymington.

(f) Wild Creatures and Forest Laws Act 1971

By this Act certain rights of Her Majesty the Queen to wild creatures were abolished and the ancient forest law repealed, subject to some exceptions.

(g) Civil Aviation Act 1949

Under section 26 of this Act the authorities may take steps to fell or reduce the height of any trees, if such action is considered to be in the interests of the safety of civil aviation.

(h) Electricity Acts 1926 and 1947

The Electricity Supply Act 1926 S.34 and the Electricity Act 1947 S.57 provide that if a tree or hedge obstructs or interferes with the construction, operation or maintenance of an electricity line, an electricity board can give notice to the owner or occupier to fell, lop or top the tree or hedge.

(i) Regulation of Railways Act 1868

Under section 24 of this Act a railway authority can take steps to obtain the removal of any tree which may endanger the railway line.

(j) Telegraph Acts 1863 and 1908

Where a tree overhangs a street or road and causes interference to an existing or proposed telegraph or telephone line, the Post Office can give notice to the owner or occupier of the land concerned, to cut back the tree. These powers are provided by the Telegraph Act 1863 S.1 and the Telegraph (Construction) Act 1908 S.5.

2. *Statutory Instruments*

In addition to Acts of Parliament, Statutory Instruments which affect trees or forestry are issued from time to time, in the form of orders and these include the following:

(a) Watermark disease

A number of orders have been made relating to this disease of which SI 437/1953—The Watermark Disease (Essex) Order, 1953 is an example. Similar orders have been made for Middlesex (1083/1953), Hertfordshire (1084/1953 and 1411/1954), Suffolk (1085/1953), Cambridgeshire (1235/1958) and Bedfordshire (2562/1962). In 1974 The Watermark Disease (Local Authorities) Order SI 1974/768 was made.

Details of this disease will be found in Chapter XII, Section 2.

(b) Elm disease

Since the elm disease epidemic occurred several Statutory Instruments have been issued and these include No. 604, The Dutch Elm Disease (Local Authorities) Order 1988 and No. 605 The Dutch Elm Disease (Restriction on Movement of Diseased Elms) 1988.

(c) Restriction of felling

The Forestry (Felling of Trees) Regulations 1951 (SI 1951/1726) forms the basis for recent orders which are concerned with the restriction of felling. Other qualifying orders under the titles of The Forestry (Exceptions from Restriction of Felling) Regulations were made in 1951, 1972, 1974 and 1977.

(d) Restriction of imports

The following orders are now in force: No. 1107, The Landing of Unbarked Coniferous Timber (Amendment) order 1973; No. 1, The Importation of Forest Trees (Prohibition) Great Britain (Amendment) Order 1974; and No. 1892, The Import and Export of Trees, Wood and Bark (Amendment) Order 1984.

(e) Tree preservation orders

Regulations made under the Town and Country Planning Act 1971 have been issued as SI 1975/148 and SI 1975/1204, the second being in respect of Scotland. Further reference to these will be found in Section 5 of this chapter.

(f) Miscellaneous

Two Instruments have been issued under the Plant Varieties and Seeds Act 1964 in respect of forest reproductive material (SI 1977/891 and SI 1977/1264).

In 1979 The Dean Forest and New Forest Acts (Amendment) Regulations were published as SI 1979/836.

3. *Trees and the Law*

(a) Dangerous trees

(i) Very briefly, the position regarding damage or injury caused by a tree or part of a tree falling is as follows. If it is proved that an owner knew, or should have known, that a tree was dangerous and was likely to fall, and he took no steps to prevent it, he will be guilty of negligence, and will be liable for such damage as results.

(ii) If negligence of the owner cannot be proved as, for instance, if the fall of the tree is caused by some extraordinary event over which he had no control, then he is not liable for the resulting damage.

(iii) Briefly, negligence consists of omitting to do what a prudent or reasonable man would do, or doing what a prudent or reasonable man would not do.

(b Poisonous trees and shrubs

(i) The following are some of the commonest: yew, laburnum, rhododendron, box.

(ii) Where the presence of poisonous trees is obvious, anyone who purchases the land must take it as he finds it—*caveat emptor*.

(iii) A person who plants poisonous trees near his boundary, and permits the branches to extend over his neighbour's land, will be liable for any consequent injury to his neighbour's cattle.

(c) Overhanging trees

(i) The whole of a tree growing on a plot of land belongs to the owner of the land, even if the roots penetrate into the soil of the adjoining plot, or if the branches overhang the adjoining land.

(ii) The natural growth of a tree over the adjoining land may constitute a trespass, and a nuisance.

(iii) The neighbouring owner, whether it inconveniences him or not, may abate the nuisance, provided he does not commit a breach of the peace, does not interfere with the owner's property in excess of what is necessary, does not interfere with the rights of an innocent party or the rights of the public, and, if there is any choice, chooses the least damaging method of abatement.

(iv) In order to abate a nuisance, entry may be made onto the land where such a nuisance emanates, *provided* notice requesting the removal of the nuisance is given in the first place.

(v) If the nuisance can be abated without trespass no notice is necessary, and an adjoining owner can cut back branches which overhang his land, but he must not enter his neighbour's land. Apart from the legal aspect, it would be common courtesy to request permission to do so before starting work.

(vi) Any person who is injured by overhanging branches or

penetrating roots of a tree belonging to an adjoining owner can bring an action for an injunction and damages. Before doing so, however, legal advice should be sought.

(vii) It should be noted that the lopped branches belong to the owner of the tree, and not to the man who lops them.

(d) Trees and highways

Trees overhanging highways are generally not nuisances, provided they do not obstruct the use of the highway.

(e) Legal definition of timber

(i) With certain exceptions, 'timber' has been held at law to be oak, ash, and elm.

(ii) The exceptions to the above include:

(1) Beech in Buckinghamshire, Bedfordshire, Gloucestershire, Hampshire, and Surrey.

(2) Birch in Cumberland and Yorkshire.

(3) Under certain legal decisions, and by custom in certain localities, other species, e.g. holly, lime, and cherry.

(iii) In some districts 'timber' refers to trees of a certain size, and this is commonly 15 cm (6 in.) diameter and above, but this has not been legally upheld (*Lord Dillon* v. *Whitty*; *Honeywood* v. *Honeywood*).

4. *Law Cases concerned with Forestry or Trees*

This section contains a list of some of the cases which have been heard in connection with trees or forestry. Details of each case may be found in the reports which have appeared in various legal and professional publications. The abbreviations which are shown after the title of the case refer to the sources of these reports and a key to these abbreviations is provided at the end of the section. The species of tree, if recorded, is given where appropriate, and summarized at the end of the subsection.

(a) Dangerous trees

Brown v. *Harrison* (1947), 177 L.T. 281 (horse chestnut)

Bruce v. *Caulfield* (1918), 34 L.T. 204 C.A. (poplar)

Caminer v. *London Investment Trust Ltd* (1951), A.C. 88 H.L. (elm)

Cunliffe v. *Bankes* (1945), 1 All E.R. 459 (elm)

Hudson v. *Bray* (1917) 1 K.B. 520 (elm)

Knight v. *Hext and Others* (1979), 253 E.G. 1227 (beech)

Lambourne v. *London Brick Co.* (1950), 156 E.G. 146 (elm)

Lane v. *Tredegar Estates Trustees* (1954), 164 E.G. 555 (horse chestnut)

Mackie v. *Western District Committee of Dunbartonshire County Council* (1927), W.N. 247 (elm)

Noble v. *Harrison* (1926), 2 K.B. 332 (beech)
Quinn v. *Scott and Another* (1964), 1 W.L.R. 1004 (beech)
Shirvell v. *Hackwood Estates Ltd.* (1938), 2 K.B. 577 C.A. (beech)
Stillwell v. *New Windsor Corporation* (1932), 147 L.T. 306 (various)
White v. *Carruthers* (1958), 172 E.G. 229 (elm)
Williams v. *Devon County Council* (1966), 200 E.G. 943 (elm)

Summary of species involved:

Beech	4
Elm	7
Horse chestnut	2
Poplar	1
Various	1
	15

(b) Overhanging trees

British Road Services Ltd. v. *Slater and Another* (1964), 1 W.L.R. 498 (oak)
Hale v. *Hants & Dorset Motor Services and Another* (1947), 2 All E.R. 628 (unspecified)
Lemmon v. *Webb* (1894), 3 Ch. 1; (1895) A.C. 1 (oak and elm)
Mills v. *Brooker* (1919), 1 K.B. 555 (apple)
Smith v. *Giddy* (1904), 2 K.B. 448 (ash and elm)

Summary of species involved:

Apple	1
Ash and elm	1
Oak and elm	1
Oak	1
Unspecified	1
	5

(c) *Poisonous trees*

Cheater v. *Cater* (1918), 1 K.B. 247, C.A.
Crowhurst v. *Amersham Burial Board* (1878), 4 Ex.D. 5.
Erskine v. *Adeane* (1873), L.R. 8 Ch. App. 756
Lawrence v. *Jenkins* (1873), 8 Q.B. 274
Ponting v. *Noakes* (1894), 2 Q.B. 281
Wilson v. *Newbury* (1871), 7 Q.B. 31

Summary of species involved:
In each of the above six cases the species concerned was yew.

(d) Damage by tree roots

Acrecrest Ltd v. *W. S. Hattrel & Partners and Another* (1979), 252 E.G. 1107 (various species)
Attfield v. *Wilson* (1949), 153 E.G. 525 (poplar)

Bridges and Others v. *Harrow London Borough Council* (1981), The Times, 18 June 1981 (oak)
Brown v. *Bateman* (1955), 165 E.G. 261 (elm)
Bunclark and Others v. *Hertfordshire County Council and Another* (1977), 243 E.G. 381 and 455 (various species)
Butler v. *Standard Telephone and Cables Ltd.* (1940), 1 K.B. 399 (poplar)
Catell v. *Bedingfield* (1946), 147 E.G. 143 (poplar)
Coupar v. *Heinrich* (1949), 153 E.G. 223 (poplar)
Daisley v. *B.S. Hall & Co.* (1972), 225 E.G. 1553 (poplar)
Davey v. *Harrow Corporation* (1957), 2 All E.R. 305 (ash and elm)
Davis v. *Artizans Estates Ltd.*, (1953), 161 E.G. 519 (poplar)
Edge v. *Briggs* (1960), 178 E.G. 261 (lime)
Jennings v. *Taverner* (1955), 2 All E.R. 769 (poplar)
King and Another v. *Taylor and Others* (1976), 238 E.G. 26 (lime)
Lemos v. *Kennedy Leigh Developments Ltd.* (1960), 105 S.J. 178 (poplar)
McCombe v. *Read and Another* (1955), 2 Q.B. 429 (poplar)
Masters v. *Brent London Borough* (1977), 246 E.G. 483 (lime)
Mayer v. *Deptford and Lewisham Borough Councils* (1959), 173 E.G. 961 (plane)
Mills v. *Smith* (1963) 2 All E.R. 1078 (oak)
Murray and Others v. *Hutchinson* (1955), 166 E.G. 467 (poplar)
Niklaus v. *Moont* (1950), 156 E.G. 93 (poplar)
Pettifer v. *Cheshunt Urban District Council* (1970), 216 E.G. 1507 (elm)
Rigby and Another v. *Sun Alliance & London Insurance Ltd.* (1979) 252 E.G. 491 (oak)
Russell and Another v. *London Borough of Barnet* (1984), 271 E.G. 699 (oak)
Solloway v. *Hampshire County Council* (1981), 258 E.G. 858 (horse chestnut)
Wallace v. *Clayton* (1961), 181 E.G. 569 (poplar)
Watson and Roberts v. *Smith and Wakeham* (1956), 167 E.G. 39 (poplar)

Summary of species involved:

Species	Number
Ash and elm	1
Elm	2
Horse chestnut	1
Lime	3
Oak	4
Plane	1
Poplar	13
Various	2
	27

(e) Tree preservation orders

Attorney General v. *Melville Construction Co. Ltd,* (1968) T.L.R. 21 August 1968.

Barnet London Borough Council v. *Eastern Electricity Board and Another* (1973), 2 All E.R. 319

Bell v. *Canterbury City Council* (1985), The Times, 11 March 1988

Bullock v. *Secretary of State for the Environment and Another* (1980), 254 E.G. 1013

Edgeborough Building Co. Ltd. v. *Woking Urban District Council* (1966) 198 E.G. 581.

Maidstone Borough Council v. *Mortimer* (1980), 256 E.G. 1013

(f) Definitions

The following cases provide a definition of the terms are given below.

(i) Coppice
Dashwood v. *Magniac* (1891), 3 Ch. 306

(ii) Underwood
R. v. *Ferrybridge (Inhabitants)* (1823), 1 B. & C. 384

(iii) Hedgerow timber
Layfield v. *Cowper* (1694), 1 Eag. & Y. 591

(iv) Lopping
Unwin v. *Hanson* (1891), 2 Q.B. 115

(v) Timber according to age and species
Honeywood v. *Honeywood* (1874), 18 Eq. 306

(vi) Timber according to size
Whitty v. *Lord Dillon* (1860), 2 F. & F. 67

(vii) Timber according to species

Beech:	*Aubrey* v. *Fisher* (1809), 10 East 446
	Bibye v. *Huxley* (1824) 1 Eag. & Y. 805
	Dashwood v. *Magniac* (1891), 3 Ch. 306
Birch:	*Countess of Cumberland's case (1610),* Moore K.B. 812
	Foster and Peacock v. *Leonard* (1581) 1 Cro. Eliz. 1.
Horse chestnut:	*R.* v. *Ferrybridge (Inhabitants)* (1823), 1 B. & C. 375
Hornbeam:	*Soby* v. *Molyns* (1575), Plowd. 470
	Turner v. *Smith* (1680), 1 Eag. & Y. 526
Larch:	*In re Harrison's Trust* (1884), 28 Ch. D. 221
Spruce:	*In re Tower's Contract* (1924), W.N. 331
Walnut:	*Duke of Chandos* v. *Talbot* (1731), 2 P.Wms 601
Willow:	*Cuffly* v. *Pindar* (1616), Hob. 219.

(g) Miscellaneous

(i) Damage by cattle to young plantations
Smith v. *Smale* (1954), 164 E.G. 436

(ii) Compensation for restriction of felling
Cardigan Timber Co. v. *Cardiganshire County Council* (1958), 9 P. & C.R. 1958, 158.

(h) Abbreviations used in reported law cases
The following abbreviations have been used in the cases referred to above. Where reference is made to the Estates Gazette, the first figure refers to the number of the volume and the second to the page number.

A.C.	Appeal Court
All E.R.	All England Law Reports
B. & C.	Barnewall and Cresswell's Reports
C.A.	Court of Appeal
Ch.	Chancery
Ch. App.	Chancery Appeal
Ch. D.	Chancery Division Reports
Cro. Eliz.	Croke, time of Elizabeth
Eag. & Y.	Eagle & Young's Collection of Tithe Cases
East	East
E.G.	Estates Gazette
Eq.	Equity
Ex.D.	Exchequer Division
F. & F.	Foster & Finlason
H.L.	House of Lords
Hob.	Hobart
K.B.	King's Bench
L.R.	Law Report
L.T.	Law Times Report
Moore	Moore
P.Wms	Peere Williams
P. & C.R.	Planning and Compensation Reports
Plowd.	Plowden
Q.B.	Queen's Bench
S.J.	Solicitor's Journal
T.L.R.	Times Law Reports
W.L.R.	Weekly Law Reports
W.N.	Weekly Notes
Wood	Wood's Tithe Causes

5. *Tree Preservation Orders*

This section is intended to provide a brief guide to tree preservation orders which are referred to in this section as 'orders', the principal source of information being the Town and Country Planning Act 1971.

(a) The object of an order

To prevent the felling or mutilation of the tree or trees covered by the order and to make provision for replanting them, if such action is considered necessary, as extended by the Town and Country Planning (Amendment) Act 1985.

(b) The extent of an order

An order can:

(i) Prohibit the felling, lopping or destruction of the trees covered by the order, unless the consent of the local planning authority has been obtained.

(ii) Be made in respect of single trees, groups of trees or entire woodlands.

(iii) Enforce the replanting of trees or woodlands which have been felled either with or without the consent of the planning authority.

(c) The making of an order

Orders are made by the local planning authority or by a local authority to which this task has been delegated. Such orders should be made in accordance with the directions contained in the following regulations:

SI 1969/17	Town and Country Planning (Tree Preservation Order) Regulations, 1969.
SI 1975/148	Town and Country Planning (Tree Preservation) Order (Amendment) and (Trees in Conservation Areas) (Exempted Cases) Regulations, 1975.
SI 1975/1204	Town and Country Planning (Tree Preservation Order and Trees in Conservation Areas) (Scotland) Regulations, 1975.

(d) Objections to an order

(i) These must be made to the appropriate Minister, in writing, setting out the reasons for the objections, the name of the authority making the order and a description of the trees or woodlands concerned.

(ii) Objections must reach the Minister within twenty-eight days of the serving of the order.

(e) Compensation

Compensation may be payable when an order is made and where the amount is not agreed, the matter can be referred to the Lands Tribunal.

(f) Exceptions to an order

(i) Trees growing on Crown lands unless consent has been

obtained, subject to Section 2 of the Town and Country Planning Act 1984.

(ii) Woodlands for which grant aid has been received under one of the Forestry Commission's schemes, unless the Commission consents to the making of the order. Where the woodlands are satisfactorily managed, consent will not normally be given.

(iii) Dead, dying and dangerous trees subject to the Town and Country Planning Act 1962 S.29(7) and the Civic Amenities Act 1967 S.13.

(vi) The felling or lopping of trees by a statutory undertaking such as an electricity authority, a river authority, the Post Office and also the Ministry of Defence.

(v) Fruit trees in a garden or orchard which are cultivated for fruit.

CHAPTER XXIV

Grants and Felling Licences

1. *Grants*

Grants for planting woodlands, shelterbelts, trees for amenity and conservation purposes, and for hedges are now available from a number of sources and information relating to these is given below. It should be borne in mind that these grants, and the conditions attached to them, may change in course of time.

(a) Forestry and Woodland Grants

(i) *Woodland Grant Scheme*

(1) Introduced in April 1988, this replaced the Forestry Grant Scheme and Broadleaved Woodland Grant Scheme.

(2) The new scheme applies to:

(a) The establishment and restocking of broadleaved, conifer and mixed woodlands by planting or natural regeneration.

(b) The restoration of neglected woodlands which are less than 20 years old.

(c) Any planting carried out under the Farm Woodland Scheme except areas which are less than 1 hectare (2·5 acres).

(3) Certain conditions are attached to the Scheme and include the following:

(a) The proportion of broadleaved species in an existing woodland must be retained or increased.

(b) When replanting or regenerating ancient woodlands, appropriate broadleaved species must be used either pure or mixed with conifers.

(c) Applications which are concerned with the replacement of broadleaved woodlands (whether pure or mixed with conifers) on ancient woodland sites must conform with the principles contained in the Forestry Commission publication *Guidelines for the Management of Broadleaved Woodlands*.

(d) In Scotland, native pinewood areas (as described by H. M. Steven and A. C. Carlisle in *The Native Pinewoods of*

Scotland) must only be planted or regenerated with native Scots pine.

(e) Where areas of conifers are to be planted which are mainly composed of a single species, a proportion of other conifer species or broadleaves must be included.

(f) Other conditions are concerned with ancient monuments, sites of special scientific interest (SSSIs), national nature reserves, public rights of way and water supplies.

(4) The rates of grants which came into force on 5 April 1988, and which are subject to review, are as shown in the table.

Area approved for planting or regeneration		*Rate of grant (£)*			
		Conifers		*Broadleaves*	
Hectares	*Acres*	*Per hectare*	*Per acre*	*Per hectare*	*Per acre*
0·25–0·9	0·6– 2·2	1,005	407	1,575	637
1·00–2·0	2·3– 7·1	880	356	1,375	556
3·0 –9·9	7·2–24·5	795	322	1,175	476
10·00 and over	24·6 and over	615	249	975	395

(5) The following conditions apply to the payment of grants.

(a) The grant band is decided according to the total area which is to be planted, restocked or naturally regenerated under the application.

(b) The rates at which grants are paid are fixed in proportion to the area which is occupied by conifers and broadleaves respectively.

(c) Grants for the planting or natural regeneration of native pinewoods will be at the same rate as for broadleaves. Reference should also be made to the Commission's leaflet *Native Pinewood Grants*.

(d) Grants for new planting and restocking will be paid in three instalments, as follows:

70% on completion of work
20% payable 5 years after completion
10% payable 10 years after completion

(e) Grants for natural regeneration are also paid in three instalments:

50% on completion of the work required to be carried out in order to encourage regeneration
30% when satisfactory stocking has been obtained, but there is no fixed time limit for this

20% payable 5 years after satisfactory stocking has been obtained.

Any existing natural regeneration which is less than 20 years of age, and for which a grant has not previously been paid, may qualify for the second and third instalments (30% and 20%).

(f) Subject to certain requirements, neglected woodlands of less than 20 years of age can also qualify for the grants of 30% and 20%.

(g) Planting distances should not exceed:
Conifers: 2·1 metres (6 ft 10 in.)
Broadleaves: (3·0 metres (9 ft 10 in.)
unless otherwise approved.

(6) A special supplement of £200 per hectare (£81 per acre) is payable where new planting is carried out on arable land or improved grassland which is less than 10 years old and does not come within the Farm Woodland Scheme. Subject to it having been agreed in the Plan of Operations, this supplement will be paid at the same time as the first instalment of the planting grant.

(7) Applications to enter the scheme must be made on form WGS1, obtainable from the Conservancy Offices of the Commission, and a Plan of Operations covering 5 years must be submitted on form WGS3. Requests for the payment of grants should be made on form WGS2.

(8) Full details relating to the Scheme will be found in a pamphlet entitled *Woodland Grant Scheme* issued by the Forestry Commission, and from which the foregoing information has been taken.

(ii) *Farm Woodland Scheme*

(1) The main objects of this Scheme, which came into effect on 1 October 1988, are:

(a) to divert land from farming so as to reduce surplus agricultural production
(b) to assist in maintaining farm incomes and rural employment
(c) to improve the appearance of the countryside
(d) to encourage timber production on farms.

(2) In the first place the Scheme will be for an experimental period of 3 years with the intention that 36,000 hectares (89,000 acres) will be planted during that period. This is the maximum area that can be planted in the course of the first 3 years.

(3) In order to encourage the removal of the most productive land from agriculture, a higher payment is made in respect

of arable land and for improved grassland which has been cultivated and reseeded within the last 10 years, than for less productive land.

(4) For the purposes of the Scheme, farm land has been classified as follows.

(a) Less Favoured Areas (LFA)

(i) These are divided into:

(1) Disadvantaged Areas (DA)

(2) Severely Disadvantaged Areas (SDA).

(ii) Each of these is again subdivided into two further classes:

(1) Arable land and improved grassland which has been cultivated and reseeded within the last 10 years.

(2) Unimproved grassland which includes rough grazing.

(b) Other areas

(i) These are referred to, under the Scheme, as 'Elsewhere' or 'Lowlands'.

(ii) They comprise arable land and improved grassland which has been cultivated and reseeded within the last 10 years.

(5) Of the total area of 36,000 hectares (89,000 acres), 3,000 hectares (7,413 acres) have been allotted for planting on unimproved grassland in Less Favoured Areas (DA and SDA) only.

(6) The following conditions apply to the Scheme.

(a) Areas to be planted must be approved by the Forestry Commission.

(b) The maximum area to be planted on a holding must not exceed 40 hectares (99 acres).

(c) The minimum area to be planted on a holding must not be less than 3 hectares (7·4 acres) except in Northern Ireland where the minimum will be 1 hectare (2·5 acres).

(d) No block of woodlands planted on the farm must be less than 1 hectare in size.

(e) The woodlands must form an integral part of the farming operations which are carried out by the applicant. For example, planting the whole farm with trees or selling it to a forestry investor, would be a disqualification.

(7) A tenant of a farm can apply to join the Scheme provided that he has obtained the written consent of his landlord.

(8) Certain categories of land are excluded from the Scheme and these include land in a National Nature Reserve, common land and existing woodlands. Full details are given in the Farm Woodland Scheme—Rules Booklet (FWS2).

(9) Subject to the conditions outlined above, and any others that are incorporated in the Scheme, the annual payments to be made are shown in the table.

Description	Grants (£)					
	SDA		*DA*		*Elsewhere*	
	Per hectare	*Per acre*	*Per hectare*	*Per acre*	*Per hectare*	*Per acre*
Arable land and improved grassland cultivated and seeded within the last 10 years	100	41	150	61	190	77
Unimproved grassland and rough grazing	30	12	30	12	—	—

Note: SDA = Severely Disadvantaged Area
DA = Disadvantaged Area

(10) These grants will be paid for periods of varying lengths in accordance with the following categories:

Category 1
Woodlands of which not less than 90% of the area consists of pedunculate oak, sessile oak or a mixture of these species, the remainder of the area comprising other broadleaved trees: 40 years.

Category 2
(a) Pure broadleaved woodlands which are not within Category 1 and are not coppiced; *or*
(b) mixed woodlands of which more than 50% of their area consist of broadleaved trees: 30 years.

Category 3
Woodlands which are not within Categories 1 or 2 and are not coppiced; that is to say, woodland of which 50% or less of their area are broadleaved trees: 20 years.

Category 4
Broadleaved woodlands which are planted for the purpose of producing coppice stools: 10 years.
Note. The species planted must be approved by the Forestry Commission as being suitable for traditional coppice, and these include hazel sweet chestnut, oak and lime.

(11) The rates of payment are to be reviewed by 30 September 1991 and thereafter at intervals not exceeding 5 years.

(12) In addition to the above annual payments, the Forestry Commission planting grants, shown in the table, will be paid, subject to the planting being approved by the Commission.

Area approved for planting		*Grant (£)*			
		Conifers		*Broadleaves*	
Hectares	*Acres*	*Per hectare*	*Per acre*	*Per hectare*	*Per acre*
1·00–2·9	2·3– 7·1	505	204	1,375	556
3·00–9·9	7·2–24·5	420	170	1,175	476
10·00 and over	24·6 and over	240	97	975	395

(13) The following are not eligible for planting grants:
- (a) Areas of less than 1·0 hectares (2·5 acres).
- (b) Crops grown for biomass, etc., on a very short rotation.
- (c) Christmas trees, fruit trees or nursery stock.

(14) Planting distances should not exceed those given below
- (a) Conifers: 2·1 metres (6 ft 10 in.)
  Broadleaves: 3·0 metres (9 ft 10 in.)
  unless otherwise approved by the Forestry Commission.

(15) Further information regarding the Scheme can be obtained from the Forest District Offices of the Forestry Commission or local Divisional Agricultural Offices in England, Wales and Scotland. Separate details are available for Northern Ireland.

(iii) *Farm Set-aside Scheme*

(1) The object of this Scheme, which was introduced in 1988, is to reduce the surpluses of arable crops, whereas the Farm Woodland Scheme is concerned with both arable and grassland.

(2) In order to achieve this, there are three options:
- (a) to fallow the land
- (b) to use it for purposes other than agriculture
- (c) to plant it with trees.

This section deals with the third option.

(3) To qualify for the Scheme, a minimum of 20% of the land used for growing certain relevant arable crops, in the base year, must be set aside. There is no maximum limit.

(4) The base year was 1987–88, and a list of the relevant crops is given in application form SA2.

(5) An agreement to enter the Scheme extends for 5 years from 1 October in the year when the application is accepted. However, it is permissible to withdraw from it at the end of 3 years.

(6) Where land is planted as woodland, the compensation paid each year for the period of the Scheme (5 years) is:
  (a) Land in Less Favoured Areas
    £180 per hectare (£73 per acre)
  (b) Elsewhere
    £200 per hectare (£81 per acre)

(7) In addition, planting grants are available from the Forestry Commission as shown in the table.

Area approved for planting		*Grant (£)*			
		Conifers		*Broadleaves*	
Hectares	*Acres*	*Per hectare*	*Per acre*	*Per hectare*	*Per acre*
0·25–0·9	0·6– 2·2	1.005	407	1,575	537
1·00–2·9	2·3– 7·1	880	356	1,375	556
3·00–9·9	7·2–24·5	795	322	1,175	476
10.0 and over	24.6 and over	615	249	975	395

Grants are paid in three instalments:
  70% on completion of planting
  20% after 5 years
  10% after 10 years.

(8) Planting grants are not payable in respect of
  (a) Areas of less than 0·25 hectares (0·6 acres).
  (b) Crops grown on very short rotations such as biomass, etc.
  (c) Christmas trees, fruit trees and nursery stock.

(9) A farm tenant who wishes to adopt the woodland option under the Scheme must obtain the written consent of his landlord.

(10) It is permissible to enter both the Set-aside and the Farm Woodland Schemes, but payments under each of these canoot be made in respect of the same area of land.

(11) Full details of the Set-aside Scheme can be obtained from local Divisional Agricultural Offices of the United Kingdom.

(b) Grants for Small Woods

(i) *The Countryside Commission*

(1) Discretionary grants, of up to 50% of the approved cost, are available for planting small areas of woodland:

(a) On sites of 0·25 hectares (0·6 acres) or less in open countryside.

(b) On sites of over 0·25 hectares if the scheme is not eligible for a grant from the Forestry Commission.

(2) The species should normally be broadleaved and appropriate to the locality.

(3) Further information can be obtained from:

(a) The Countryside Commission, John Dower House, Crescent Place, Cheltenham, Glos. GL50 3RA.

(b) The Countryside Commission for Scotland, Battleby, Redgorton, Perth PH1 3EW.

(ii) *The National Parks*

(1) Assistance of up to 75% of the approved cost is available for private landowners or occupiers who wish to plant bare land or rehabilitate broadleaved woodland within a National Park.

(2) Such support may take the form of cash, a supply of trees and material or a contribution by the applicant towards the cost of the work.

(3) The area to be planted must not exceed 0·25 hectares (0·6 acres).

(4) Details are available from the appropriate National Park Authority, which can be located through the telephone directory for the area.

(c) Grants for Individual Trees or Small Groups

(i) *Local authorities*

(1) Some local authorities provide assistance for planting individual trees. For example, the Devon County Council will supply individuals, parish councils and other organizations with free trees subject to certain conditions as to the site, planting, protection and maintenance. Private individuals are limited to twenty-five trees in any one planting season.

(2) Enquiries should be addressed to the appropriate local authority.

(ii) *Ministry of Agriculture, Fisheries and Food*

(1) Grants are available for planting, staking and protecting trees which are intended to provide shade for stock. These could be in hedgerows or on other approved sites.

(2) Further information can be obtained from:

(a) The Agricultural Development and Advisory Service (ADAS) of the Ministry of Agriculture, Great Westminster House, Horseferry Road, London SW1P 2AE, or from the Divisional Offices of the Ministry (addresses can be traced through the local telephone directory).

(b) The Department of Agriculture and Fisheries for Scotland, Chesser House, 500 Gorgie Road, Edinburgh EH11 3AW.

(iii) *The Tree Council*

(1) The Council will consider providing a certain amount of limited financial help for planting trees.

(2) Applications for assistance which is limited to half of the total cost of planting, should be made to the Secretary, The Tree Council, 35 Belgrave Square, London SW1X 8QN.

(d) Grants for Shelterbelts

(i) Grants are available for planting and protecting shelterbelts and shelter hedges, and for their maintenance during the first 3 years.

(ii) Details can be obtained from the Agricultural Development and Advisory Service or from the Department of Agriculture for Scotland at the addresses given under section (*c*)(ii) which deals with individual trees.

(e) Grants for Amenity Planting

(i) Assistance towards the cost of planting trees for amenity purposes (subject to certain conditions) may be obtained from the sources given below.

(ii) In some cases, planting for amenity may coincide with planting for other purposes, as for example, individual trees.

(iii) Enquiries may be made to:

The Agricultural Development and Advisory Service
The Department of Agriculture for Scotland
The Countryside Commissions
The National Parks
The Tree Council
Local Authorities

at the addresses given above.

(f) Grants in Relation to Conservation

(i) The Nature Conservancy Council will consider making grants for projects which it considers to be a worthwhile contribution to nature conservation.

(ii) As regards trees, the following would be considered.

(1) The planting of individual trees or small woods:

(a) in areas designated as Sites of Special Scientific Interest

(b) on sites considered to be important wildlife habitats

(c) in locations which are managed as nature reserves

(d) on sites recorded in the Council's inventory of ancient woodlands.

(2) The management of existing trees or woodlands situated on any of the sites referred to above.

(iii) All grants are discretionary and usually amount to 50% of the total cost.

(iv) Enquiries should be addressed to the nearest Regional Office of the Nature Conservancy, which can be obtained from the local telephone directory. Failing this, the Headquarters of the Council at Northminster House, Peterborough PE1 1UA, should be approached.

2. *Felling Licences*

(*a*) Under the Forestry Act 1967 as amended by the Forestry Act 1979 and modified by Statutory Instrument No. 1958 of 1985, a licence is required to fell growing trees or to sell them for felling.

(*b*) However it is not necessary to obtain a licence for:

(i) felling trees not exceeding 8 cm (3 in.) dia.; coppice or underwood not exceeding 15 cm (6 in.) dia.; thinnings not exceeding 10 cm (4 in.) dia.—such measurements to be taken over bark at 1·3 m (5 ft) above ground level;

(ii) felling fruit trees and trees growing in gardens, orchards, churchyards or public open spaces;

(iii) lopping or topping trees or trimming hedges;

(iv) felling a tree which is a danger or nuisance;

(v) felling a tree in order to comply with the requirements of an Act of Parliament;

(vi) felling a tree, at the request of an Electricity Board, which obstructs or interferes with transmission lines;

(vii) felling a tree where such action is necessary for carrying out development authorized under the Town and Country Planning Act 1971;

(viii) felling trees growing on land in the occupation of the owner of the land or his tenant, provided that:

(1) the cubic contents of the trees felled without a licence shall not exceed 5 cubic metres (138 Hoppus feet) in any one quarter.

(2) of this quantity not more than 2 cubic metres (55 Hoppus feet) are sold in any quarter;

(ix) Managed woodlands, provided that any felling which is carried out is in accordance with the agreed Plan of Operations for those woodlands.

(*c*) An application for a felling licence should be sent to the conservator for the conservancy in which the estate lies. The addresses of the conservators, and the extent of each conservancy, will be found in Chapter XXV.

(*d*) When granting a licence, the Forestry Commission can require replanting to be carried out as a condition of its issue.

(*e*) If the trees concerned are the subject of a tree preservation order it is necessary to consult the planning authority that made the order.

(*f*) The following Statutory Instruments are concerned with felling licences and restrictions.

791 (1979): The Forestry (Felling of Trees) Regulations 1979

1958 (1985): The Forestry (Modification of Felling Restrictions) Regulations 1985

1572 (1985): The Forestry (Exceptions from Restriction of Felling) (Amendment) Regulations 1985

632 (1987): The Forestry (Felling of Trees) (Amendment) Regulations 1987

CHAPTER XXV

The Forestry Commission

1. *The Formation of the Forestry Commission*

(*a*) Although the management of the Forest and Land Revenues were transferred to the Commissioners of Woods and Forests in 1810, their duties were largely concerned with the ancient royal forests of which the New Forest and the Forest of Dean were the most important. It was not until 1924 that the forest areas held by the Commissioners of Woods were transferred to the Forestry Commissioners under the Forestry (Transfer of Woods) Act 1923.

(*b*) After the outbreak of war in 1914, the need for adequate supplies of home-grown timber was soon realized. As submarine warfare gained momentum and the losses of allied shipping mounted, the country became increasingly dependent on home-grown timber. As a result large areas were felled, but since the national forests were so limited in extent the heaviest demands were made on privately owned woodlands.

(*c*) In 1916 a Forestry Sub-Committee of the Reconstruction Committee was appointed under the chairmanship of the Rt Hon. F. D. Acland, and 10 months later its report was published. This is generally referred to as the Acland Report and it was in the light of the Committee's recommendations that the Forestry Commission was established after the passing of the Forestry Act 1919.

2. *The Development of the Commission*

(*a*) Under the chairmanship of Lord Lovat the Commission made steady progress and in 1927 another Forestry Act was passed which increased the number of Commissioners from eight to ten.

(*b*) During the 1939–45 war history repeated itself and further heavy fellings were necessary, the majority of which, once again, occurred in private woodlands. In 1943 the Forestry Commissioners prepared and presented a report to the Chancellor of the Exchequer entitled *Post-War Forest Policy*, and this was followed by a supplementary report, *Post-War Forest Policy, Private Woodlands*, in

1944. These reports laid the foundations of the forest policy for this country during the first 20 years after the war.

(*c*) The Forestry Act 1945 reconstituted the Commission, enacted certain provisions as to the acquisition of land and made certain amendments to the Forestry Acts 1919 to 1927.

(*d*) In 1947 a further Forestry Act was passed which covered certain aspects of forestry dedication covenants and the restriction of compulsory powers regarding the acquisition of dedicated land.

(*e*) Four years later the Forestry Act 1951 set out the law regarding the felling of trees and the licences which were necessary, with a view to safeguarding adequate stocks of standing timber. It also reconstituted Regional Advisory Committees and the Home-Grown Timber Advisory Committee as statutory committees.

(*f*) In 1965 the Forestry Commission was reorganized to a considerable extent and this was followed by the Forestry Act 1967 which consolidated the provisions of the earlier Forestry Acts and repealed those of 1919, 1923, 1927, 1945, 1947 and 1951.

(*g*) On 24 October 1973 new proposals were announced relating to the payment of grants, a new Dedication Scheme and the membership of the Regional Advisory Committees while a statement made on 5 July 1974 gave further details of these proposals. Subsequently the Commission redefined its objectives which were set out in the Fifty-Fourth Annual Report.

(*h*) The Forestry Act 1979 restated the powers of the Commissioners to make grants and loans, amended parts of S.9 and S.43 of the Forestry Act 1967 by substituting metric measure for Imperial and repealed part of S.9(6).

(*i*) The Forestry Act, 1981, dealt with the disposal of the Commissioners' property, certain financial matters and an increase in the number of Forestry Commissioners from nine to ten excluding the Chairman. In October 1981 the Basis III Dedication Scheme and the Small Woods Scheme were replaced by the Forestry Grant Scheme.

(*j*) A new Government policy for broadleaved woodlands was announced in July 1985 and the Broadleaved Woodland Grant Scheme was introduced in October of that year. It also became the duty of the Commission, under the Wildlife and Countryside (Amendment) Act 1985 (which amended S.1 of the Forestry Act 1967), to try to reach a satisfactory balance between the interests of forestry and the environment.

(*k*) In April 1988 the Woodland Grant Scheme was introduced, which replaced the two schemes referred to in the previous paragraphs.

3. *The Organization of the Commission*

The following is a brief account of the organization of the Forestry Commission as on 1 April 1988.

(a) Ministerial responsibility
Responsibility for forest policy is shared by the Minister of Agriculture, Fisheries and Food, the Secretary of State for Scotland and the Secretary of State for Wales.

(b) The Commissioners

(i) Under the Forestry Act 1967, as amended by the Forestry Act 1981, there are eleven Commissioners of whom seven including the Chairman, are only part-time. The remaining four, who are full-time, are the Director-General and three senior officers of the Commission.
   (1) At least three should have special knowledge and experience of forestry.
   (2) At least one should have scientific attainments and a technical knowledge of forestry.
   (3) At least one should have a special knowledge and experience of the timber trade.

(ii) The names of the Commissioners, senior members of the staff, conservators and members of the committees and other bodies appointed by the Commissioners are published in the Annual Report and Accounts of the Forestry Commission.

(c) Headquarters organization
Chairman
Deputy Chairman and Director-General
Three Executive Commissioners responsible respectively for:
  Administration and Finance
  Operations
  Private Forestry and Development
Secretary
Director, Harvesting and Marketing
Director, Research
Director, Planning and Surveys
Director, Estate Management
Director, Private Forestry and Services
Director, Personnel
Controller of Finance
Head of Silviculture
Head of Data Processing
Chief Engineer
Head of Information.

Note: Early in 1975 the headquarters of the Commission was transferred from London and Basingstoke to Edinburgh. The new Headquarters Office at 231 Corstorphine Road, Edinburgh EH2 7AT (telephone 031 334 0303) was formally opened by the Secretary of State for Scotland on 16 May 1975.

(d) Forest Research Stations

The Commission has two research stations:

(i) Forestry Commission Research Station, Alice Holt Lodge, Wrecclesham, Farnham, Surrey GU10 4LH (telephone 0420 22255).

(ii) Forestry Commission Northern Research Station, Roslin, Midlothian EH25 9SY (telephone 031 445 2176).

(e) Conservancies

For purposes of administration, England, Scotland and Wales are divided into regions known as conservancies and until April 1985 there was a total of eleven, of which five were in England, four in Scotland and two in Wales. Prior to 1969 the New Forest and Dean Forest formed two separate charges under their own Deputy Surveyors but in that year they became part of the South East and South West Conservancies, respectively. However, from 1 April 1985 these eleven conservancies were reduced to seven, while in April 1988 further minor alterations were made to the Mid Scotland and South Scotland Conservancies in respect of the Motherwell District. Every conservancy is sub-divided into Forest Districts which vary in number from seven in the South Scotland Conservancy to fourteen in the Wales Conservancy, each having its own District Office. The extent of the seven conservancies, with the location of the Conservancy Offices, as in April 1988, are given below.

(1) *North England*

Extent: The counties of Northumberland, Tyne and Wear, Durham, Cleveland, Cumbria, Lancashire, Cheshire, Merseyside, Greater Manchester, West Yorkshire, North Yorkshire, South Yorkshire and Humberside except the districts of Glanford, Scunthorpe, Grimsby and Cleethorpes.

Office: 1A Grosvenor Terrace, York YO3 7BD.

(2) *East England*

Extent: The counties of Lincolnshire, Bedfordshire, Norfolk, Suffolk, Essex, Hertfordshire, Buckinghamshire, Northamptonshire, Cambridgeshire, Oxfordshire and Leicestershire. That part of the Staffordshire Moorlands District of Staffordshire which falls within the Peak District National Park. That part of Humberside comprising the districts of Glanford, Scunthorpe, Grimsby and Cleethorpes. Greater London,

Nottinghamshire, Derbyshire, Berkshire, Hampshire, Kent, Surrey, East Sussex, West Sussex and Isle of Wight.

Office: Great Eastern House, Tenison Road, Cambridge CB1 2DU.

(3) *West England*

Extent: The counties of Cornwall, Devon, Somerset, Dorset, Wiltshire, Avon, Gloucestershire, Hereford and Worcestershire, Warwickshire, West Midlands, Shropshire and the whole of Staffordshire except that part of the Staffordshire Moorlands District which falls within the Peak District National Park.

Office: Avon Fields House, Somerdale, Keynsham, Bristol BS18 2BD.

(4) *Wales*

Office: Victoria House, Victoria Terrace, Aberystwyth, Dyfed SY23 2DQ.

(5) *North Scotland*

Extent: The whole of the Western Isles Authority area, Shetland Isles Authority area and Orkney Isles Authority area. The whole of the Highland Region area with the exception of that portion of Lochaber District east of Loch Linnhe and south of Loch Leven, the River Leven, the Blackwater Reservoir and the Blackwater, to where the Highland Region boundary reaches the river of Lochan A'chlaidheimh. Strathclyde Region —the Isles of Mull, Iona, Coll and Tiree only. The whole of the Grampian region.

Office: 21 Church Street, Inverness IV1 1EL.

(6) *Mid Scotland*

Extent: That portion of the Lochaber District of Highland Region east of Loch Linnhe and south of Loch Leven, the River Leven, the Blackwater Reservoir and the Blackwater, to where the Highland Region boundary reaches the river at Lochan A'chlaidheimh. Central Region, Tayside Region and Fife Region. That part of Strathclyde Region comprising the districts of Argyll and Bute—except the Isles of Mull, Iona, Coll and Tiree—Dumbarton, Clydebank, Bearsden and Milngavie, Strathkelvin, Cumbernauld, Monklands, part of Motherwell (see South Scotland), Hamilton, City of Glasgow, Inverclyde, Renfrew, that portion of East Kilbride District north of a line from Routen Burn to Eaglesham, and that portion of Eastwood District north and west of the B764 from Eaglesham to the district Boundary.

Office: Portcullis House, 21 India Street, Glasgow G2 4PL.

(7) *South Scotland*

Extent: The regions of Lothian, Borders and Dumfries and Galloway. That part of Strathclyde Region comprising the districts of Lanark, Cumnock and Doon Valley, Kyle and

Carrick, Cunninghame, Kilmarnock and Loudoun, the portion of East Kilbride District south of a line from Routen Burn to Eaglesham, that portion of Eastwood District south and east of the B764 from Eaglesham to the district boundary, and part of Motherwell District including Shotts, Hartwood, Allanton and the area east of the 'C' road between Allanton and Carluke.

4. *The Committees of the Commission*

The following are the principal committees appointed by or in conjunction with the Commission.

(a) National Committees

(i) Three National Committees, for England, Scotland and Wales respectively, were appointed under the provisions of the Forestry Act 1945 when they replaced the earlier Consultative Committees. Their functions are now purely advisory.

(ii) In 1987 the Committee for England consisted of seven members of whom four were Commissioners and the remainder chairmen of the three English Regional Advisory Committees. The Committee for Scotland was composed of three Commissioners and three chairmen of the Advisory Committees while the Committee for Wales comprised two Commissioners and four independent members.

(b) Regional Advisory Committees

(i) These were formed in 1946, one Committee being set up in each conservancy, the object being to provide a link between the Conservator and those in the conservancy who are interested in forestry.

(ii) In October 1974 the membership of the Committees was enlarged so as to include agricultural, amenity and local planning interests as well as those of woodland owners and timber merchants.

(c) Home Grown Timber Advisory Committee

(i) This Committee was originally formed in 1939 and in 1987 it numbered twenty-five members, seven of whom were appointed independently. The remaining eighteen were representatives of woodland owners, timber merchants, British Coal, the particleboard and pulpwood industries and timber research and development.

(ii) The function of the Committee is to advise the Commissioners on all matters relating to home-grown timber.

(iii) The Committee can also appoint sub-committees to report on any particular aspect of home timber production, and in 1987 two had been appointed—the Supply and Demand Sub-Committee and the Technical Sub-Committee.

(d) Advisory Committee on Forest Research
The Committee which was appointed in 1929 is an internal committee of the Forestry Commission and advises the Director of Research on the quality and direction of research carried out by the Commission.

(e) Forestry Research Coordination Committee
This Committee was established in 1982 and its terms of reference may be summarized as follows:

(i) To identify and define forestry research needs.
(ii) To advise on research requirements and priorities.
(iii) To stimulate forest research, the exchange of information and collaboration between research organizations and individuals.
(iv) To publish the results of such research.
(v) To encourage the financing of research proposals.

(f) Forestry Training Council

(i) Although this body is not a committee, it has been included since it is appointed by the Commission.
(ii) It was set up in 1971 after forestry interests had withdrawn from the Agricultural, Horticultural and Forestry Industry Training Board, and is now responsible for providing training courses for personnel both in the Commission and the private sector.

(g) Forestry Safety Council

(i) The Council occupies a similar position to that of the Forestry Training Council in that it is not a committee but at the same time is appointed by the Forestry Commission.
(ii) It was established in 1974 for the purpose of promoting safety in forestry.

5. *The Objectives of the Commission*

The Forestry Commission has two distinct parts to play. First, as the Forestry Enterprise, it is responsible for the management of the forests and land under its control and second, it is the Forest Authority. As such it advises on forest policy, carries out research, controls felling, deals with grants and so on. Its objectives, which are set out in *Forest Facts 2* issued by the Commission, are as follows:

(a) As Forestry Enterprise

(i) To develop its forests for the production of wood for industry, by extending and improving the forest estate.
(ii) To manage its estate economically and efficiently and to account for its activities to Ministers and Parliament.
(iii) To protect and enhance the environment.
(iv) To provide recreational facilities.
(v) To stimulate and support employment and the local economy in rural areas by the development of forests, including the establishment of new plantations, and of the wood-using industry.
(vi) To foster a harmonious relationship between forestry and other land-use interests, including agriculture.

(b) As Forestry Authority

(i) To advance knowledge and understanding of forestry and trees in the countryside.
(ii) To develop and ensure the best use of the country's forest resources and to promote the development of the wood-using industry and its efficiency.
(iii) To endeavour to achieve a reasonable balance between the interests of forestry and those of the environment.
(iv) To undertake research relevant to the needs of forestry.
(v) To combat forest and tree pests and diseases.
(vi) To advise and assist with safety and training in forestry.
(vii) To encourage good forestry practice in private woodlands through advice and schemes of financial assistance and by controls on felling.

6. *The Publications of the Commission*

One of the first steps to be taken by the Commission after its formation in 1919 was to publish information on forestry matters, an early example being a leaflet on pine weevils which appeared in February 1920. Since then, the many publications issued in the Commission's various series have provided an outstanding source of reliable information. A further account of these will be found in Chapter XXX.

CHAPTER XXVI

The State Forest Service in Northern Ireland

1. *The Formation of the Forestry Service*

(*a*) In 1921 authority was given to the Government of Northern Ireland to implement a separate forest policy and thereafter the Ministry of Agriculture, now known as the Department of Agriculture, assumed responsibility for forestry.

(*b*) Under the Forestry Act (Northern Ireland) 1953, powers were granted to the Department of Agriculture to acquire and manage land for forestry purposes, to encourage private forestry and to protect any forests which were thus established. This Act replaced earlier legislation.

2. *The Development of State Forests*

(*a*) Although State Forests only extended to a few hundred acres in 1921, the area planted had increased to 58,600 hectares (145,000 acres) by the end of 1987.

(*b*) This achievement has been due largely to an expanding programme of planting, particularly since 1946. The current rate of planting, including replanting (1987), is approximately 600 hectares (1,480 acres) per year.

(*c*) Timber production resulting from this afforestation programme is now running at 125,000 tonnes in 1987.

3. *Present Organization*

(a) General

(i) The State Forest Service forms one of the Divisions of the Department of Agriculture and has its Headquarters in Belfast.

(ii) In addition to Headquarters there are five District Offices throughout Northern Ireland with administrative support.

(iii) The forest area, which comprises nineteen forest charges, is staffed by Forest Officers Grades I, II, III and IV.

(b) Headquarters Organization

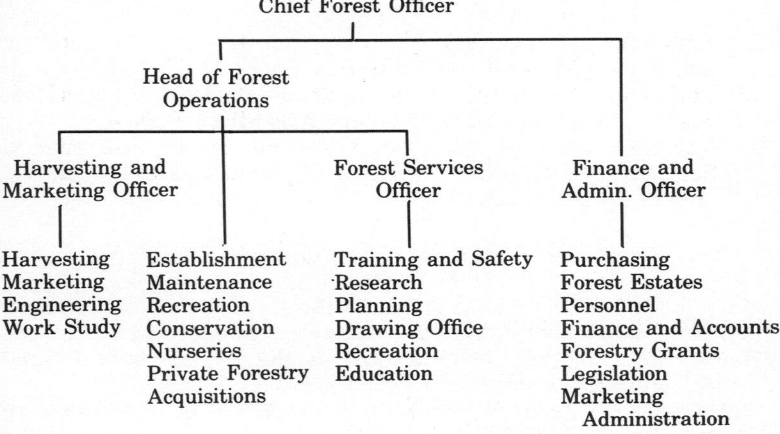

(c) Field Organization

Forest operations and administration in the field are organized on a basis of five districts. Each district is headed by a Forest Officer I, who is responsible for the execution and administration of government policy.

(d) Staff

The total Forestry Staff consists of 83 Professional and Technical staff, 62 Administrative and 354 Industrial staff as at 1988.

4. *Recruitment and Training*

The recruitment of Forest Officers is carried out at two levels.

(a) Forest Officer II

(i) The usual qualification is an Honours Degree in Forestry from a recognized university, or a lengthy period of service as a Forest Officer III.

(ii) Vacancies are filled by the Civil Service Commission Selection Boards when required. Opportunities exist within the Service for advancement to higher grades.

(b) Forest Officer IV

(i) The usual qualifications are:

(1) Business and Technician Education Council (BTEC) National Diploma from the Cumbria College of Agriculture and Forestry, Penrith.

(2) Scottish Vocational Educational Council (SCOTVEC) from the Scottish School of Forestry and the Inverness Technical College, Inverness.

(ii) Both Colleges require 2 years of pre-college work experience and courses are of 3 years duration.

(iii) The Forest Service can provide approximately three places each year for those provisionally accepted by either College.

(iv) Vacancies are also filled by the Civil Service Commission Selection Boards when required. Opportunities also exist for advancement to higher grades.

5. *Research*

(*a*) The Research Officer, assisted by Field Officers, is responsible for the administration, maintenance and analysis of active experiments. The major areas of research are:

(i) the effects of ground preparation and drainage treatments on tree growth and stability;

(ii) the effects of spacing and thinning on forest stands.

(*b*) Contact is maintained with Research Officers working in similar fields in the British Forestry Commission and the Forest Service of the Republic of Ireland.

(*c*) Close co-operation exists with Research Officers in the Food and Agricultural Chemistry, Biometrics, Plant Pathology and Agricultural Botany Research Divisions of the Department of Agriculture, working principally on forest soils and nutrition, forest modelling, pathology and vegetative propagation techniques.

6. *Amenity and Recreation*

(*a*) Amenity is considered to be an important aspect of forest management.

(*b*) The first National Forest Park was established at Tollymore, Newcastle, Co. Down in 1955. Since then eight other Forest Parks and five Forest Drives have been opened. All counties, with the exception of Londonderry, have at lest one Forest Park and one Forest Drive.

(*c*) All forests are open to the public on foot, although access for vehicles is limited.

7. *Conservation*

Some fifty-two Forest Nature Reserves, of which fifteen have national status, have been established and are managed jointly by agreement with the Department of the Environment (Northern Ireland). The object is to protect wildlife, natural vegetation and sites of geological interest and to preserve them for scientific and educational purposes.

8. *Private Forestry*

(*a*) Private forestry is aided and encouraged.

(*b*) Practical assistance takes the form of free advice, planting and maintenance grants and the sale and supply of young trees.

(*c*) Further details may be obtained from Room 22, Dundonald House, Upper Newtonards Road, Belfast BT4 3SB.

CHAPTER XXVII

Societies, Organizations, Establishments and Trusts Concerned with Forestry

1. *Societies*

(a) Royal Forestry Society of England, Wales and Northern Ireland
Founded 1882.
Membership:
Woodland owners, professional members, corporate bodies, foresters, woodmen, students, non-professional members, honorary members.
Publication:
Quarterly Journal of Forestry.
Director's address:
102 High Street, Tring, Herts. HP23 4AH.

(b) Royal Scottish Forestry Society
Founded 1854.
Membership:
Ordinary members (two classes), honorary members and associate members (three classes).
Publication:
Scottish Forestry (quarterly).
Secretary's address:
11 Atholl Crescent, Edinburgh EH3 8HE.

(c) Commonwealth Forestry Association
Incorporated by Royal Charter 1921.
Membership:
Ordinary members, associate members, honorary members, life members, affiliated members, foreign members.
Publications:
Commonwealth Forestry Review (quarterly).
Commonwealth Forestry Handbook (irregular).
Editor Secretary's address:
c/o The Oxford Forestry Institute, South Parks Road, Oxford OX1 3RB.

(d) Institute of Chartered Foresters
Founded as a learned society in 1926, its status was changed in 1973 to that of a professional Institute for those who are engaged in forestry, in a professional capacity. It was incorporated by Royal Charter in 1982.
Membership:
Fellows, ordinary members, associates, students, affiliated members.
Publications:
Forestry (quarterly).
Newsletter (quarterly).
Secretary's address:
22 Walker Street, Edinburgh EH3 7HR.

(e) Association of Professional Foresters
Founded 1960.
Membership:
Individuals (five classes), forestry companies, trade companies.
Publication:
Newsletter (quarterly).
Secretary's address:
Brokerswood House, Brokerswood, nr. Westbury, Wilts BA13 4EH.

(f) Society of Consultant Foresters of Scotland
Founded 1953.
Membership:
Full members only.
Publication:
Half-yearly report (April and October) only issued to members.
Secretary's address:
Belses Mill, Ancrum, Roxburghshire TD8 6UP.

(g) Society of Irish Foresters
Founded 1942.
Membership:
Technical members, associates, students.
Publication:
Irish Forestry (twice yearly).
Honorary Secretary's address:
c/o The Royal Dublin Society, Ballsbridge, Dublin 4, Eire.

(h) Aberdeen University Forestry Society
Membership:
Members of the University.
Publication:
Arbor (annually).

Secretary's address:
c/o The Department of Forestry, University of Aberdeen, Old Aberdeen AB9 2UU.

(i) The Forestry and Wood Science Society of the University College of North Wales
Membership:
Membership of the University College.
Publication:
Y Coedwigwr—The Forester (annually).
Secretary's address:
c/o School of Agricultural and Forest Sciences, University College of North Wales, Bangor, Gwynedd LL57 2UW.

(j) Men of the Trees
Founded 1922.
Membership:
Members and life members.
Publications:
Trees (twice yearly—April and October) and Newsletters (February and July).
Secretary's address:
Crawley Down, Crawley, Sussex RH10 4HL.

2. *Bodies concerned with Special Aspects of Forestry*

(a) Commonwealth Forestry Bureau
Established in 1938 under the Commonwealth Agricultural Bureau (now the Commonwealth Agricultural Bureau International) from the Information Section of the Commonwealth Forestry Institute and funded mainly by Commonwealth Governments.

The Bureau functions as a clearing-house of information for field and research officers in forestry, including the utilization of forest products. Its main activities are the publication, from current world literature, of the monthly *Forestry Abstracts* and *Forestry Products Abstracts* (available in paper and microform editions, on cards and on-line as part of the CAB Abstracts database), the publication of reviews and annotated bibliographies on selected forestry and forest products subjects, and its Information Service. The main part of the Commonwealth Forestry Bureau is now housed at Commonwealth Agricultural Bureau International headquarters in Wallingford, with some staff remaining at the Oxford Forestry Institute.
Address:
Commonwealth Agricultural Bureau International, Wallingford, Oxon OX10 8DE.

(b) Oxford Forestry Institute

(i) Founded in 1924 as the Imperial (later the Commonwealth) Forestry Institute and renamed the Oxford Forestry Institute in 1986, to reflect the University inputs and global coverage.

(ii) The Institute houses:

(1) The forestry lecturers of the Department of Plant Sciences, which provides education and facilities for research in the sciences on which forestry and land use are based.

(2) The Institute's library, which is recognized as the western world's library of deposit for forestry and related literature.

(3) The Commonwealth and Tropical Forestry Unit which provides training, research and advisory services in tropical forestry.

(4) A range of research activities funded by various concerns including the Forestry Commission, while courses are offered in Forestry Planning and Management; Social and Community Forestry and Forest Research Methods.

Address:

South Parks Road, Oxford OX1 3RB.

(c) The Tree Council

(i) Established in 1974, the Council has the following objectives:

(1) To improve the environment by promoting the planting and proper maintenance of trees.

(2) To spread a knowledge of trees and their care.

(3) To act as a forum for organizations concerned with trees.

(4) To identify national problems relating to trees and to encourage co-operation.

(ii) In 1988 the Council was composed of twenty bodies known as Council Members and eleven bodies known as Consultative Members.

Address:

35 Belgrave Square, London SW1X 8QN.

3. *Associations primarily concerned with Timber*

(a) *British Timber Merchants' Association (England and Wales)*

The Association represents the home-grown timber trade in England and Wales. It maintains regular contact with the Forestry Commission, with private woodland owners, with the home-grown timber trade in Scotland and with the trade's principal customers. Its members are engaged in the harvesting, conversion, sale and export of home-grown timber and roundwood.

Membership:

Limited to timber merchants but associate membership is open to ancillary trades such as the manufacturers of sawmill equipment.

Publications:

Annual Report.

Newsletter for members (monthly).

BTMA Handbook.

Advisory Notes to Contractors.

Secretary's address:

Ridgeway House, 6 Ridgeway Road, Long Ashton, Bristol BS18 9EU.

(b) Home Timber Merchants' Association of Northern Ireland

The object of the Association is to promote and further the common interests of the timber trade generally and particularly those of the timber trade in Northern Ireland.

Membership:

Firms or individuals engaged either in felling trees for sale in the round or in the conversion of home-grown timber in a sawmill in Northern Ireland, and associate members.

Publications:

None.

Secretary's address:

c/o 87, University Street, Belfast BT7 1HP.

(c) Home Timber Merchants' Association of Scotland

The Association is concerned with the numerous aspects of sawmilling and timber conversion in Scotland.

Membership:

Members of the timber trade.

Publications:

None.

Secretary's address:

16 Gordon Street, Glasgow G1 3QE.

(d) Timber Research and Development Association

This Association was originally known as the Timber Development Association.

Membership:

Ordinary members, associate members.

Publications:

Annual Report and *Concept in Wood.*

Secretary's address:

Stocking Lane, Hughenden Valley, High Wycombe, Bucks HP14

(e) British Wood Preserving Association

A scientific and advisory Association concerned with the preservation of timber in all its aspects.

Membership:

Commercial and non-commercial members.

Publications:
BWPA Manual.
Bulletin.
Record of Annual Convention.
Technical leaflets.
Secretary's address:
Premier House, 150 Southampton Row, London WC1B 5AL.

(f) Building Research Establishment—Timber Division
The Princes Risborough Laboratory, formerly the Forest Products Research Laboratory, was transferred to the Department of the Environment in 1971 and became part of the Building Research Establishment of which it now forms the Timber Division. The Division deals with all aspects of the use of timber and wood-based panels in buildings. These include the material and structural properties, durability and grading of timber, preservatives and protective finishes under adverse climatic conditions.
Address:
The Building Research Establishment, Timber Division, Garston, Watford WD2 7JR.

4. *Organizations concerned with the Business Aspects of Forestry*

(a) Timber Growers United Kingdom Ltd.
This body has its origins in the Timber Growers Organization which, in 1981, became Timber Growers England and Wales. At the same time the Scottish Woodland Owners Association changed its title to Timber Growers Scotland, and in 1983 the two concerns amalgamated to form Timber Growers United Kingdom Ltd.
Membership:
There are three classes: Woodland Owners, Associate Members and Company Members.
Addresses:
London Office: Agriculture House, Knightsbridge, London SW1X 7NJ.
Edinburgh Office: 5, Dublin Street Lane South, Edinburgh EH1 3PX.

(b) Scottish Woodlands Ltd.
Area covered:
This is divided into five regions: namely, Central (based in Lochgilphead), East (Perth), North (Inverness), South-East (Edinburgh) and South-West (Castle Douglas).
Secretary's address:
NCR House, 2 Roseburn Gardens, Edinburgh EH12 5NJ.

(c) Dwyfor Woodlands Ltd.
Area covered:
Lleyn Peninsula.
Secretary's address:
c/o Glynllivon Estate Office, Llanwnda, Caernarvon, Gwynedd LL54 5SP.

(d) Flintshire Woodlands Ltd.
Area covered:
Wales and North West and Central England.
Secretary's address:
Winston House, Bailey Hill, Mold, Clwyd CH7 1BR.

(e) Welsh Agricultural Organization Society Ltd
Area covered:
Wales.
Secretary's address:
P.O. Box 8, Brynawel, Great Darkgate Street, Aberystwyth, Dyfed SY23 1DR.

(f) British Christmas Tree Growers' Association
The objectives of the Association, which was formed in 1980, are:
(i) To promote home-grown Christmas trees.
(ii) To provide marketing assistance for members.
(iii) To give advice to members on the growing and care of Christmas trees.
(iv) To carry out market research so as to determine market prospects.
(v) To act as a forum for the exchange of ideas.
Membership:
Open to all growers of Christmas trees.
Secretary's address:
12 Lauriston Road, Wimbledon, London SW19 4TQ.

(g) Forestry Industry Committee of Great Britain
(i) This Committee was formed in January 1987 as a comprehensive grouping of enterprises, organizations and professional associations within the private sector of the forestry industry. In 1988 it was composed of sixteen constituent bodies.
(ii) It covers all forestry industry activities from silvicultural research to the commercial processing of timber, and affords the industry the means to debate and plan its future development.
(iii) Its objectives are:
  (1) To ensure the effective development of the forestry industry.
  (2) To promote a better and more informed understanding of the role of the industry in Great Britain and overseas.

(iv) In December 1987 the Committee published a document entitled *Beyond 2000*, which considered the anticipated developments of the industry up to the year 2000.

Secretary's address:
Agriculture House, Knightsbridge, London SW1X 7NJ.

5. *Bodies concerned with Conservation, Amenity and Similar Matters*

(a) *British Trust for Conservation Volunteers*

(i) The Trust was established in 1959 to involve and educate people in the practical conservation of wildlife and nature, both in countryside and urban areas.
(ii) It has developed a particular interest and skill in the management of small woods and larger woodland areas where amenity and conservation are management aims.
(iii) The Trust also runs training courses in conservation management, woodland crafts and similar skills.
(iv) A number of well-illustrated practical handbooks have been published by the Trust.

Address:
36 St Mary's Street, Wallingford, Oxfordshire OX10 OEU.

(b) *Countryside Commission*

(i) The Commission was set up in 1968 and is responsible for the conservation of the natural beauty of the English and Welsh countryside and for improving the facilities for its enjoyment. It is funded by the Department of the Environment.
(ii) It acts as the Government's adviser on countryside matters, designates national parks and areas of outstanding beauty and is concerned with national policies regarding forestry.
(iii) The Commission also:
  (1) Makes grants for tree planting and woodland management.
  (2) Provides funds for research into some aspects of forestry.
  (3) Comments on afforestation proposals in designated areas.
  (4) Promotes public access to woodlands.
(iv) After the great storm of 16 October 1987 the Commission set up a special unit, under the title of 'Task Force Trees', to deal with the damage.
(v) The Commission has issued a number of publications which deal with various aspects of the countryside.

Address:
John Dower House, Crescent Place, Cheltenham, Gloucestershire GL50 3RA.

(c) Countryside Commission for Scotland

(i) Established under the Countryside (Scotland) Act 1967, the Commission works to conserve the natural beauty of Scotland and to safeguard access for its enjoyment.

(ii) It encourages the conservation and management of old semi-natural and policy woodlands around country houses, and at the same time seeks to influence the siting, design and composition of new forests.

(iii) Farm woodland management is encouraged through advisory publications and advice which is largely provided through Farming, Forestry and Wildlife Group advisers.

(iv) Grants are available from the Commission for planting small areas of woodland, single trees, groups, avenues and other amenity features.

Address:
Battleby, Redgorton, Perth PH1 3EW.

(d) Farming and Wildlife Advisory Group

(i) Known in Scotland and Wales as the Farming, Forestry and Wildlife Advisory Group, it was formed on a national basis in 1970. During the next 12–14 years local or county groups were set up, and by 1988 there were sixty-five groups in the United Kingdom.

(ii) The objectives of the groups are to bring together all countryside interests—commercial, sporting and conservation—in order to reconcile their differences.

(iii) More than forty of the groups have full-time Farm Conservation Advisers who can advise farmers and landowners on conservation in the light of farming practices. This includes the management of farm woodlands with special reference to conservation.

(iv) The Group publishes a series of information booklets.

(v) Information on the Farming and Wildlife Trust will be found in the following section.

Address:
National Agricultural Centre, Stoneleigh, Kenilworth, Warwickshire CV8 2RX.

(e) The Game Conservancy Advisory Service

(i) Originating as the Eley Game Advisory Service, which was formed shortly after the Second World War, it is now part of The Game Conservancy.

(ii) Advice can be obtained on game management in all its aspects, including its integration with forestry and agriculture. This has become increasingly important in view of the growing demands on the countryside for public access and recreation, as well as the need to supplement farm incomes.

(iii) Information regarding the Game Conservancy Trust will be found in the next section.

Address:

The Advisory Service, The Game Conservancy, Fordingbridge, Hampshire SP6 1EF.

(f) Institute of Terrestrial Ecology

The Institute of Terrestrial Ecology (ITE) is one of the component institutes of the Natural Environment Research Council (NERC). The Institute studies the factors determining the structure, composition and processes of land and freshwater systems, and of individual plant and animal species. The research of the Institute is used to develop a sounder scientific basis for predicting and modelling environment trends arising from natural or man-made change, including forestry. The results of this research are available to those responsible for the protection, management and wise use of our natural resources. Nearly half of ITE's research is commissioned by Government and other agencies. The remainder is fundamental research supported by NERC. ITE's expertise is widely used by international organizations in overseas projects and programmes of research.

Addresses:

(i) Director, Terrestrial Ecology (North), Institute of Terrestrial Eclogy, Edinburgh Research Station, Bush Estate, Penicuik, Midlothian EH26 0QB.

(ii) Director, Terrestrial Ecology (South), Institute of Terrestrial Ecology, Monkswood Experimental Station, Abbots Ripton, Huntingdon PE17 2LS.

(g) Nature Conservancy Council

(i) The Council, which is the Government agency responsible for nature conservation, was established under the Nature Conservancy Council Act 1973.

(ii) Its duties include:

(1) The selection, establishment and management of National Nature Reserves.

(2) Advising the Government on matters affecting nature conservation.

(3) The notification of areas of special scientific interest for conservation.

(4) Giving advice and supplying information on nature conservation.

(5) Commissioning or supporting research into matters relevant to the above.

(iii) In the case of forestry, the Council has been very active in connection with the following:

(1) The conduct of forestry in National Nature Reserves.

(2) Reconciling forestry with conservation in areas of special scientific interest.
(3) Preparing a provisional inventory of ancient, semi-natural woodlands in Britain.
(4) Advising on many forestry topics such as the Farm Woodlands Scheme and Planning locations for forestry.

(iv) The Council has issued numerous publications on various aspects of conservation.

Address:
The Nature Conservancy Council, Northminster House, Peterborough PE1 1UA.

6. *Trusts for Research and Education in Forestry and other Related Subjects*

(a) The Scottish Forestry Trust
(i) Founded in 1983 by Timber Growers Scotland Ltd, which now forms a constituent part of Timber Growers United Kingdom Ltd.
(ii) The aim of the Trust is to further 'the objects of education, training, research and other allied matters relative to forestry in the United Kingdom'.
(iii) Grants are made for approved research and educational training projects.
(iv) Full details can be obtained from the Director, 5 Dublin Street Lane South, Edinburgh EH1 3PX.

(b) The Forestry Trust for Conservation and Education
(i) Set up by the Royal Forestry Society of England, Wales and Northern Ireland in 1988.
(ii) The purpose of the Trust is to demonstrate to the general public, schools and other professions, that productive forestry is not only compatible with the conservation of wildlife but can be of the greatest assistance by providing valuable wildlife habitats.
(iii) Further information can be obtained from the General Administrator, 102 High Street, Tring, Hertfordshire HP23 4AH.

(c) The Game Conservancy Trust
(i) Established as a Registered Charity in 1980 following the merger of the Game Research Association and the Eley Game Advisory Service.
(ii) The objects of the Trust are:
(1) To advance the education of the public in game biology.
(2) To conduct research into various aspects of game including breeding, feeding, habits and diseases.

(3) To study the effect of game on the environment, including its bearing on forestry and woodland management.
(4) To publish the results of such investigations where appropriate.

(iii) Details of the Trust are available from the Director, The Game Conservancy Trust, Fordingbridge, Hampshire SP6 1EF.

(d) The Farming and Wildlife Trust Ltd

(i) Formed in 1984 for the purpose of promoting and supporting the Farming and Wildlife Advisory Groups throughout the United Kingdom.

(ii) The main functions of the Trust are:
(1) To raise and administer funds for this purpose, and especially for the appointment of Farm Conservation Advisers.
(2) To provide a national focus for the advisory groups.
(3) To provide a framework for the farming, forestry and conservation interests that are involved.

(iii) Additional information is obtainable from the Director, the Farming and Wildlife Trust Ltd, National Agricultural Centre, Stoneleigh, Kenilworth, Warwickshire CV8 2RX.

CHAPTER XXVIII

Forest Gardens and Forest Parks

1. *Forest Gardens*

FOREST gardens may be defined as areas which have been laid out in plots or groups in each of which a different species or a predetermined mixture of species has been established. The plots are usually between 0·1 and 0·8 hectares (¼ and 2 acres) in size.

(a) Bedgebury

(i) In 1929 a forest garden was established next to the National Pinetum at Bedgebury, Kent, between Cranbrook, Goudhurst and Hawkhurst.

(ii) The site was originally part of Bedgebury Forest and in 1972 the garden covered approximately 18 hectares (45 acres) on which 97 species had been planted in 151 plots.

(iii) However, the great storm in October 1987 caused very considerable damage and approximately 70% of the Forest Plots were blown down while between 25% and 30% of the specimen trees in the Pinetum were lost.

(iv) In 1988 action was taken to replace the losses in the Pinetum, and it was hoped that the Forest Plots would eventually be replanted.

(v) Further information on the Pinetum will be found in Forestry Commission publication *A Guide to Bedgebury National Pinetum* (1986).

(b) Ceiriog

(i) This forest garden, which lies some 4·8 km (3 miles) west of Chirk, between Oswestry and Llangollen on the London–Holyhead road (A5), covers an area of about 20 hectares (50 acres). It was laid out between 1907 and 1910 and comprised some 51 plots.

(ii) Extensive damage was caused by a severe ice storm in February 1940 and consequently the plots were almost completely clear felled. Replanting, mainly with commercial conifers, was completed in 1949, and in 1965 there were 36 plots and three shelter belts. The area is the property of the Clwyd County

Council but is managed in co-operation with the Department of Forestry and Wood Sciences of the University College of North Wales, Bangor.

(iii) The garden was originally described in Forestry Commission Bulletin No. 12, *Forest Gardens*, which was issued in 1931, but a more recent account has been given in *Y Coedwigwr* (*The Forester*) vol. 4, no. 2 (1961–62) published by The Forestry and Wood Science Society of The University College of North Wales.

(c) Cirencester

(i) Also known as the Rough Hills Experimental Plots, this forest garden is situated about 4·8 km (3 miles) west of Cirencester on the Cirencester–Stroud road (A419).

(ii) It was established between 1903 and 1905 under the supervision of F. C. M'Clellan who was then Lecturer in Forestry at the Royal Agricultural College, Cirencester. The site extends to about 4·0 hectares (10 acres), of which half is covered by shelter belts. Although since 1947 some of the plots have been felled on account of damage by wind and disease, replanting has been carried out as required. The management plan for the garden, which is the property of the Bathurst Estate, is agreed between the Estate and the Lecturer in Forestry at the College.

(iii) A guide to the garden was published in 1951 under the title of *An Experiment in Forestry*.

(d) Coed Mor

(i) This is an experimental area of about 12 hectares (30 acres) which is situated in Anglesey between the Britannia Bridge and the Suspension Bridge about 6·4 km (4 miles) from Bangor.

(ii) It was previously a devastated woodland area and was replanted between 1961 and 1964. It is owned by the University College, Bangor. There is also an arboretum containing 150 species of trees in 1988.

(e) Crarae

(i) The forest garden and arboretum are adjacent to Crarae House, which stands on the northern bank of Loch Fyne. The village of Crarae lies on the Inverary–Lochgilphead road (A83) about 19 km (12 miles) south-west of Inverary.

(ii) Planting was begun by Sir George Campbell of Succouth, Bt, in 1933, and the property was subsequently presented by him to the Forestry Commission in 1955. In 1980 there were 38 plots and 132 groups of exotic trees covering 13·7 hectares (34 acres), several plots having been blown down in the gales of 1968.

(iii) Full details can be obtained from Sir Ilay Campbell, Bt, Cumlodden Estate Office, Crarae, Inveraray, Argyll PA32 8YA (telephone no. 05466 633).

(f) Kilmun

(i) Kilmun forest garden is situated some 4·8 km (3 miles) due north of Dunoon and adjoins the A880 road on the north-east side of Holy Loch which opens into the Firth of Clyde.

(ii) Extending to 48 hectares (120 acres), it was established by the Forestry Commission in 1930 with the object of testing the suitability of species for the west coast of Scotland. In 1980 there were 146 plots and 213 groups containing altogether 214 different species.

(iii) Further information is available from the Forest District Manager, Cowal Forest District, Kilmun, Dunoon, Argyll PA23 8SE (telephone no. 036984 666).

2. *National Forest Parks*

(*a*) The origin of the National Forest Parks can be traced to *The Report of the Committee on National Parks 1931* and to the appointment of a Committee, in March 1935, to advise on the use of surplus land which the Commission owned in Argyllshire. The Committee's recommendations, which were contained in *The Report of the National Forest Park Committee 1935*, were followed by the opening of the first park—the Argyll National Forest Park—in the same year.

(*b*) Another Committee was appointed in 1936 to consider the formation of a forest park in Snowdonia, while in the following year a further Committee was set up to report on the feasibility of the Forest of Dean being designated a Forest Park.

(*c*) Since then other National Forest Parks have been set up and by 1988 the following had been formed.

Argyll Forest Park
(between Loch Long and Loch Fyne)
Border Forest Park
(parts of Cumbria, Dumfriesshire, Northumberland and Roxburghshire)
Dean Forest Park
Delamere Forest Park
(between Chester and Northwich)
Galloway Forest Park
Glenmore Forest Park
(The Cairngorms)
Grizedale Forest Park
(between Lake Windermere and Coniston Water)
New Forest
North Riding Forest Park
(between Pickering and Scarborough)

Queen Elizabeth Forest Park
(Loch Lomond–Aberfoyle–Loch Achray)
Snowdonia Forest Park
Tummel Forest Park
(Loch Rannoch–Pitlochry–Aberfeldy)

(*d*) In 1988, guides to the following localities were available from the Forestry Commission:

Explore the New Forest.
Glenmore Forest Park.
Kielder Forests.
The Secret Forest of Dean.

CHAPTER XXIX

Education and Training

1. *The Forestry Training Council*

(*a*) The Council is the non-statutory training organization for forestry and was reconstituted in 1987 to fill this role.

(*b*) It co-ordinates all requests for training and also certifies Approved Instructors who operate both independently and on behalf of the Council.

(*c*) Administrative matters are dealt with by the Forestry Commission on behalf of the Council, which is located in the Commission's headquarters at 231 Corstorphine Road, Edinburgh EH12 7AT.

2. *Training for Forest Workers*

(*a*) Training for young people can be obtained through the Youth Training Scheme which is administered by the Manpower Services Commission. It consists of two years with an approved employer and further education on block release.

(*b*) Technical education can follow, and is in accordance with the City and Guilds examinations, the regulations and syllabus of which can be obtained from the City and Guilds of London Institute, 76 Portland Place, London W1N 4AA. In Scotland the forestry certificate and diploma of the Scottish Vocational Education Council (SCOTVEC) are the equivalents.

(*c*) In England and Wales the examinations are divided into three stages, while in Scotland they are composed of a series of modules.

Stage I
This consists of two block-release courses of 6 weeks, which are held at the Cumbria College of Agriculture and Forestry, Newton Rigg, Penrith, Cumbria.

Stage II
This can be taken after a further block-release course of not less than 6 weeks, which may be taken in or after the third year. It is

also possible to specialize in certain subjects such as felling and conversion, during or after the fourth year.

Stage III
This exam, which can be taken later, is designed for those who hope to become foresters, and gives the holder the opportunity to proceed to the National Diploma of the Business and Technician Educational Council (BTECH).

3. *Training for Head Foresters*

(*a*) The definition of the title 'head forester' varies to some extent, but in this section it is used to denote a 'supervisor responsible for labour management and for technical decisions'.

(*b*) Whether for service in the Commission or on private estates, head foresters now qualify by taking the National Diploma in Forestry of the Business and Technician Educational Council (BTECH). For this a 3-year 'sandwich' course, commencing each year in September, is provided by the Cumbria College of Agriculture and Forestry. In Scotland the equivalent is the Scottish Vocational Educational Council's forestry diploma.

(*c*) Those wishing to undertake these courses must:

(i) be in possession of four 'O' levels in the General Certificate of Education or in the Scottish Certificate of Education, which must include English, mathematics and a biological or physical science;

(ii) have 2 years practical experience.

(*d*) Applications for the course should be made either to the principal of the Cumbria College of Agriculture and Forestry or to the Principal of the Scottish School of Forestry, Inverness Technical College, Inverness.

4. *Central Forestry Examination Board*

(*a*) Formed in 1951, its members are appointed by the following constituent bodies: the Forestry Commission; the Royal Scottish Forestry Society; the Royal Forestry Society of England, Wales and Northern Ireland; the Institute of Chartered Foresters and the Society of Irish Foresters.

(*b*) The Board holds examinations every year and awards the National Diploma in Forestry to successful candidates.

(*c*) Further details can be obtained from the Secretary, 52 Carr Lane, Acomb, York YO2 5HX.

5. *Training for Forest Managers*

(*a*) The qualifications required for forest managers are a degree from one of the universities referred to below, or the National Diploma of Forestry of the Central Forestry Examination Board.

(b) University of Aberdeen

(i) Two courses in forestry are available for either a 3-year ordinary degree or a 4-year honours degree.

(ii) Applicants should possess five 'O' levels in the General Certificate of Education or the Scottish Certificate of Education, including the following subjects: English, mathematics, chemistry and physics and two or three 'A' levels or four or five Scottish Highers. In both cases at least two of the passes must be in science subjects, and required grades of pass are specified.

(c) University of Edinburgh

(i) The following degrees are available:

(1) a 3-year ordinary degree in ecological science;

(2) a 4-year honours degree in ecological science with honours in forestry in the final year;

(3) a 4-year joint honours degree in ecological science with honours in agriculture, forestry and rural economy in the final year;

(4) at postgraduate level: a 1-year taught course leading to an M.Sc. or diploma in resource management or a Ph.D. and M.Phil. degrees by dissertation in forestry topics.

(ii) Entry requirements for undergraduate courses are: Scottish Certificate of Education or General Certificate of Education 'O'level passes in English and either four Scottish Certificate Higher or three General Certificate 'A'-level passes. The 'H' and 'A' subjects must include chemistry and any two of biology, mathematics and physics, provided that biology, mathematics and physics have all been passed at least at 'O' level.

(iii) Entry requirement for postgraduate courses is a good honours degree in an acceptable discipline.

(d) University of Oxford

(i) A 3-year honours degree in pure and applied biology with a heavy emphasis on agricultural and forest production, conservation, protection, soils and economics.

(ii) Candidates must be accepted by a College of the University. Most places are given on the results of the Oxford Colleges' Entrance Examination held in November and December each year. The examination is usually based on the candidate's 'A'-level subjects with a general paper and an interview.

(iii) A 1-year M.Sc. course in 'Forestry and its Relation to Land Use' is open to those with acceptable degrees, usually of the minimum standard of an upper second class honours first degree, in appropriate subjects.

(iv) Postgraduate research degrees (M.Sc. and D.Phil.) are offered in a range of biological, environmental, sociological and technical topics related to forestry.

(e) University College of North Wales, Bangor

(i) Three-year courses are offered in forestry at honours degree level. Courses are also available in agroforestry, wood science, soils and forest science, and in forestry and applied zoology. An optional 'sandwich' year is available between the second and third year of the forestry course and the wood science course.

(ii) Those wishing to enter must matriculate in the University of Wales in English and have either three 'A' levels or two 'A' levels and two 'AS' levels in specified subjects. There are special matriculation conditions for those who are over 21 years of age.

CHAPTER XXX

Publications, Periodicals and Libraries

1. *Publications*

Two developments have become apparent, in the case of forestry publications, since 1982. In the first place many more booklets and leaflets dealing with specialized aspects of forestry have been published rather than books which cover a wider field. Secondly, several bodies have begun to produce their own publicatons on matters which concern trees or forestry, and in which they have a particular interest. Information on some of these is given below.

(a) British Trust for Conservation Volunteers

(ii) The Trust issues several very practical and well-illustrated publications and these include *Woodlands*, *Hedging* and *Fencing*.

(ii) A catalogue of publications is available from the Trust at 36 St Mary's Street, Wallingford, Oxfordshire OX10 0EU.

(b) Countryside Commission

(i) The Commission's publications as regards forestry include *Forestry in the Countryside* and a series of leaflets on such matters as trees, hedges, game habitats on the farm and the management of small woodlands.

(ii) A catalogue can be obtained from Countryside Commission publications, 19/23 Albert Road, Manchester M19 2EQ.

(c) Farming and Wildlife Advisory Group

(i) The Group has published a number of information leaflets on matters connected with farming, forestry and wildlife, and among these are the following titles: *A Guide to Planting Trees and Shrubs for Wildlife and the Landscape*, *Farm Woodland* and *Trees on Farms in the Lowlands*.

(ii) A list of these leaflets, which are divided into three categories—those for use in England, those for Scotland and those for Northern Ireland—can be obtained from the Group at the National Agricultural Centre, Stoneleigh, Kenilworth, CV8 2RH.

(d) The Forestry Commission

(i) The publications of the Commission have provided an invaluable source of accurate and up-to-date information on forestry matters since 1920.

(ii) As the number of publications increased it was found to be more satisfactory to issue them in different formats, and these ultimately included bulletins, booklets, forest records, leaflets, and research and development papers.

(iii) In November 1986 it was decided to reorganize these categories, and that in future the majority of the Commission's priced technical publications would appear as bulletins, handbooks or field books. Booklets, forest records, leaflets and research and development papers would be discontinued as from this date, although they would still be available as long as stocks remained. However, Arboricultural Leaflets and Occasional Papers will still be issued. Research Information Notes are unpriced and single copies are available on application; all new issues can be sent on payment of an annual handling charge.

(iv) A catalogue of the Commission's publications is issued each year and is available from the Publications Section, Forestry Commission, Forest Research Station, Alice Holt Lodge, Wrecclesham, Farnham, Surrey GU10 4LH.

(e) Forestry Industry Committee of Great Britain

Set up in January 1987, the Committee published a booklet entitled *Beyond 2000* in December of that year. This examines the present position in forestry and the anticipated developments, future opportunities and challenges which face it.

(f) Nature Conservancy Council

(i) The Council has produced a variety of publications, some of which are concerned with trees and forestry.

(ii) A catalogue is available from Department LA, Publications, Nature Conservancy Council, Northminster House, Peterborough PE1 1UA.

(g) The Royal Forestry Society of England, Wales and Northern Ireland

(i) The Society's publications include *Oceanic Forestry*, *Forestry and Conservation* and *Birds and Coniferous Plantations*.

(ii) These can be obtained from the Society at 102 High Street, Tring, Hertfordshire HP23 4AH.

2. *Periodicals*

The following forestry periodicals were published in 1988.

(a) Arbor
(i) Published annually by the Aberdeen University Forestry Society.
(ii) Editor's address: c/o The Department of Forestry, The University of Aberdeen, Old Aberdeen AB9 2UU.

(b) Commonwealth Forestry Review
(i) Published quarterly by the Commonwealth Forestry Association.
(ii) Editor's address: c/o The Oxford Forestry Institute, South Parks Road, Oxford OX1 3RB.

(c) Forestry
(i) Published quarterly by the Institute of Chartered Foresters.
(ii) Editor's address: 22 Walker Street, Edinburgh EH3 7HR.

(d) Forestry Abstracts, Forest Products Abstracts and Agroforestry Abstracts
(i) These three publications are prepared by the Commonwealth Forestry Bureau and published by Commonwealth Agricultural Bureau International (CABI).
(ii) Editor's address: Commonwealth Agricultural Bureau International, Wallingford, Oxfordshire OX10 8DE.

(e) Forestry and British Timber
(i) Published monthly by Benn Publications plc.
(ii) Editor's address: Benn Publications plc, Sovereign Way, Tonbridge, Kent TN9 1RW.

(f) Irish Forestry
(i) Published half-yearly by the Society of Irish Foresters.
(ii) Editor's address: c/o The Royal Dublin Society, Ballsbridge, Dublin 4, Eire.

(g) Quarterly Journal of Forestry
(i) Published quarterly by the Royal Forestry Society of England, Wales and Northern Ireland.
(ii) Editor's address: 102 High Street, Tring, Herts HP23 4AH.

(h) Scottish Forestry
(i) Published quarterly by the Royal Scottish Forestry Society.
(ii) Editor's address: 11 Atholl Crescent, Edinburgh EH3 8HE.

(i) Slasher
(i) Published six times a year by the Forestry Commission.
(ii) Editor's address: 231 Corstorphine Road, Edinburgh EH12 7AT.

Note. Although published for members of the Forestry Commission, copies can be obtained for those who are not members on application to the Information Branch at the above address.

(j) Timber Grower
(i) Published quarterly by Timber Growers United Kingdom Ltd.
(ii) Editor's address: Agriculture House, Knightsbridge, London SW1X 7NJ.

(k) Timber Trades Journal
(i) Published weekly by Benn Publications plc.
(ii) Editor's address: Benn Publications plc, Sovereign Way, Tonbridge, Kent TN9 1RW.

(l) Trees
(i) Published half-yearly by the Men of the Trees.
(ii) Editor's address: Crawley Down, Crawley, Sussex RH10 4HL.

(m) Y Coedwigw (The Forester)
(i) Published annually by The Forestry and Wood Science Society of the University College of North Wales.
(ii) Editor's address: c/o School of Agricultural and Forest Sciences, University College of North Wales, Bangor, Gwynedd LL57 2UW.

3. *Libraries*

The following bodies and societies have established libraries which are concerned with forestry and its allied subjects, at the address given below. Those who wish to visit one of these libraries should get in touch with the librarian beforehand.

The Forestry Commission at Alice Holt Lodge, Wrecclesham, Farnham, Surrey CU10 4LH.

The Oxford Forestry Institute at South Parks Road, Oxford OX1 3RB.

The Building Research Establishment, Timber Division, Garston, Watford WD2 7JR.

The Department of Forestry at The University of Aberdeen, Old Aberdeen AB9 2UU.

The Central Science Library, The University College of North Wales, Bangor, Gwynedd LL57 2UW.

The Department of Forestry and Natural Resources, The University of Edinburgh at The Darwin Library, The King's Buildings, Mayfield Road, Edinburgh EH9 3JU.

The Royal Scottish Forestry Society. The Society's library has now been merged with that of the University of Edinburgh, Department of Forestry and Natural Resources at the address given above.

The Royal Forestry Society of England, Wales and Northern Ireland, at 102 High Street, Tring, Herts HP23 4AH.

The Timber Research and Development Association at Hughenden Valley, High Wycombe, Bucks HP14 4ND.

CHAPTER XXXI

Machinery and Equipment

1. *Introduction*

(*a*) During the first 10 years or so which followed the Second World War, few machines or implements were produced which were specifically designed for forestry work. Since then, the position has changed considerably and a large amount of machinery and equipment is now available.

(*b*) However, much of this has been designed for use in timber harvesting and utilization and is of foreign origin or manufacture.

(*c*) In the following sections, lists are given of the types of machines and equipment which are available at the present time. These are arranged in groups according to the forest operation for which they were designed or for which they may be used.

2. *Preparation, Planting and Weeding*

(a) Preparatory work

The following are some of the machines which are available:

Bulldozers for road or ride construction

Graders for road-making

Post drivers and post-hole diggers for fencing

Flail and rotary cutters for scrub and undergrowth clearing

Brush cutters and clearing saws

Tractors (usually on tracks) fitted with hydraulically operated tines (in place of a bucket) for scrub clearance

Ditching machines

Ploughs. The Forestry Commission has carried out a great deal of research on the production of ploughs for use in planting moorland and upland sites. For further information reference should be made to Forestry Commission Leaflet No. 70, *Forest Ploughs*.

(b) Planting

(i) Although planting machines designed for use in forestry are to be seen occasionally at demonstrations of forestry machinery, these are invariably of foreign manufacture. Experiments in this country have not resulted in a planting machine being placed on the market during recent years.

(ii) There are undoubtedly considerable difficulties in designing a machine that can operate on land which may either contain the stumps of the previous crop or be a moorland site which, after ploughing, consists of a succession of large ridges and deep furrows.

(c) Weeding

(i) In recent years herbicides have largely replaced mechanical methods for weeding plantations although the following are still in use to some extent:

Brush cutters carried by the operator by means of a body harness
Strimmers
Tractor-mounted swipes.

(ii) Further information on weeding will be found in Forestry Commission Handbook No. 2, *Trees and Weeds*, and Bulletin No. 51, *The Use of Herbicides in the Forest.*

3. *Felling and Extraction*

(a) Felling

(i) Power saws have now replaced hand felling for all practical purposes.

(ii) Further information on chain saws will be found in Chapter XIV.

(b) Extraction

The following is a list of machines and equipment which can be used in the extraction of timber and thinnings.

(i) *Skidders, forwarders and cablecranes*
These are described in Chapter XIV.

(ii) *Loaders and crane loaders*
The term loader can be used to describe two entirely different types of equipment which may be described as follows:

(1) Tractors fitted with an hydraulically operated front-end mounted grab. These are known as independent loaders, and after a log has been lifted by the grab the tractor moves to the point where the log is to be loaded onto a vehicle or placed on a stack.

(2) Hydraulically operated equipment, which is also known as a grapple crane or hoist. This can be fixed to a lorry or

tractor unit and is able to load material independently of any other vehicle or tractor.

(3) Further information on extraction and loading will be found in Bulletin No. 14, *Forestry Practice.*

(iii) *Helicopters*

The extraction of timber and thinnings from sites where access is especially difficult can be carried out by helicopter, and several air-operating firms offer such services.

4. *Processing and Harvesting*

(*a*) Two types of machine, known respectively as processors and harvesters, have been designed for use in the forest.

(*b*) Processors, also known as limber–buckers, can remove the branches of felled trees and cross-cut them to length. There are three main types: bed processors, grapple processors and sliding boom processors.

(*c*) Harvesters which are also termed feller–limber–buckers, are designed to fell trees as well as delimbing and cross-cutting them.

5. *Preparation of Produce*

The following are some of the machines and equipment which are available for converting forest material into more saleable produce:

Portable saw benches. The most suitable type is fitted with three-point linkage and is driven from the tractor-power take/off.

De-barking or peeling machines. These are essential when converting thinnings which are to be impregnated.

Chipping machines. These are available as tractor-mounted machines which can deal with small trees and crooked material as well as the usual waste, irrespective of species.

Log-splitting machines. Their use has been encouraged by the increasing popularity of log-burning stoves.

6. *Nursery Work*

(*a*) A number of specialized machines and accessories have been developed by the Forestry Commission for nursery work although the use of some of these may not be economically justified in the smaller estate nurseries.

(*b*) The following is a list of the machines concerned:

Nursery ploughs
Cultivators
Seed-sowing machines

Tractor hauled seed rollers
Lining-out ploughs
Transplanting machines
Root pruners for undercutting seedlings
Plant lifters.

(c) Further information on these will be found in Forestry Commission Bulletin No. 43, *Nursery Practice*.

7. *Miscellaneous*

Other items which may be of assistance in woodland management include the following:

(a) Cross-country vehicles

There are now an increasing number of cross-country vehicles being manufactured and these can be divided into three categories:

(i) The Land Rover and those vehicles which are built after the style of the Land Rover.

(ii) Four-wheel-drive cars.

(iii) Specialized 'all-terrain' vehicles, some of which are fitted with light tracks or sets of multiple wheels, while others are in the form of bicycles or tricycles. They can operate in snow, over bogs or under exceptionally difficult conditions, in addition to the usual cross-country work.

(b) Stump removers

These can either be of the type which is operated through a tractor-power take-off or are fitted with their own self-contained power unit.

(c) Hedge trimmers

Hedge trimmers are now generally fitted with a flail cutting mechanism.

CHAPTER XXXII

Safety in Forestry

1. *General Considerations*

(*a*) The increased emphasis which is now being placed on safety is due, to a large extent, to the major changes which have taken place in forestry operations during recent years. The slower movements of the axe, the cross-cut saw and the horse have been replaced by the speed and comparative complexity of the power saw, the forwarder and the lorry.

(*b*) The need for greater safety precautions has been brought about mainly by the following:

(i) The greater use of machinery in the woods, particularly in connection with felling and extraction.

(ii) The extension of piece-work in some operations which encourages work to be carried out more quickly and in so doing can increase the risk of accidents.

(iii) The employment and application of chemicals especially in the case of herbicides.

2. *The Forestry Safety Council*

(*a*) This body was set up by the Forestry Commission on 1 April 1974 with the following terms of reference:

(i) To promote safety in forestry by every means including the encouragement of co-operation and consultation at all levels within the industry.

(ii) To make representations to the Health and Safety Commission Executive on the special problems of forestry and be consulted by them on proposed legislation, regulations and other revelant matters.

(iii) To sponsor the production and maintenance of forest industry safety guides.

(iv) To co-ordinate publicity and the collection of statistics on health and safety matters and to encourage research into health and safety.

(v) To liaise with the Forestry Training Council and other appropriate bodies on education and training in forestry.

(vi) To review and report progress annually to the Minister of Agriculture, Fisheries and Food and the Secretary of State for Scotland, through the Forestry Commissioners, who will submit the report to the Home Grown Timber Advisory Committee.

(*b*) One important function of the Forestry Safety Council has been the preparation and publication of leaflets covering the safety aspects of the use of certain machinery and equipment and the carrying out of a selection of operations. These are known as 'Forest Industry Safety Guides' and the following is a list of those which were available in April 1988. Copies can be obtained free of charge from The Secretary, Forestry Safety Council, Forestry Commission, 231 Corstorphine Road, Edinburgh EH12 7AT.

1. Clearing Saw
2. Ultra Low Volume Herbicide Spraying
3. Application of Herbicides by Knapsack Spraying
4. Application of Granular Herbicide
6. Tractor Mounted Weeding Machines
7. Planting
8. Hand Weeding
9. Brashing and Pruning with Handsaw
10. The Chain Saw
11. Felling by Chain Saw
12. Chain Saw Snedding
13. Cross-Cutting and Stacking
14. Takedown of Hung-up Trees
15. Chain Saw Clearance of Windblow
17. Felling Large Hardwoods
18. Tree Climbing and Pruning
21. Forest Tractors
22. Extraction by Skidder
23. Extaction by Forwarder
24. Processor (Limber Bucker)
25. Extraction by Cablecrane
26. Use of Tractors with Winches in Directional Felling and Takedown
30. Mobile Saw Bench
31. Mobile Pelling Machine
32. Fencing
33. Hand Held Power Posthole Borer
34. First Aid
35. All-Terrain Cycles

N. Noise and Hearing Conservation

(*c*) All employees should be completely conversant with those guides that apply to the type of work on which they are employed.

They should also be given training in their work, as explained in the guides. Those who are self-employed should also become fully acquainted with the contents.

(*d*) Attention has already been drawn to a number of these leaflets in earlier chapters where appropriate.

(*e*) Where protective clothing is considered to be necessary for the operation concerned, details are given in the appropriate leaflet.

3. *Health and Safety at Work Act 1974*

(a) General

(i) This Act, which received the Royal Assent on 31 July 1974, sets out the law relating to the health, safety and welfare of those working in the forest, whether employed or self-employed, and also of members of the public who might consequently be affected.

(ii) On 1 October 1974 the Health and Safety Commission was set up under th Act. This body has the duty of developing health and safety and of drawing up new regulations when necessary.

(b) Duties imposed by the Act

(i) Employers must, so far as is reasonably practical, safeguard their employees by:
  (1) providing safe plant and machinery
  (2) adopting safe systems of work
  (3) ensuring proper training, instruction and supervision.

(ii) Employees and self-employed persons must take reasonable care of their own health and safety and also that of members of the public who may be affected by their work.

(iii) Manufacturers and suppliers must provide machinery and equipment which is safe to use.

(c) Notices and inspectors

(i) Two types of notices may be served by inspectors appointed under the Act:
  (1) Improvement Notices which state what action should be taken.
  (2) Prohibition Notices which require a complete or partial stoppage of work, if the action required by an Improvement Notice is not taken within a given time. The Notice can require an immediate stoppage if there is a serious safety hazard.

(ii) Appeals against notices can be made to an Industrial Tribunal.

(iii) The authority which is concerned with the enforcement of health and safety regulations relating to forestry, is the

Agricultural Inspectorate of the Health and Safety Executive, St Hugh's House, Stanley Precinct, Bootle L20 3QY.

(d) Codes of practice
(i) Regulations may be supplemented by codes of practice which can be used in criminal proceedings, as evidence of the infringement of a statutory requirement.
(ii) The Health and Safety Commission can prepare codes of practice and approve those which have been drawn up by other authorities.

4. *Safety Committees and Representatives*

Regulations relating to safety committees and safety representatives came into force on 1 October 1974 and the effect of these may be summarized as follows:

(a) Safety representatives
A recognized trade union can appoint safety representatives from amongst the employees of an employer who recognizes it. Such representatives should have at least 2 years experience in their particular work.

(b) Safety committees
(i) These can be set up where two or more employees ask their employer to do so.
(ii) The membership of the committee should be agreed by the management and the union members.

Further information will be found in the Health and Safety Council's booklet *Safety Representatives and Safety Committees*, which can be obtained from H.M. Stationery Office.

5. *Statutory Instruments concerning Safety*

The following Statutory Instruments should be noted.

SI 1957/1386	The Agriculture (Power Take-off) Regulations 1957.
SI 1959/427	The Agriculture (Circular Saw) Regulations 1959.
SI 1959/1216	The Agriculture (Stationary Machinery) Regulations 1959.
SI 1962/1472	The Agriculture (Field Machinery) Regulations 1962.
SI 1971/694	The Road Vehicles (Lighting) Regulations 1961.

SI 1973/24	The Motor Vehicular (Construction and Use) Regulations 1973.
SI 1974/2034	The Agriculture (Tractor Cabs) Regulations 1974.
SI 1980/1036	The Agriculture (Tractor Cabs) (Amendment) Regulations 1980.
SI 1981/917	Health and Safety (First Aid) Regulations 1981.
SI 1984/605	The Agriculture (Tractor Cabs) Regulations 1984.
SI 1985/2023	The Reporting of Injuries, Disease and Dangerous Occurrences Regulations 1985.

CHAPTER XXXIII

A Calendar of Forestry Work

THE following suggestions as to the work which may be put in hand each month depend on various factors, such as the season, the locality, and weather conditions. For details of the operations referred to, reference should be made to the appropriate chapter on the subject. It should be emphasized, however, that operations such as brashing, cleaning, pruning, and thinning can, if necessary, be done at most times of the year. Although traditionally, felling was restricted to the winter months, thinning, more particularly of conifers often continues throughout the year, especially if there is a large area to cover.

1. *January*

(a) Woodlands

(i) If the weather is open, planting should continue if it has not yet been completed, with the exception of Corsican pine, which should not be planted until March, if possible. On no account should planting take place in frosty weather, or cold drying winds.

(ii) Thinning of plantations and felling generally can be carried out. Less damage will be done to rides, gateways, and field if extraction is deferred until a hard frost.

(iii) When conifers are felled the cones should be collected if the seed is required, and if the trees are of a suitable type.

(iv) General maintenance work in the woods should be put in hand. This will include cleaning ditches, repairing gates and fences, trimming hedges, and making up rides. The usual steps should be taken to keep down rabbits, and after the first fall of snow the opportunity should be taken to see if any rabbit tracks occur inside areas surrounded by wire netting. Snow also assists in following the movements of deer.

(b) Nursery

(i) As transplants are lifted and despatched to the woods for planting, the vacant beds should be cultivated if the weather and soil permit.

(ii) Consider the reallocation of the nursery area for the spring, whether new seed beds should be laid out, and which areas are to be fallowed or manured.

(iii) Transplanting of hawthorn should be completed this month, if possible.

2. *February*

(a) Woodlands

(i) Continue planting so long as the weather is suitable.

(ii) Settle the details of next season's planting programme, so that if transplants are to be ordered from nurserymen ample notice may be given of one's requirement.

(iii) Continue thinning and felling.

(iv) Continue general maintenance work.

(b) Nursery

(i) Seedlings may be lifted and lined out.

(ii) Where seedlings are purchased from commercial nurseries these should be lined out as soon as they arrive.

(iii) Poplar cuttings should now be taken, and planted in the nursery.

3. *March*

(a) Woodlands

(i) Corsican pine should be planted during this month for preference, although planting may have to start earlier if a large area is to be completed. The planting of all species should be completed by the end of this month.

(ii) March is a particularly dangerous month for forest fires. Fire equipment should be checked over, patrols organized, and where ploughed rides or firebreaks have been laid out, these should be scarified. Unploughed rides should be cut.

(iii) The cutting of coppice should be completed by the end of the month.

(b) Nursery

(i) Transplanting and lining out should be finished by the end of this month, or early April.

(ii) If the seed beds are to be moved to another part of the nursery, work on the new site should be put in hand.

4. *April*

(a) Woodlands

(i) Particular attention should still be paid to fire hazards, until young green growth of surface vegetation is well developed.

(ii) If all other work in the woods and nursery is completed, a start may be made on clearing the areas to be planted next season.

(iii) Bark for tanning should be peeled as soon as the sap rises. This is normally from mid-April to mid-June.

(b) Nursery

(i) Lining out should be finished early this month.

(ii) The nursery should be put in order, hedges trimmed, and the whole tied up.

5. *May*

(a) Woodlands

(i) This month should be considered primarily as an opportunity to take stock of the season's work. It can provide a breathing space between the winter's planting and the summer's weeding of plantations. In particular, the following work should be put in hand:

(1) Check over and repair all tools and equipment.

(2) Order any new tools, wire netting, etc.

(3) Take stock in the nursery, and order any young trees if these have not been ordered already.

(ii) Grey squirrels must not be overlooked. They are active at this time of year.

(b) Nursery

Special attention should be given to weed control.

6. *June*

(a) Woodlands

(i) Weeding of young plantations should start this month.

(ii) General maintenance of gates and fences.

(iii) A careful watch should be kept for pine weevils (*Hylobius* and *Pissodes*) from now until the end of September.

(b) Nursery

Work in the nursery will now consist largely of weed control. The seed beds may require protection from the sun in hot weather. Watering may have to be undertaken.

7. *July*

(a) Woodlands

(i) Weed young plantations.
(ii) Cut and trim rides, if necessary.

(b) Nursery

Ensure that weeds are kept in check.

8. *August*

(a) Woodlands

(i) Continue weeding of young plantations. Where weed growth is rapid, a second weeding may be necessary.
(ii) Cleaning and brashing of plantations can be put in hand.
(iii) Work on preparing the areas to be planted during the coming winter should be started.

(b) Nursery

Weed control is still necessary.

9. *September*

(a) Woodlands

(i) Work on the new planting areas should be well in hand before the end of the month. The area may have to be cleared, ditches cleaned out and rabbit fences erected if necessary.
(ii) Weeding of young plantations should now be completed.

(b) Nursery

Continue weeding, if necessary.

10. *October*

(a) Woodlands

(i) Complete the work on the planting areas.
(ii) Beating up in young plantations may start towards the end of the month if conditions are suitable.

(b) Nursery

If the season permits, and the nursery stock has hardened off, lifting and planting may be started at the end of the month.

11. *November*

(a) Woodlands

(i) Planting and beating up should be put in hand, unless a start has already been made.

(ii) If the weather is unsuitable for planting other work such as thinning, felling, pruning or brashing may be carried out.

(b) Nursery

(i) Transplants should be lifted ready for planting.

(ii) Where transplants are bought from a nurseryman they should be heeled in as soon as they arrive. It is essential to see that the bundles are opened up, so as to prevent heating.

12. *December*

(a) Woodlands

(i) Continue planting so long as the weather permits.

(ii) In hard winter, fell, thin, prune, and brash.

(iii) If heavy rain reveals areas in young plantations which need draining, grips should be cut and drains opened up.

(b) Nursery

(i) Examine young seedlings for damage by 'frost-lift'.

(ii) Lift transplants as required for planting.

APPENDIX: Abbreviations

ADAS	Agricultural Development and Advisory Service
AONB	Area of Outstanding Natural Beauty
APF	Association of Professional Foresters
BCTGA	British Christmas Tree Growers Association
BDS	British Deer Society
BFSS	British Field Sports Society
BRE	Building Research Establishment
BTCV	British Trust for Conservation Volunteers
BTECH	Business and Technician Education Council
BTMA(EW)	British Timber Merchants Association (England and Wales)
BWPA	British Wood Preserving Association
CABI	Commonwealth Agricultural Bureaux International
CAS	Centre for Agricultural Strategy
CC	Countryside Commission
CCS	Countryside Commission for Scotland
CFA	Commonwealth Forestry Association
CFB	Commonwealth Forestry Bureau
CFEB	Central Forestry Examination Board
CLA	Country Landowners' Association
COSIRA	Council for Small Industries in Rural Areas
CPRE	Council for the Protection of Rural England
DA	Disadvantaged Areas
DOE	Department of the Environment
EEC	European Economic Community
EFG	Economic Forestry Group
ESA	Environmentally Sensitive Area
FAO	Food and Agriculture Organization of the United Nations
FC	Forestry Commission
FFWAG	Farming, Forestry and Wildlife Advisory Group
FICGB	Forestry Industry Committee of Great Britain
FRCC	Forestry Research Co-ordination Committee (of the Forestry Commission)
FSC	Forestry Safety Council
FTC	Forestry Training Council

FUW	Farmers' Union of Wales
FWAG	Farming and Wildlife Advisory Group
FWS	Farm Woodland Scheme
GC	Game Conservancy
HSE	Health and Safety Executive
HTMANI	Home Timber Merchants Association of Northern Ireland
HTMAS	Home Timber Merchants Association of Scotland
ICF	Institute of Chartered Foresters
ITE	Institute of Terrestrial Ecology
IUFRO	International Union of Forestry Research Organizations
LVA	Less Favoured Areas
MAFF	Ministry of Agriculture, Fisheries and Food
MSC	Manpower Services Commission
NCC	Nature Conservancy Council
NERC	Natural Environment Research Council
NFU	National Farmers' Union
NFUS	National Farmers' Union of Scotland
NIFS	Northern Ireland Forestry Service
NNR	National Nature Reserve
NPA	National Parks Authority
NT	National Trust
NTS	National Trust for Scotland
OFI	Oxford Forestry Institute
PDO	Potentially Damaging Operation
RAC	Regional Advisory Committee (of the Forestry Commission)
RAW	Register of Ancient Woodlands
RFSEWNI	Royal Forestry Society of England, Wales and Northern Ireland
RICS	Royal Institution of Chartered Surveyors
RSFS	Royal Scottish Forestry Society
RSPB	Royal Society for the Protection of Birds
SCOTVEC	Scottish Vocational Educational Council
SDA	Severely Disadvantaged Areas
SIF	Society of Irish Foresters
SLF	Scottish Landowners Federation
SSSI	Site of Special Scientific Interest
SWL	Scottish Woodlands Ltd
TC	Tree Council
TGUK	Timber Growers United Kingdom Ltd
TPO	Tree Preservation Order
TRADA	Timber Research and Development Association
WGS	Woodland Grant Scheme
YTS	Youth Training Scheme

Index

In compiling this index the following procedure has been adopted. Fungi, bacteria, viruses and insects are arranged in alphabetical order of English names in Chapter XII and are not specifically mentioned in the index. In order to save space, the publications of the Forestry Commission and the Forestry Safety Council are not indexed but reference is made to many of them under the various matters to which they refer. A list of the current publications of the Commission can be obtained from the Publications Officer at the Forest Research Station, Alice Holt Lodge, Wrecclesham, Farnham, Surrey GU10 4LH, while Sectional List 31, which also deals with the Commission's literature, may be obtained from HM Stationery Office. Statutes, statutory instruments and law cases which are given in Chapter XXIII are not repeated in this index.